THE BRITISH INVASION

HOW THE BEATLES AND OTHER UK BANDS CONQUERED A[MERICA]

Bill Harry

BRITISH INVASION

HOW THE BEATLES AND OTHER UK BANDS CONQUERED AMERICA

by Bill Harry

A CHROME DREAMS PUBLICATION

WWW.CHROMEDREAMS.CO.UK

FIRST EDITION 2004

ISBN 1 84240 247 1

COPYRIGHT © 2004 Bill Harry

EDITOR   Rob Johnstone

DESIGN   Sylvia Grzeszczuk

Published by

CHROME DREAMS
PO BOX 230
NEW MALDEN
SURREY
KT3 6YY
UK

A catalogue record for this book is available from the British Library.

Printed and Bound in the UK

THE BRITISH INVASION

HOW THE BEATLES AND OTHER UK BANDS CONQUERED AMERICA

BILL HARRY

I *was* there and I *do* remember the sixties (well, there was so much happening that I admit to at least remembering part of it!).

In August 2003, Rod Murray and I unveiled a plaque to the Dissenters at Ye Cracke pub in Rice Street, Liverpool. This all harked back to early 1960 when John Lennon, Stuart Sutcliffe, Rod and myself had been to Liverpool University to attend a recital by British poet Royston Ellis.

At the time we were all students at Liverpool College of Art. Rod was Stu's best friend and they shared a flat together in Gambier Terrace, which John then moved into. The four of us used to hang around together in pubs and parties and at the Gambier Terrace flat and on this particular evening we decided to see Ellis perform his poetry.

Following the recital we retired to Ye Cracke, our art college watering hole, and a discussion began. We had noticed that Royston had written his poetry in the style of the San Francisco poets, who we were all aware of. In fact, we had copies from the City Lights Bookshop of poems by Ginsberg, Ferlighetti and Corso and Ellis seemed to be copying their style.

In those days the major films were all American, the music we all loved was American, even the 'in' books such as *On The Road* and *The Catcher In The Rye* were American as were the current icons such as James Dean and Marilyn Monroe. We all were fascinated by 'The Beat Generation' depicted by Jack Kerouac and Co, and admired the American president John F. Kennedy.

The conversation touched on the fact that there was a degree of American popular culture domination in Britain and people seemed to be copying it. At the time reporters from

THIS PLAQUE COMMEMORATES JOHN LENNON'S 'OTHER BAND' (WHICH NEVER PLAYED A NOTE)

THE DISSENTERS

WRITER MUSICIAN ARTIST ARTIST

BILL HARRY (1939-) JOHN LENNON (1940-80) STUART SUTCLIFFE (1940-62) ROD MURRAY (1937-)

IN JUNE 1960, THESE 4 ART STUDENTS ATTENDED A POETRY READING BY ROYSTON ELLIS (THE 'PAPERBACK WRITER' IN PAUL McCARTNEY'S SONG 1966); ELLIS'S WORK WAS HEAVILY INFLUENCED BY ALLEN GINSBERG AND OTHER AMERICANS. AFTERWARDS, THE 4 CAME HERE TO DISCUSS WHAT THEY'D HEARD. THEY WERE UNIMPRESSED AND DECIDED TO PUT LIVERPOOL 'ON THE MAP' EACH IN THEIR OWN WAY AS 'THE DISSENTERS': THE REST IS...

PLAQUE UNVEILED BY BILL HARRY AND ROD MURRAY 24 AUGUST 2003

the *Sunday People* newspaper had swarmed over the Gambier Terrace flat trying to do a story on Beatniks (the flat was described in the paper under the heading 'Beatnik Horror!') and Beatniks, of course, were examples of British youth copying the American Beats.

I pointed out that any creative person is better off expressing themselves with the familiarity of their own experience and environment. To me, the Liverpool area was an exciting place with lots of creative people and I did not see why anyone should bother trying to write, paint or make music based on something outside their own experience, i.e. someone else's environment rather than their own.

A positive example was John himself. He was a poet, but he did not copy the San Francisco poets. His influences were Lewis Carroll, the Goons and Stanley Unwin. His writings in the *Daily Howl* had been comic pieces about the teachers and pupils he was familiar with. He was English and his English background was obvious in his work.

We began to talk about Liverpool itself, a city with a proud heritage and lots of interesting things going on. Over the pints of bitter we all decided to take a vow – we would use our talents to make Liverpool famous. John would do it with his music, Stuart and Rod with their painting and myself with my writing.

I suggested we call ourselves the Dissenters.

The idea that was spawned in our minds that night was to grow, and it must be admitted that John succeeded in that promise far beyond

MERSEYSIDE'S OWN ENTERTAINMENTS PAPER

MERSEY BEAT

l. 1 No. 13   JANUARY 4-18, 1962   Price THREEPENCE

of an entire album on their Liverpool roots, although one cannot complain when it turned into 'Sgt Pepper' instead!

Sadly and tragically, Stuart was to die so young. I am convinced that if he had lived he would have become one of the world's acclaimed artists.

As for myself, my creation was the coining of the phrase 'Mersey Beat' and the founding of the newspaper of that name to promote the Beatles and all the other Liverpool groups and artists. That name I created has now become part of the English language. My girlfriend Virginia and I had borrowed £50 to start the newspaper. We had a little attic office costing £5 a week situated above a wine merchant in Renshaw Street and I initially took no salary but lived on a grant I had received for a Senior City Art Scholar-

ship. In the early hours one morning, preparing items for the first issue, I realised that I had to come up with an appropriate name for the paper. It was going to be a sort of 'what's on of music in Liverpool,' promoting the local musicians and the venues.

I had to establish the area I would cover and began to consider what we called 'over the water', across the Mersey. This included Birkenhead, the Wirral and New Brighton. On our side of the river I thought I would take in the area up to Southport, all of Liverpool and some surrounding towns such as Widnes, Warrington and St. Helens. In my mind I visualised a map of the area I would be covering and suddenly, into the picture I saw a policeman – a policeman's beat. The name Mersey Beat popped into my head.

The author with the Beatles

Mersey Beat

our wildest dreams. In the years to come I was particularly pleased with *Strawberry Fields Forever* and *Penny Lane* because that was one of the things we discussed - why could not songs be written about the places we were familiar with? All the songs we listened to were about American locations and we often heard people saying that songs could not be written about British places because they had unglamorous names. They always quoted names such as Scunthorpe. It was a pity that John and Paul could not carry out their original intention

Liverpool 1960

What happened on Merseyside caused a revolution in Britain music. Groups from the provinces began to descend on Liverpool to perform at venues such as the Cavern. the Hollies and Herman's Hermits from Manchester, the Animals from Newcastle, Dave Berry & the Cruisers from Sheffield and groups from Birmingham and other major cities. Mersey Beat also began to cover groups in Birmingham, Sheffield, Manchester and then those cities began to spawn newspapers of their own based on Mersey Beat such as Midland Beat and Scottish Beat. The London dominated music scene then began to have input from all over the British Isles.

One of the highlights of the period was when Alan Ginsberg sat next to me in the Blue Angel club and related how exciting Liverpool was. He was to make a quote about Liverpool being the centre of the universe at that time. Suddenly the world was coming to us, I was taking Bob Dylan round Liverpool, entertaining Judy Garland at the Blue Angel, involved in the making of TV documentaries such as 'The Mersey Sound' and 'Beat City'. It was a miraculous, magical string of memorable moments.

Could it ever be repeated?

It could!

In 1966 the scene had changed and Virginia and I decided to move down to London where I initially carried on writing for the music papers including Record Mirror, Music Now and Record Retailer. We were literally then hurled into the centre of the Swinging London scene.

We settled in a flat in Charing Cross Road and were spending seven days a week, from morning to night, involved in all the exciting events which were occurring. I would go out drinking with Keith Moon and Peter Noone, would visit artist Alan Aldridge in his studio, would drop into 'Top Of The Pops' and the 'Ready Steady Go' studios every week and visit the clubs and venues every night. Highlights included being invited to stay at his rented house with Bobby Darin, giving the Bee Gees their very first interview in a British music paper, taking Pink Floyd to visit the BBC radiophonic workshop where the boffins created intriguing new sounds, spending time at the Playboy club with stars such as

Mickie Most

Telly Savalas, enjoying evenings at Jimi Hendrix's flat playing board games, sitting at the next table to Paul when he was first introduced to Linda at the Bag O' Nails club. And Virginia, apart from working for a show business agency, loved shopping at Biba's and the other boutiques, witness to the latest and rapidly changing fashions, experiencing the fashion trends in the Swinging City.

So much was happening. I was asked to become press agent to the Kinks and the Hollies, then Pink Floyd. During the following years I became press agent for Chicken Shack (with singer Christine Perfect, who was later to join Fleetwood Mac), Ten Years After, Jethro Tull, David Bowie and many others. Still at the heart of Swinging London I was also aware of the effect the groups were having with The British Invasion although I did not begin to travel to America with the bands until 1968.

In addition to writing for the music press (using lots of pen names), I became press agent for the 'in' clubs Tiles, the Speakeasy, the Revolution and Blaises. The clubs were the gathering places for the artists. When we first arrived in London we visited the Ad Lib club and then became regulars at the Scotch Of St James. I remember one night we were sitting in a packed corner of the Scotch with the Beatles, the Rolling Stones, Marlon Brando and I was chatting to a hero of mine, author James Baldwin. At that time the artists, managers, PRs, DJs formed part of a community in which he socialised together on a regular basis.

Music also dominated our lives and we attended the Marquee club a few nights each week, the Lyceum, the Saville Theatre, in addition to concerts and all the major festivals, plus attending the gigs with the bands I was publicising. We saw virtually every visiting American band, with Derek Taylor inviting us to attend the Byrds first concert in London.

We also saw Jimi Hendrix's very first London performance and experienced so many other memorable musical moments.

I even became PR for a time for American bands such as the Beach Boys and the Electric Prunes.

When I began to publicise groups for Chris Wright and Terry Ellis, I was asked to rent an office on the floor of a small building they had moved into in Oxford Street. Music publisher Mike Berry, who was also in the building, said it could be compared to the Brill Building in New York. On the first floor were Ellis, Wright and Harry Simmonds. For them I represented, among others, Ten Years After, Jethro Tull, Chicken Shack, Savoy Brown and later, Procol Harum. On the next floor was Shroeder Music with Mike Berry and also Island Music and for Island Records I was to handle artists such as Free and Mott the Hoople.

On the top floor Mickie Most and Peter Grant shared an office. I had known Peter since 1963 when he had arrived in Liverpool with Gene Vincent and he had later had me act as PR for the New Vaudeville Band. He then asked me to represent his artists Stone the Crows and Led Zeppelin. Mickie had me become press agent for all his acts, beginning with Terry Reid and Suzi Quatro.

I was to work with Mickie Most for the next fourteen years, publicising all his acts, together with the label Rak Records that he was to launch.

Mickie is one of the unsung heroes of the British Invasion and recorded many of the hits associated with it including 'House Of the Rising Sun', 'I'm Into Something Good', 'To Sir With Love' and 'Sunshine Superman'. The artists he recorded included the Animals, Herman's Hermits, Lulu, the Yardbirds, Donovan, the Nashville Teens and Mary Hopkin. Between 1964 and 1984 he had 22 No.1 hits in America and 15 in Britain.

The most famous recording manager in the world is Sir George Martin because he recorded the Beatles. However, apart from the other Liverpool acts who came with the Epstein package, he is not know for discovering and recording other major stars. Mickie, on the other hand, was one of the most successful recording managers on the planet, discovering hit artist after hit artist and recording an astonishing string of hit records over two decades which included 37 No. 1 hits worldwide and sales of 400,000,000 records.

His hits in the 1960s were numerous, but he proved to be even more successful in the following decade after forming Rak Records in 1969. The number ones came from Suzi Quatro, Jeff Beck, Cozy Powell, Hot Chocolate and stretched right up to Kim Wilde in the early 1980s shortly before he sold Rak for £20,000,000.

He was born Michael Peter Hayes in June 1938 in Aldershot and after leaving school at the age of 15 had a number of jobs, including park keeper, bricklayer, dustman and sheet metal worker.

His introduction to show business came when he formed a duo called the Most Brothers and travelled to South Africa. There he met a 16 year old called Christina and fell in love. They were married and their relationship, which lasted for life, brought them one son Calvin and two daughters Cristalle and Nathalie.

Mickie's first taste of success came with the Animals, a group from New-

castle-on-Tyne, and he produced their second single 'House Of the Rising Sun' in 15 minutes at a cost of £1.50. He recalled, "They were working by 8am and by quarter past they had recorded one song. When they finished that, we had time to spare before they caught the 12.15pm train for a Southampton concert. Plenty of time to make an album. And we did".

Sadly, Mickie died of a rare form of lung cancer on May 30th 2003, said to have been caused by exposure to asbestos in South Africa forty years earlier.

His best friend Johnny Gold, owner of Tramps nightclub said, "He never got the recognition he was due. He was the best and most successful record producer of his day, selling more records than the Beatles. When I look at some people in the music industry who receive knighthoods, OBEs and MBEs I think it's disgusting he never got one".

The last artist I represented for Mickie was Kim Wilde, who entered the American charts with 'Kids in America' in 1982.

So, from my perspective, although I was press agent for several of the British Invasion artists, I observed it all from this side of the pond.

My mind often goes back to that night in Ye Cracke in 1960 when we discussed the vow of John (with his group) making Liverpool famous with his music. Was this the spark that was to set alight the beginning of 'the British Invasion'?

Bill Harry, London, October 2003

Matthew Street, Liverpool 1960

Lonnie Donegan was the main inspiration for the huge popularity of skiffle throughout the British Isles that produced literally thousands of skiffle groups between 1954-1958.

Adam Faith, also inspired by Donegan's *Rock Island Line* to form his own skiffle group the Worried Men, said, "Skiffle hit Britain with all the fury of Asian flu. Everyone went down with it."

Artists ranging from Mick Jagger to John Lennon all began their musical careers in skiffle groups.

There are various explanations for the term, some say it was a type of music originated in New Orleans in 1900, others that term originally came from Afro-Americans in the 1920s. It has also been suggested that artists playing such music were originally called spasm bands. Charlie Spanel originally used the term on record in 1929 on his recording of *Hometown Skiffle*.

The music was initially performed by poor black musicians who couldn't afford to buy expensive musical instruments and used washboards, handmade banjos and acoustic guitars. In many ways they held parties playing music in which they charged a nominal fee in order to pay their rent. Lonnie Donegan was to say, "Skiffle is part of the phrase skiffle party which is a way of saying 'home rent party'."

Following Donegan's success, the world's biggest skiffle movement took place in Britain where youngsters also found that they could produce music with affordable basic instruments such as kazoo, tea-chest-bass, washboard and acoustic guitars.

The movement literally took Britain by storm and apart from Donegan there were a series of chart hits by skiffle artists ranging from the Vipers to Chas McDevitt and Nancy Whiskey.

British skiffle artists generally played numbers that were early American folk ballads and railroad songs such as *Jesse James, Railroad Bill, Casey Joes* and *St James Infirmary*. In fact, some Liverpool groups actually believe the latter number had been written about the St James Infirmary in Liverpool. Those early American folk numbers had, in their turn, been originally inspired by British folk songs.

It is interesting to note the rapid progression of popular music trend in Britain between 1954-1960. They began with the influence of early American folk music (skiffle), then there was a Trad Jazz boom, inspired by New Orleans jazz, followed by a rock 'n' roll boom. In six years Britain had run through a hundred years of American popular music!

The Beatles and the British Invasion

John F. Kennedy International Airport, Friday, February 7th 1964

What was known in musical terms as The British Invasion started with the American release of *I Want To Hold Your Hand*, which topped the U.S. charts on January 25th 1964. For the rest of the decade British bands and artists stormed the American charts and airwaves with rebellious reinterpretations of American rock 'n' roll.

This is the general impression, yet although it is basically accurate, it does need some refining. The Beatles heralded The British Invasion and due to them the American charts did receive a steady flow of British hits throughout the decade, although they were not strictly limited to groups as they included both male and female solo singers.

The British Invasion did not exactly swamp the American charts either and American artists continued to hold sway, although the music scene changed completely, with American hits generally comprising more home grown groups than previously, many of whom had been inspired by the Beatles and British bands. The British Invasion has become a time of nostalgia for the Baby Boomers and the Beatles still retain their crown as the greatest group in the history of popular music.

What were the British Invasion's origins? A Scottish musician named Anthony Donegan was the person who kick-started it all. Born in Glasgow on April 29th 1931, he first joined a local group and was then called up for National Service. It was during his two year stint with the army that he developed his musical skills, playing drums with the Wolverines Jazz Band. When he was demobbed he moved down to London. In 1952 when he appeared on a bill with the legendary blues guitarist Lonnie Johnson in London, the compere mistakenly announced him as 'Lonnie Donegan'– and he decided to keep the name.

Donegan joined Ken Colyer's Jazzmen, playing guitar and banjo. He was given his own spot in the show and teamed up with Chris Barber on bass and Bill Colyer on washboard to perform a style of music generally known as Skiffle.

He appeared in Liverpool featuring at concerts at the Pavilion and Empire Theatres in 1956. It was at the Empire Theatre that a young schoolboy,

Paul McCartney, became inspired. As a member of the audience he was so thrilled with Donegan's sound that during school lunchtime he returned to the theatre for a glimpse of his idol. He was impressed by the way Donegan treated his fans, chatting to them and signing autographs.

It was Donegan's appearance that sparked Paul's desire to buy a guitar and his father bought him one for £15.

The fourteen-year old George Harrison also found inspiration from the Donegan performance and he also decided he wanted a guitar, which his mum bought him for £3.

George's brother Harry was to recall, "Lonnie Donegan was appearing at the Empire and of course George just had to go. In fact, he borrowed the money from our parents so that he could see every single show! Anyway, he found out where Lonnie was staying, which happened to be in a house in Speke, so George went round and hammered on the door until he came out and gave George his autograph. Of course, he immediately

raced home to show everyone."

Years later, George was to recall, "Lonnie and Skiffle seemed made for me. It was easy music to play if you knew two or three chords, and you'd have a tea-chest as bass and washboard and you were on your way."

He also told Beatles biographer Hunter Davies that Donegan was the first person to make an impression on him musically: "I'd been aware of pop singers before him, like Frankie Laine and Johnny Ray, but never really taken much interest in them. I don't think I was old enough for them. But Lonnie Donegan and Skiffle just seemed made for me".

'Rock Island Line' was a traditional American railroad song that became a major hit for Donegan, not only in Britain, but also in the United States. The track was issued in Britain on Decca F 10647 and reached No. 8 in the charts in January 1956. It was issued in America on London 1650 and reached No. 8 in March of that year.

Donegan was also a seminal influence on the sixteen-year-old John Lennon. Although he did not have much money to spend on records, John bought a 78rpm record of 'Rock Island Line'. He played the song until it was nearly worn out, then sold it to Rod Davis, a school friend, also inspired by Donegan, who was to join him in his first Skiffle group, the Quarry Men.

Their repertoire comprised several Skiffle numbers popularised by Donegan, including *Rock Island Line, Cumberland Gap, Midnight Special, Railroad Bill* and *Worried Man Blues*. Incidentally, Donegan's influence on Lennon can actually be heard. Donegan had a chart hit with the traditional *Stewball*. Listen to John's '*Happy Xmas (War Is Over)*' and the influence becomes apparent.

Ringo Starr also became interested in music during the Skiffle boom and he joined the Eddie Clayton Skiffle Group in 1957.

The music scene that grew and developed on Merseyside in the 1950s was unique, although this was not the case for the Skiffle boom that spawned it.

Skiffle was a national phenomenon in Britain following the huge chart success of Donegan's *Rock Island Line*. Skiffle groups sprang up throughout the country, although the boom burst after a couple of years. In Liverpool, however, the groups turned to rock 'n' roll with literally hundreds of groups performing in clubs, cellars, church halls, synagogues, ice rinks, swimming baths, ferry boats, department stores, youth clubs, seaside piers, coffee bars, cinemas, social clubs, colleges and pubs.

The James Boys developed into Kingsize Taylor & the Dominoes, the Ralph Ellis Skiffle Group became the Swinging Bluegenes (later, the Swinging Bluejeans), the Raving Texans became Rory Storm & the Hurricanes (with drummer Ringo Starr) and the Quarry Men evolved into the Beatles.

Like other Skiffle groups who had abandoned the simplistic Skiffle sounds and turned to rock 'n' roll, the Quarry Men's repertoire comprised compositions by Buddy Holly & the Crickets, Elvis Presley, Chuck Berry, Eddie Cochran, Jerry Lee Lewis,

the Coasters, Carl Perkins, Larry Williams, the Isley Brothers, Ray Charles, Little Richard, the Olympics, Lloyd Price, Gene Vincent, Larry Williams and the Everly Brothers. By 1960 the sole Skiffle tune they performed was 'Midnight Special', which had been made popular in the U.K. by Donegan.

The numbers they played were all available on records in local record stores in Liverpool and the Quarry Men, competing for a suitable repertoire in competition with the other Mersey bands, in common with the other groups, often paid attention to the B sides of records.

There was a myth that Liverpool had the edge over other British cities because, being a seaport, sailors and 'Cunard Yanks' (Liverpool seamen who plied the Atlantic between America and Britain) brought in American records unavailable in Britain. This was not the case. One or two musicians, such as John McNally of the Searchers, had brothers who went to sea and brought them records as gifts, but the records were still those readily available at home (the Searchers repertoire actually came from drummer Chris Curtis's excellent record collection). Some of the Country bands such as Hank Walters & His Dusty Road Ramblers sought Country Records from relatives who went to sea, but that was about the extent of the 'Cunard Yanks' story. The hundreds of local groups drew their material from records obtained at the record stores.

Buddy Holly was the next major influence following Donegan. The Quarry Men selected several of his

Buddy Holly

numbers for their repertoire, including *It's So Easy*, *Maybe Baby*, *Peggy Sue*, *That'll Be The Day*, *Think It Over*, *Words Of Love* and *Crying, Waiting, Hoping*.

Just as Paul and George had gone to see their idol Donegan perform at the Empire, John and Paul went to see Buddy Holly & the Crickets when they appeared at the Philharmonic Hall, Liverpool on March 20th 1958. Years later, Paul was to comment, "I had always said I liked Buddy, he was one of my big influences when I started writing."

The Crickets also inspired the Beatles name. After abandoning the Quarry Men title, John Lennon, Paul

McCartney, George Harrison and Stuart Sutcliffe temporarily toyed with a number of names such as Johnny & The Moondogs. Early in 1960, while John and Stuart were sharing a flat in Gambier Terrace, they sat down to think of an appropriate name. Stuart suggested that they consider something similar to that of the Crickets. Why not the name of another insect? The name Beetles seemed appropriate. This was altered slightly over the next few months with names such as Beatals, the Silver Beats, the Silver Beetles, the Silver Beatles and finally, in August 1960, simply the Beatles.

While the youngsters on Merseyside honed their talent in the halls and cellars of the conurbation, developing their own style of rock 'n' roll, the situation in America was changing.

In many quarters in the United States, including the media of radio and television, rock 'n' roll was looked down on. It was considered 'black music' or 'the devil's music' and, although it had its champions such as Alan Freed, who promoted it on radio and in major concerts in New York, it was still considered *persona non grata.* Freed himself was hounded and accused of payola until his career was in tatters. (Freed, incidentally, was the man who coined the phrase 'rock 'n' roll).

There were also major problems concerning the great rock 'n' roll stars that had helped to create the new sound. Elvis Presley had been tamed. The rock 'n' roll star had returned from his stint in the army to appear in evening suit and dickie bow, duetting with Frank Sinatra on television.

Carl Perkins had been involved in a car accident in which his brother had died and his injuries had caused him to pause his career. Little Richard had turned his back on rock 'n' roll and was involved in gospel music. Chuck Berry had been jailed for taking a minor across a state line. Jerry Lee Lewis was in disgrace for marrying his fourteen-year-old cousin and Buddy Holly, the Big Bopper and Ritchie Valens had died in an air crash.

Their places had been taken by clean-cut, handsome white youngsters such as Fabian, Frankie Avalon, Dion, Ricky Nelson, Conway Twitty, Bobby Vee, Brian Hyland, Bobby Vinton, Tab Hunter and James Darren, singing teen songs of love and romance. Rather than *Short Fat Fanny*, you had *Young Love*; rather than *Memphis, Tennessee* you had *Itsy Bitsy Teenie Weenie Yellow Polkadot Bikini*; rather than *Blue Suede Shoes* you had *Roses Are Red* (*My Love*); rather than *Rave On* you had *The Story Of My Love*; rather than *Whole Lotta Shakin* you had *Rubber Ball* and so on.

In Liverpool rock 'n' roll survived. With over three hundred venues on Merseyside the groups numbered in the hundreds. Among the basic repertoires were songs such as 'Some Other Guy', 'Little Egypt', 'Love Potion Number 9', 'Skinnie Minnie', 'Memphis Tennessee', 'Bony Moronie', 'Dizzy Miss Lizzy', 'Good Golly Miss Molly', 'High School Confidential', 'Hully Gully', 'Jailhouse Rock' 'Johnny B. Goode', 'Lawdy Miss Clawdy', 'Long Tall Sally', 'Lucille', 'Reelin' And Rockin'' 'Rock And Roll Is Here To Stay', 'Roll Over Beethoven', 'Searchin'', 'Shout'; 'Slow Down', 'Sweet Little Sixteen', 'Tutti Frutti', 'Twenty Flight Rock' and 'Yakety Yak'.

Chuck Berry

They honed their talents in competition with all the other bands in venues that sometimes booked two or three different outfits each night. A basic line-up of many of the bands was that of a quartet – a lead, bass, and rhythm guitarist, with a drummer, while the guitarists also performed vocal harmony in addition to individuals taking on lead vocals. It is this particular style that became known as 'The Liverpool Sound', or 'The Mersey Sound', and its exponents included the Beatles, the Searchers, Gerry & the Pacemakers, the Strangers, Billy Kramer & the Coasters, Ian & the Zodiacs, the Fourmost, the Swinging Bluejeans and many others.

However, over the years this has tended to overshadow the huge musical melting pot that Merseyside was during those years. There was a thriving Country Music scene, the biggest in Europe, which led to Liverpool being dubbed 'the Nashville of the North'. They had their own Grand Ole Opry at the Philharmonic Hall and even a Country Music Association. There was a major Folk Music scene, led by the Spinners, Britain's leading folk outfit. The poetry scene led by Roger McGough, Adrian Henri and Brian Patten also became the major national poetry movement of the 1960s and there were black vocal groups such as the Chants.

Another influence was Tamla Motown. At the time Oriole Records distributed Motown Records in Britain and their biggest market was Merseyside. This led to Liverpool groups adapting Motown numbers to their own style in what I loosely termed the 'Mersey Motown Sound'.

The Searchers

There were lots of girl singers and even all-female rock 'n' roll bands and there were duos, trios, quintets, and groups of various differing line-ups.

The template for what happened with the British Invasion occurred with the Mersey music breakthrough in the U.K. The British scene was controlled from London. The national press, the music press, magazines and the BBC with its radio and television were all based in the capitol. There was no commercial radio, no pirate radio stations at the time, simply BBC radio with programmes such as 'Worker's Playtime' and

'Family Favourites' supplying music for an older generation. ITV, the commercial television channel, also had its main stations in London.

The Grade Organisation, led by Lew and Leslie Grade, owned television stations such as ATV, their brother Bernard Delfont ran Moss Empires and Britain's major TV shows such as 'Sunday Night At the London Palladium' and 'The Royal Variety Show'. Their associate Harold Davidson had the leading agency and management company for artists and virtually all show business agents were based in London, as were all the record companies and music publishers.

Commenting on the Beatles' initial success in America, George Harrison was to say, "Apart from the odd singer, nobody had ever made it. So we definitely felt the pressure. But we knew we'd had sufficient success in Europe and Britain to have a bit of confidence."

The Beatles were not in fact the first British artists to enter the American charts, although prior to the British Invasion, only a trickle of artists ever cracked the American record market.

One of the Beatles' seminal influences, Lonnie Donegan had a chart hit with *Rock Island Line*, which reached No. 8 on March 31st 1956, and a second hit *Does Your Chewing Gum Lose Its Flavour On The Bedpost Overnight* reached No. 5 on August 14th 1961. Donegan appeared on two American trips and discussing his appearance in New York on his second trip, he recalled, "I was terrified. They put me on Madison Square Garden and I was very aware of the fact that 17,000 people had come along to see the Harlem Globetrotters. But don't be misled by the stories you've read. They yelled for more when we finished."

The same month that Donegan rose to his highest position in the American charts, another British artist actually topped the charts in the U.S. Laurie London reached No. 1 on March 24th 1958.

The Beatles were also not the first act from Liverpool to make their mark in the U.S. Amazingly, of the small handful of British artists who managed to enter the American charts prior to the British Invasion, two of them were from Liverpool – a sign of things to come?

The first was Russ Hamilton, who was born in the Everton district of Liverpool in 1932. He became a Butlin's Redcoat (a holiday camp entertainer) and, on completing his National Service, formed a skiffle group. His self-penned debut record *We Will Make Love* was a British top ten, but it was the B-side *Rainbow* which became a hit in America, reaching No. 4 in the charts on August 5th 1957. Hamilton made a number of appearances in America and also wrote his follow-up record *Wedding Ring*, which became his second and final Top 20 entry, although he was to record seventeen singles.

Frankie Vaughan was the second artist from Liverpool to hit the American music scene on July 28th 1958 when his recording of *Judy* reached No 22 in the Billboard charts. Vaughn appeared in several films and his 1957 movie 'These Dangerous Years' was filmed in Liver-

Frankie Vaughan with Marilyn Monroe

pool. It was about a local tearaway who is called up for his National Service, goes AWOL and hides out on the Cast Iron Shore (John Lennon sings *Standing on the Cast-Iron Shore* in *Glass Onion*). In 1960 Vaughan starred in *Let's Make Love*'opposite Marilyn Monroe.

He was born Frank Ephrain Abelson in Liverpool on February 3rd 1929 and was the first Liverpool artist ever to top the British charts with 'Garden Of Eden' in 1957. He made his chart debut with *My Sweetie Went Away* and among almost three dozen successful singles for him between 1954 and 1968 was another No. 1 record *Tower Of Strength,* and hits such as *the Green Door, Hello Dolly* and his theme tune *Give Me The Moonlight.*

Vaughan became a popular cabaret performer in Britain. He also devoted much of his spare time to working with the National Association of Boys' Clubs, in particular the Merseyside and North Wales Variety Club, based in Liverpool, for which he was awarded an O.B.E. In 1997, almost thirty years later, when he was sixty-eight, he was awarded a C.B.E.

Three years later he died at his home in High Wycombe on September 17th 1999 at the age of seventy-one.

The next major impact on the American charts was by Laurie London with *He's Got The Whole World In His Hands.* Laurie was born in London on January 19th 1944. In 1958, at the age of 13 he visited the Radio Show and appeared on the '6.5 Special' sec-

tion of the closed circuit television of the BBC stand, where he sang. The BBC producer John Warrinton was so impressed he invited Laurie to sing at the stand each day. This brought him to the attention of EMI Records who engaged producer Norman Newall to make a record with the youngster. Geoff Love arranged the gospel number *He's Got the Whole World In His Hands,* which Mahalia Jackson had recorded in 1946. It was released on Parlophone, the label the Beatles were to sign with a few years later.

On its release the record reached No. 12 in the British charts, but it proved a sensation in America where it topped the Billboard charts in 1958, making Laurie the most successful British male vocalist in America during the 1950s.

Laurie's father Will then left his job as a sales manager to manage his son. However, he turned down the prospect of an American tour in 1958 and Laurie had no further success in the States.

In Britain, Laurie recorded some further gospel titles, including *Joshua, The Gospel Truth* and *I Got A Robe* but he was never to chart again and later joined the clothing trade in London.

Another Brit to make his mark was Matt Monro who reached No. 18 in the American charts on 26th June 1961 with *My Kind Of Girl* and returned to the American charts on December 26th 1964 with *Walk Away.*

His real name was Terry Parson and he was a former London bus driver who first came to fame impersonating Frank Sinatra on Peter Sellers' album *Songs for Swinging*

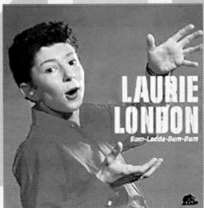

Laurie London

Sellers. Later on in the decade Monro was to beat Marianne Faithful in the chart race with his version of Paul McCartney's 'Yesterday'. Although he had no further American hits, he had several more in Britain, including *Portrait Of My Love, My Kind Of Girl, Softly As I Leave You, From Russia With Love,* and *Born Free.*

He died from cancer on February 7th 1985.

The Tornados were actually the first British group ever to top the American charts. They were an instrumental outfit originally formed by British independent producer Joe Meek and consisted of Alan Caddy and George Bellamy (guitars), Clem Cattini (drums), Roger LaVern (keyboards) and Heinz Burt (bass).

Their debut record 'Telstar' was also their biggest hit and on its release, following its chart-topping performance on both sides of the Atlantic, became the biggest selling instrumental of all time. Despite other releases such as 'Globetrotter', 'Robot', 'The Ice Cream Man' and 'Dragonfly', they never had another Stateside hit.

For a British group to top the American charts with their debut disc was an incredible achievement, yet the Tornados never enjoyed any financial success as a result. At the height of their fame they were earning just £25 each per week and their legal battle to win their rights took 29 years and lasted until 1991! They received scant royalties for the chart-topper and were continually involved in legal wrangles. In fact, LaVern went bankrupt in an attempt to wrest his royalties from Joe Meek's publishing company.

In 1967 Meek had shot his landlady with a shotgun, which he then turned on himself. Soon after, the group disbanded.

Bellamy, Burt, Cattini and LaVern were to reform a decade later under the name of the Original Tornados and re-recorded 'Telstar', but without success and disbanded once again.

Clem Cattini went on to become one of the major British session drummers with more than 40 Number One records behind him. Once again, he re-formed the Tornados, this time in 1989, introducing a female into the line-up, Lynn Alice on keyboards and vocals. The other members were Dave Harvey, bass, Dave Graham lead and vocals and Bip Weatherell on keyboards and vocals.

Pianist Roger LaVern married eight times and had children with another four women. In the mid 1970s he moved to Mexico where he appeared in numerous television commercials and played piano in leading hotels and nightclubs. He was to

The Tornados

comment, "I was known as El lobo Plateado, the Silver Wolf." In 1986 his hands seized up with a crippling disease and he could no longer play. He then married his eighth wife Maria-Esther, who was 20 years his junior.

Heinz Burt, who was born in Germany on July 24th 1942, was discovered by Meek slicing bacon in a grocery when he signed him up at the age of nineteen in 1962. After seeing the film *Village Of The Damned*, Meek encouraged Heinz to dye his hair blonde and launched him on a solo career in which he had a hit record *Just Like Eddie*. After a short career as a musician, Heinz then worked on the assembly line at the Ford car plant in Dagenham and painted trains for British Rail. He then succumbed to multiple sclerosis and died on April 7th 2000.

George Bellamy became a builder in Devon.

Alan Caddy also passed away at a relatively young age. He was sixty when he died on February 2nd 1990.

The Springfields were a folk trio who hit No. 2 in the American charts on September 22nd 1963 with *Silver Threads And Golden Needles*. The record became a million-seller in the States, but failed to make an impact on the British charts.

They had formed in 1960 when Mary O'Brien and her brother Dion teamed up with Tim Field. Mary changed her name to Dusty Springfield and Dion to Tom Springfield. Their second record *Breakaway* entered the UK chart and they followed up with the hits *Bambino*, *Island Of Dreams*, *Say I Won't Be There* and *Come On Home*. Tim Field left the trio in 1962 and Mike Hurst replaced him.

Despite being voted Best UK Vocal Group the Springfields broke up in 1963 when Dusty embarked on her solo career.

These were the British artists who had all dipped their toes into the American chart waters prior to the Beatles.

Interestingly enough, when listing the countries of origin of various chart artists, Billboard lists one artist, Valerie Carr as 'English'. She is actually African-American and was born in New York. The mistake may have arisen because her hit *When The Boys talk About the Girls* was a success in Britain before it entered the American charts in 1958.

The Springfileds

It was a controlled scene, that was, until the emergence of the Beatles. The breakthrough they made transformed the British music scene irrevocably and groups from the provinces were able to benefit from opportunities they had never had before. There was the Animals from Newcastle, the Hollies from Manchester, Dave Berry & the Cruisers from Sheffield, the Moody Blues from Birmingham, an invasion of young artists playing their own type of music revolutionised the stale musical scene in Britain.

Apart from a handful of artists such as Cliff Richard & the Shadows and the Larry Parnes stable of acts and TV programmes such as *Oh Boy!* – all of them London based anyway – the music scene in Britain had not really catered for teenagers, which is probably why Lonnie Donegan's hits sparked such a boom in Skiffle music. After the emergence of the Beatles, the music scene in Britain was never the same and they were to create exactly the same effect in America.

Once Beatlemania swept Britain and the Continent, EMI Records approached Capitol Records in America to release the British hits in the United States.

Like many other British artists, despite their success on their home territory, American record executives did not consider the Beatles suitable for the American record buying public. Only a handful of British artists had ever achieved an American chart entry and generally were unable to follow up with a string of further hits or establish themselves on the American market.

Therefore, the climate still did not seem right for a British artist to make waves on the America hit parade.

The Beatles British record company, EMI Records, actually owned Capitol Records in America. They had bought the American label outright in 1955 for nine million dollars. Despite this they did not want to pressurise the label into accepting British artists. However, EMI gave Capitol the right of first and second refusal on British recordings.

When *Please Please Me* topped the British charts, Sir Joseph Lockwood, EMI's managing director, offered the

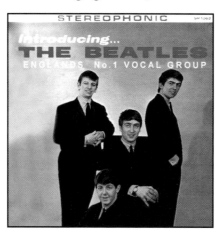

record to Capitol. He recalled, "They wouldn't take it at any price." In fact, it was the job of Dave Dexter Jr, based at Capitol's Los Angeles head quarters, to listen to all records from EMI companies around the world and decide whether any would be suitable for the American market. He originally listened to *Love Me Do* and rejected it. After also rejecting *Please Please Me* he said, "I couldn't count the number of times a British artist was a smash over there and then

came over here and died."

When *From Me To You* topped the British charts it was George Martin who approached Capitol to take the single. They refused it. Alan Livingston, President of Capitol Records then sent a memo to EMI, "We don't think the Beatles will do anything in this market".

When the Beatles *She Loves You* topped the British charts George Martin tried once again and told Capitol, "For God's sake, do something about this. These boys are breaking it, they're going to be fantastic throughout the world. So for heaven's sake, latch on to them." For the third time Capitol told EMI that the Beatles had no prospects in America.

Frustrated that their own American arm would not accept their biggest British and European act, EMI then contacted Transglobal, another of their American subsidiaries and a company that fixed deals for EMI Records which had been rejected by Capitol. Arrangements were made for a small label Vee Jay Records to issue the 'Please Please Me' single, which they released on February 25th 1963. It did not chart. They next issued *From Me To You*, but considered its highest placing in Billboard at No. 116 was unsuccessful, even though it was also made *Pick Of The Week* in *Cashbox* magazine.

The final Vee Jay Beatles release of that year was the album *Introducing the Beatles* This also failed to register. It was rumoured that Vee Jay then turned down *She Loves You*. However, this was denied because Transglobal, the licensing firm in

New York, cancelled Vee Jay's rights to release products on August 8th 1963 due to the fact that the record company had not paid royalties for the first two Beatles releases. This caused problems for Vee Jay, who had already pressed the album *Introducing The Beatles* which contained the two numbers. To have destroyed all the albums would have caused the company to go bankrupt, so they went ahead with the release, but did not list any of the tracks on the back cover of the album.

Swan Records, an independent label from Philadelphia next entered the picture. When Swan's President was in London at the beginning of September 1963 he asked EMI if they had a reciprocal license for him as EMI had released Swan's artist Freddie Cannon. EMI asked if he would be interested in the Beatles latest release *She Loves You.*

A license was set up and Swan released *She Loves You* on September 16th 1963, with *I'll Get By* on the flip. *Cashbox* reviewed the record calling *She Loves You* 'a robust romantic rocker that the crew works over with solid sales authority' and *I'll Get You* as 'a catchy cha-cha twist handclapper'.

The single did not sell well and was soon relegated to the bargain bins and Swan received no more offers as Capitol were about to agree to issue *I Want To Hold Your Hand.*

These examples might have pointed out that Capitol had been correct in their opinion, but then a series of happenings, coupled with a strong streak of luck, finally turned the fortunes of the Beatles.

The timing of a number of events, which coalesced in February 1964 to boost the popularity of the Beatles even further in America, came about as a result of a number of coincidences. One concerned Ed Sullivan who was the host of America's biggest television entertainment series *The Ed Sullivan Show*. On October 31st 1963 Sullivan happened to be at Heathrow Airport. At the time the Beatles were returning from their tour of Sweden and the roof of Queen's Building was absolutely crammed with screaming fans.

Sullivan was to recall, "My wife Sylvia and I were in London, at Heathrow Airport. There was the biggest crowd I'd ever seen in my life. I asked someone what was going on, and he said, 'The Beatles'. Who the hell are the Beatles? I asked. But I went back to my hotel, got the name of their manager, and arranged for them to do three shows."

Brian Epstein then travelled to America and met with Sullivan at his offices in the Delmonico Hotel on several occasions. Although the usual fee for an appearance on the show was $7,500, Epstein agreed to $10,000 for the three appearances.

Bob Precht, Sullivan's son-in-law was the show's producer and he was apprehensive about booking an unknown group from Britain for three shows and tackled Sullivan about it. Sullivan told him, "I think they're worth the investment."

Another of the unique coincidences that added to the impact of the Beatles' initial trip to America resulted from the actions of Sid Bernstein,

a former ballroom manager who was earning $200 a week working as an independent promoter/agent for General Artists Corporation (GAC), America's largest theatrical agency. In 1963 Bernstein was completing a night school course at the New School for Social Research in New York. He had originally begun the course the previous year and part of the course required him to read English newspapers on a weekly basis.

By the time he had completed the course in February 1963 he had noted the rise of 'Beatlemania' in the British press. Seeing the potential of the group he recommended them to GAC, but could not interest anyone at the agency in the Beatles. As a result he decided to strike out on his own and managed to locate Brian Epstein's phone number in Liverpool. In February 1963 he contacted Epstein, having decided on promoting the Beatles independently in New York. He suggested to him that he would like to book them to appear at the Carnegie Hall.

Epstein was obviously impressed by the possibility of appearing at such a prestigious venue, but he still remained cautious.

Bernstein had suggested booking the Beatles in June or July of that year, but Epstein realised that they did not have any airplay in America, that they also did not have any audience there and he felt that a concert in those circumstances would be premature. However, Bernstein persisted, asking Brian how much the Beatles were currently being paid. He was told they received $2,000 a night, so he offered Brian $6,500 for them to appear on two concerts on the one day at Carnegie Hall.

Appreciating Epstein's concern that a mid-1963 appearance might be too early, he suggested the booking should take place on Abraham Lincoln's birthday the following year, February 12th 1964. Brian agreed to this on the condition that the contract would become null and void if the Beatles did not have an American hit by the close of 1963.

Fortunately for Bernstein, his gamble paid off when it was announced that Ed Sullivan had booked them for his TV show, which was to take place shortly prior to the Carnegie Hall appearance.

In the meantime, Brian Epstein was becoming so increasingly annoyed at the negative response from Capitol that he instructed EMI to use their clout, after all, they did own the American record company. Epstein also made a personal phone call to Livingston and said, "Mr Livingston, we just don't understand it. The Beatles are doing very well in England, why don't you release them over there?" Livingston told Epstein he would listen to the records and call him back.

Other pressure was being put on the record company with EMI's Senior Executive L. G. Wood calling Lloyd Dunn, Capitol's Vice President in charge of Merchandising and Sales and asking him to use his influence. Wood told him, "We have this record we really *must* release in the States. It seems your lads in A&R refuse to accept it, which is frightfully embar-rassing, because the group is really selling here in a most gratifying fashion."

Dunn recalled, "I told Dexter to put it on the release schedule simply as a favour to a friend and colleague from whom one day I would probably have to ask the same in return."

In fact, Dexter was to say that he had already made his mind up to release the Beatles single. He had been in London on his annual trip to EMI and Tony Palmer had been asking him to listen to the record before he returned to Hollywood. He agreed to listen "under protest" but remembers, "The first four bars of the song, that guitar just grabbed me. A five-year-old kid, an eighty-year-old man would have picked that record."

Brian Epstein also flew to New York to meet with Brown Meggs, who was Director of Eastern Operations for Capitol. He brought with him a copy of *I Want To Hold Your Hand* and played it to him. Although Capitol had already turned down three of the Beatles British chart records, Meggs thought the number was suitable for release in America. Livingston then made his promised call to Epstein and said he would be prepared to release a single and an album by the Beatles. Brian then told him, "I'm not going to give them to you unless you agree to spend $40,000 promoting this song."

The song in question was *I Want to Hold Your Hand.*

Although he was the man who claimed, "We don't think the Beatles will do anything in this market," Livingston did not have to live with the stigma as Dick Rowe did as 'the man who turned down the Beatles'."

The group he had rejected three times transformed *Capitol*'s fortunes and Livingston, who was married to film actress Nancy Olsen, was to invite the Beatles to a spectacular party at his Hollywood home that August with guests who included Edward G. Robinson, Jack Palance, Tony Bennett, Gene Barry, Jane Fonda, Richard Chamberlain, Rock Hudson, Groucho Marx, Dean Martin, Hayley Mills, James Stewart and Lloyd Bridges.

In 1963 $40,000 was a vast amount of money to spend on a promotion, as the record amount spent up to that time on a particular record was just $5,000. Livingston decided to take the gamble and launch what would be the biggest single promotional campaign in the history of the record industry.

Capitol's marketing and merchandising department came up with the slogan 'The Beatles Are Coming!' (Just like the cry of 'The British Are Coming! in the first British Invasion) and five million stickers with the message were ordered, with the instruction: "It may sound funny, but we literally want your salesmen to be plastering these stickers on any friendly surface. Involve your friends and relatives. Remember the 'Kilroy Was Here!' cartoon that appeared everywhere about ten years ago? Well, now it's going to be 'The Beatles Are Coming!' stickers that are everywhere you look".

They also announced, "Until further notice, all Capitol sales and promotion staff are ordered to wear the Beatle wigs during the business day. Get those Beatle wigs around properly, and you'll find you're helping to start the Beatle Hair-Do Craze that should be sweeping the country soon."

In the meantime yet another twist of fate had occurred which was to help consolidate the Beatles' massive impact on the American market.

Carroll James was a disc jockey at WWDC-AM, the Washington DC radio station. He received a letter from a listener, fifteen-year-old Marsha Albert Thompson requesting that he play *I Want to Hold Your Hand* by the Beatles. As the record had not been released in America he requested a stewardess with BOAC (British Overseas Airways) to bring him a copy of the record from England.

On December 17th 1963 he invited Marsha into the studio to introduce it. He recalled, "We played the record and I said to the radio audience, 'We'd like to know what you think about the record. Don't call. Please write.'

Despite the particular request to write, listeners began phoning straight away and the switchboard became jammed. James played the single again, an hour later.

Capitol Records had intended issuing *I Want To Hold Your Hand* in America in late January 1964 as a build-up to the Ed Sullivan appearance, but the response in Washington

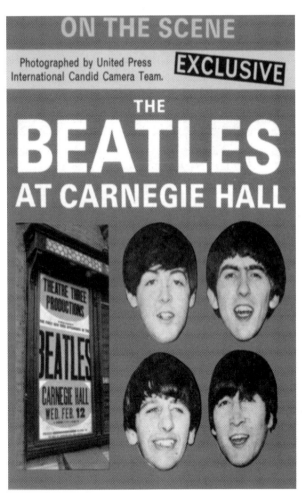

was confusing them. It proved to be so popular that it was being played every day, once an hour. Initially, Capitol considered taking an injunction against the station for playing it when it had not been officially released, but they decided to bring forward the release date to December 27th 1963.

Meanwhile, one of James' friends had taped the number and sent it to a disc jockey in Chicago, who also began having an immediate response – and he sent a tape along to a disc jockey in St Louis. With this entire situation going on, Capitol seemed to have little choice but to bring the release date forward.

Within two weeks of *I Want To Hold your Hand* being released on *Capitol* 5112 on January 13th 1964, with *I Saw Her Standing There* on the flip, there were orders for more than a million copies. *Capitol*'s pressing plant staff were put on overtime, working on shifts around the clock, but they still could not cope with the demand. Capitol had to hire *RCA Records* to press additional copies for them as the number became the fastest selling single in the history of recorded music and was the biggest record that any record company had ever released. Capitol also released the album *Meet The Beatles* on Capitol ST 2047 on January 20th.

Sid Bernstein had also been active. Booking the Beatles for Carnegie Hall was no simple matter. No pop group had ever appeared at the world-famous concert hall and Bernstein knew he would be turned down if it were discovered exactly who the Beatles were. When he phoned to make the booking, a Polish lady asked him who the Beatles were. He told her they were a phenomenon. "Oh, that's all right, then," she said.

Bernstein, who came from the East Bronx and only had a low income, had to borrow the $500 required for the deposit. He had taken a gamble

John Fitzgerald Kennedy

on his hunch because he had booked them without even hearing one of their records and he had no idea what they sounded like.

Another disc jockey who latched on to the Beatles sound earlier than many was Murray Kaufman, known as Murray the K, a New York DJ who had received a copy of *She Loves You* in October 1963 from a promotion man, Bud Helliwell.

Murray recalled that he included it in a contest in which he played five records and asked listeners to vote on them. *She Loves You* came third to *Coney Island Baby* by the Excellents and a Four Seasons single. Murray continued to play the Beatles single for two and a half weeks. Nothing seemed to happen so he dropped it and went off to Miami in mid-January for his vacation. Suddenly, while

listening to the radio there, it seemed as if every other record being played was the Beatles' *I Want To Hold Your Hand*. Then he received a phone call from his programme director Joel Chaseman at 1010 WINS, telling him to return to the station as the Beatles were coming.

"Get yourself an exterminator," Kaufman told him, but his director was firm. Murray's job was on the line, so he cut short his holiday to attend the Beatles' airport press conference.

The bringing forward of the release date resulted in the Beatles being in the No 1 position in the American charts shortly prior to their *Ed Sullivan Show* appearance. The coincidence of Sullivan being at Heathrow when he was ensured they were on America's major entertainment television show at exactly the right time. The far-sightedness of Bernstein ensured that they would become the first pop act ever to appear at the prestigious Carnegie Hall, shortly after the impact of their Sullivan show.

Another element was a tragic one. President John F. Kennedy had been assassinated on November 24th 1963 and America had been in mourning. The emergence of the Beatles was to help put a smile back on America's face after such a devastating tragedy.

The build up began when *The Jack Parr Show* broadcast a short clip of the Beatles performing *She Loves You* on the evening of Friday January 3rd 1964. It was a highly rated NBC show and the clip had been filmed at the Beatles' Manchester concert on November 20th 1963.

Jack Parr may take the credit for being the first person to introduce the Beatles on a major American television entertainments show, but he marred the historic occasion by making snide remarks about their haircuts and the fans they attracted, with comments such as, "I understand scientists are working on a cure for this." Despite this unnecessary flippancy, when the Beatles appeared on the *Ed Sullivan Show* on February 9th 1964 their first three numbers were dedicated to Parr's daughter, Randy.

JFK airport

The Beatles were at the George V Hotel in Paris on the evening of January 17th when they were given the news that *I Want To Hold Your Hand* was No. 1 in the American charts. Road manager Mal Evans was to describe the excitement the Beatles displayed at the news: "They always act this way when anything big happens – just a bunch of kids, jumping up and down with sheer delight. Paul climbed on my back demanding a piggyback. They felt that this was the biggest thing that could have happened. And who could blame them? Gradually they quietened down, ordered some more drinks and sat down to appreciate fully what had happened. It was a wonderful, marvellous night for all of them. I was knocked out".

The Beatles continued their celebration until 5am.

Norman Weiss, Vice President of General Artists Corporation was also in Paris, and met Brian Epstein to confirm the Carnegie Hall concerts on behalf of Bernstein. The agreement now was for a payment of $7,000 against 60% of the gross receipts.

A week before they left for America, the Beatles first met Phil Spector at a party at Decca promotion man Tony Hall's London house. They were somewhat apprehensive about their forthcoming trip to America, a country only George had visited, and then only briefly, and were asking the American recording man what they should expect when they arrived in New York. It ended up where the

The Beatles at the Cavern before their success in America

Beatles asked Spector if he would fly over with them.

Although Spector was actually afraid of flying, he was to recall that the flight was: "A lot of fun. It was probably the only time I flew that I wasn't afraid, because I knew that they weren't going to get killed in a plane.

"That plane was really an awful trip. I mean there were twenty-eight or thirty minutes where the plane dropped thousands of feet over the ocean. It scared the shit out of me, but there were 140 people on board who were all press and Beatles right-hand men and left hand men, and we just sat together and talked about the Apollo and all that jive. Lennon was with his first wife, and he was very quiet. Paul asked a lot of questions.

George was wonderful. It was a nice trip."

When they landed the Beatles turned to Spector and asked a favour. He said, "It's really funny but they were terribly frightened to get off the plane. They were really frightened of America. They said 'you go first'. Because the whole thing about Kennedy scared them very, very much. They really thought it would be possible for somebody to be there and want to kill them".

They had flown out of Heathrow Airport on Pan Am Flight 101, on 'Clipper Defiance' in the First Class section of the plane. Apart from Spector the other First Class passengers were Cynthia Lennon, Brian Epstein and George Harrison of the Liverpool Echo. They were present-

JFK - the press conference

ed with a lavish lunch of champagne, caviar, lobster and smoked salmon and Paul McCartney mused, "Since America has always had everything, why should we be over there making money? They've got their own groups. What are we going to give them that they don't already have?"

Other passengers included photographer Dezo Hoffmann and Cavern club boss Ray McFall, who alighted wearing a fur hat he had bought in Hamburg. Businessmen who were trying to obtain Beatles merchandising rights occupied other seats in the plane, along with the representatives of the press. The businessmen kept sending notes to Epstein, who ignored them. Neil Aspinall and Mal Evans, the Beatles' road managers, spent a great deal of time forging the Beatles' signatures on photographs.

They arrived at John F. Kennedy Airport in New York City at 1.35 pm on Friday, February 7th 1964.

There were 5,000 fans gathered at the airport, mainly on the balcony above the customs hall, waving banners with messages such as 'Welcome to Beatlesville USA' and singing 'We love you Beatles, Oh yes we do".

As the passengers alighted, each was given a Beatle kit with the compliments of Capitol Records. This comprised a 'signed' photograph, and 'I like the Beatles' badge and a Beatles wig.

There was a 100-man police cordon holding back the crowds and escorting the Beatles to the customs hall and one policeman said, "I think the world has gone mad," while another commented, "Boy, can they use a haircut."

All their luggage was thoroughly examined in the customs hall while airport officials said that they had experienced nothing like it since General MacArthur had returned from Korea.

Brian Sommerville, the group's press agent, had arrived a few days earlier to co-ordinate the press and there were two hundred press representatives waiting for them on the first floor of the main terminal. "The two hundred journalists and photographers were almost impossible to control and they ignored Sommerville's request for order – until John Lennon shouted at them to "Shut up!" This was greeted with applause, followed by a quiet spell during which Sommerville was able to introduce each member of the group and the question and answer session began.

Q: "Are you in favour of lunacy?"
Paul: "Yeah. It's healthy."
Q: "Will you be getting a haircut?"
George: "We had one yesterday"
Q: "Will you sing something?"
John: "No, we need money first."
Q: "Which one of you is really bald?"
Paul: "I'm bald."
John: "We're all bald."
Q: "Is there any truth to the rumour that you're really just four Elvis Presleys?"
Ringo: "No, nah, we're not". (His voice mimicking Elvis).
Q: "What is the secret of your success?"
Ringo: "We have a press agent."
Q: "What do you think of the campaign in Detroit to 'Stamp out the Beatles'?"
John: "We have a campaign to stamp out Detroit."
Q: "Are you part of a social rebellion against the older generation?"
Paul: "No, it's a dirty lie."
All: "Yeah, a dirty lie."
Q: "Ringo, why do you wear two rings on each hand?"
Ringo: "Because I can't fit them through my nose."
Q: "Do you think it's wrong to set such a bad example to teenagers, smoking the way you do?"
Ringo: "It's better than being alcoholics."
Q: "What do you think of the criticism that you are not very good?"
George: "We're not."
Q: "What do you believe is the reason you are the most popular singing group today?"
John: "We've no idea. If we did we'd get four long-haired boys, put them together, and become their managers."
Q: "What do you miss most now that your fame prohibits your freedom?"
Ringo: "Going to the movies."
George: "Having nothing to do."
John: "School, because you don't have much to do there."
Paul: "Going on buses."
Q: "What do you do when you're cooped up in a hotel room between shows?"
George: "We ice skate."
Q: "How did you find America?"
Ringo: "We went to Greenland and made a left turn?"
Q: "Would you like to walk down the street without being recognised?"

John: "We used to do that with no money in our pockets. There's no point in it".

Q: "How do you keep your psychic balance?"

Ringo: "The important thing is not to get potty. There's four of us, so whenever one of us gets a little potty, the other three bring him back to earth"

Q: "Does all the adulation from teenage girls affect you?"

John: "When I feel my head start to swell, I look at Ringo and know perfectly well we're not supermen."

Q: "How do you feel about the invasion of your privacy all the time?"

Ringo: "The only time it bothers us is when they get us to the floor and really mangle us".

Q: "Do you speak French?"

Paul: "*Non.*"

Q: "Do you have any special advice for teenagers?"

John: "Don't get pimples."

Q: "What would you do if the fans got past the police lines?"

George: "We'd die laughing."

Q: "What will you do when the bubble bursts?"

George: "Take up ice-hockey."

Paul: "Play baseball."

Q: "Has success spoiled the Beatles?"

John: "Well, you don't see us running out and buying bowler hats. Do you? I think we've pretty well succeeded in remaining ourselves"

Paul: "The great thing about it is that you don't have big worries anymore when you've got where we are, only little ones – like whether the plane is going to crash"

Q: "What is the biggest threat to your careers, the atom bomb or dandruff?"

Ringo: "The atom bomb. We've already got dandruff".

At the press conference the questions about their hairstyle were numerous because the 'moptop' seemed to fascinate Americans. Throughout their press conferences they were asked questions such as "What excuse do you have for your collar-length hair?" "What do you do with your long hair in the shower?" "Do you have any plans for a haircut?" "Does your hair require any special care" and so on. When Paul was asked, "Do you ever go unnoticed?" he replied, "When we take off our wigs".

On their arrival the New York Herald Tribune reported, "The Beatles' hairstyle is a mop effect that covers the forehead, some of the ears and most of the back of the neck".

The Beatles never wore wigs, of course, but Beatle wigs were manufactured in vast quantities in America, although they looked more like the hair style of Mo Howard of the Three Stooges than the Beatles style. On their arrival American photographers and journalists kept tugging their hair, asking them if they were wearing wigs.

It was a case of wigmania! The media seemed obsessed with the hairstyle. New York radio station WMCA ran a competition for listeners to paint or draw someone in a Beatlewig – either celebrity pictures clipped from newspapers or photos of friends. The most popular subjects were: Nikita Krushchev, Mayor Wagner, Alfred E. Newman (of Mad magazine), Brigitte Bardot and the Jolly Green Giant.

Capitol Records instructed all their sales staff to wear Beatles wigs during the working day until further notice and issued a memo, "Get these Beatle wigs around properly, and you'll find yourself helping to start the Beatle Hair-Do craze that should be sweeping the country soon.

An example of the way in which the Beatles altered the style and fashions of the 60s is provided by the fact that the male youth of America began to grow their hair long, in contrast to the almost military short back and sides of previous years. Paul McCartney was to say, "There they were in America, all getting housetrained for adulthood with their indisputable principle of life: short hair equals men; long hair equals women. Well, we got rid of that small convention for them. And a few others too."

MURRAY THE K

Over the years Murray Kaufman kept in touch with the Beatles and visited them in London where he attended their appearance at the *New Musical Express Award* winner's concert at Wembley Stadium and interviewed them during the filming of *A Hard Day's Night*. He also travelled to the Queen Elizabeth Hotel, Montreal, some years later when John and Yoko had a 'Bed-In' and was one of the celebrities present who provided the background clapping to *Give Peace A Chance*.

The interviews he conducted with the Beatles in London, New York, Miami and Washington were issued as an EP (Extended Player) called *The Beatles And Murray The K.*

As It Happened and George Harrison penned an introduction to his autobiography *Murray The K Tells It Like It Is, Baby*, published in America in 1966.

The disc jockey also appeared as himself in the 1978 film *I Wanna Hold Your Hand* which followed the adventures of a bunch of youngster attempting to see the Beatles on their first American visit.

Kaufman was also technical adviser to the *Beatlemania* stage show and participated in a major Beatles Festival at Knotts Berry Farm in 1981.

He died of cancer in Los Angeles on February 21st 1982.

Despite the unprecedented interest by the media, a handful seemingly remained unimpressed if the statement by Chet Huntley of *NBC Evening News* was anything to go by: "Like a good little news organisation, we sent three cameramen out to Kennedy Airport today to cover the arrival of a group from England known as the Beatles. However, after surveying the film our men returned with, and the subject of that film, I feel there is absolutely no need to show any of that film."

An editorial in the New York World Telegram read: "Having got rich off 'teenage lunacy' in their home stompings, these fantastic characters now have come to tap the jackpot – New York, Washington, Miami, American Television. Their shrewdness in assaying a market is evidenced by the 4000 screaming, hookey-playing school-age adulators who swooned all over the airport when the Beatles arrived in New York."

"These lads cultivate a vague allusion to being musicians, in a gurgling sort of way. They tote instruments but blandly assure their fans they know not a note. (All their notes are in the bank). Their production seems to be a haunting combination of rock 'n' roll, the shimmy, a hungry cat riot and Fidel Castro on a harangue."

After the press reception the Beatles were driven in air-conditioned Cadillac limousines to the famous Plaza Hotel, a very conservative establishment on West 58th Street. Writer Tom Wolfe, then writing for the *New York Herald Tribune*, accompanied them and reported; "The Beatles left the airport in four Cadillac limousines, one Beatle to a limousine, heading for the Plaza Hotel in Manhattan. The first sortie came almost immediately. Five kinds in a powder blue Ford overtook the caravan on the expressway, and as they passed each Beatle, one guy hung out the back window and waved a red blanket."

"A white convertible came up second, with the word BEETLES scratched on both sides in the dust. A police car was close behind that one with the siren going and the alarm light rolling, but the kids, a girl at the wheel and two guys in the back seat, waved at each Beatle before pulling over to exit with the cops gesturing at them."

As they arrived the Beatles discovered that the hotel was surrounded by crowds of fans, held in check by one hundred New York City cops with a squad of mounted police.

The management issued a statement that the hotel would not have accepted the bookings if they had known who the Beatles were. They had assumed they were English businessmen. There has been some doubt cast upon this story, as the hotel certainly knew who the Beatles were, and the hotel staff queued up for autographs. However, the Plaza had previously banned Elvis Presley and Chubby Checker.

Later, when George was asked, "What made you pick the Plaza?" He replied, "I didn't. Our manager did. All I can tell you is I don't like the food."

The Beatles were taken to the ten-room Presidential suite (Suites 1209 to 1216) on the twelfth floor, which overlooked 58th Street. Guards from the Burns Detective Agency sealed one of the corridors off and there were two guards on duty around the clock. The suites contained expensive modern furniture in creams, browns and turquoise. Fan mail was brought to them there, and there was also camera and radio equipment stored there by the various media who came for interviews. While the Beatles were sitting around they took a call from Brian Matthew in London for an interview on *Saturday Club*.

Matthew was a BBC radio host who worked with the Beatles more than any other radio personality in Britain and *Saturday Club* was a prestigious radio show which was originally launched in 1958 as a showcase for up-and-coming talent.

Persistent disc jockey Murray the K had returned from Miami and before the Beatles arrived began announcing on his station the airline, flight number and approximate time that the Beatles would be arriving.

At the airport press conference he had managed to attract their attention. He was wearing a hat with a straw brim and was at the forefront of the reporters. He started a conversation with George who said, "I love your hat" and Murray said, "Here, you can have it".

A CBS cameraman said, "Tell Murray the K to cut the crap".

Quick as a flash, Ringo said, "Cut the crap! Yeah, Murray".

He contacted the Beatles at the Plaza and conducted a radio interview with them over the phone. This tickled their interest and they did not object when he turned up at the hotel the next day. They were apparently aware of him from the sleeve notes he had made on various record albums, and he told them: 'You're what's happening, baby'. Murray was to become the omnipresent disc jockey during their first trip.

The next day, a Saturday, found George in bed with a throat problem, strep throat. His sister Louise had arrived at the hotel and moved in to nurse him. The hotel doctor, Dr Gordon, told George, "I'll have to get you fit, otherwise my young relatives will blunt all my needles". He did, however, insist on a signed photograph before starting treatment.

The rest of the group attended another press reception in the Plaza's Baroque Room during which one female reporter noticed Ringo smoking and told him that it set a bad example for teenagers. Ringo said, "Who's a teenager? I'm twenty-three', and an angry John Lennon rounded on her, "We're not here to set examples for teenagers."

The Q and A session between the Beatles and the press began:

Q: "John, is the reaction to the group the same here as in England?"
John: "I find it's very similar, only over here they go wilder quicker, you know."
Q: "Will you sing a song for us?"
John: "No. Sorry, we need money first."
Q: "How much money do you expect to make here?"
John: "About half a crown. Depends on the tax. How much have you got?"
Q: "Some of your detractors allege that you are bald and those haircuts are wigs. Is that true?"
John: "Oh, we're all bald. Yeah. And deaf and dumb too."
Q: What is the Beatle sound?"
John; "Well, as far as we are concerned, there's no such thing as a Liverpool or even a Beatles sound. It's just a name that people tag on."
Q: "One of your hits is 'Roll Over Beethoven'. What do you think of

Beethoven as a composer?"
Ringo: "He's great. Especially his poems."
Q: "Are these your real names?"
Paul: "Yeah, except Ringo. His name's Richard Starkey. He's called Ringo because of his rings, you know. And Starr, he didn't like Starkey."
Q: "Do all the Beatles write songs?"
John: "Paul and I do most of the writing. George has written a few. Ringo hasn't, because it's hard to write something on the drums, isn't it?"
Ringo: "Yes" Q: "How do you account for your fantastic success?"
Paul: "Wish we knew."
John: "Good press agent."
Q: "Why do millions of Beatles fans buy millions of Beatles records?"
John: "If we knew, we'd form another group and become their managers"
Q: "What do you think of American girls compared to British girls?"
Paul: "The accents are different, of course. In films American women always seem to be bossing the men, being superior in big business and things. But from what I've seen, they're not. They're very similar to British women, just ordinary people, very nice."
Q: "Where did the name 'Beatle' come from?"
George: "We were just racking our brains and John came up with the name Beatle. It was good because it was an insect and it was also a pun, you know, 'beat', on the beat. We liked the name and we kept it."
Q: "Have you been influenced by any one American artist?"
George: "In the early days it was Elvis Presley, Carl Perkins, Chuck Berry, Little Richard and Buddy Holly. But there's no one we tried to copy."
Q: "Why do you wear your hair in such an unusual style?"
George: "Well, I went to the swimming baths and when I came out my hair dried and it was just all forward like a mop. I left it like that. When Ringo joined the group we got him to get his hair like this because by then people were calling it the Beatles cut."
Q: "Do you contemplate becoming permanent residents of the US?"

George: "I love the States, but if we came to live over here everybody would go mad. It's like Elvis, if he went to, say, Australia and then suddenly decided to live there. What would all the American people think?"

Q: "Paul, what are your ambitions?"

Paul: "We used to have lots of ambitions. Like number one records, 'Sunday Night At The Palladium', 'The Ed Sullivan Show', to go to America. A thousand ambitions like that. I can't really think of any more. We've lived an awful lot of them."

Q: "Paul, what is your aim in life?"

Paul: "To have a laugh, you know, to be happy."

Q: "John, is it a fad?"

John: Obviously. Anything in this business is a fad. We don't think we're going to last forever. We're just going to have a good time while it lasts."

Murray the K breezed into their suite with the Ronettes, still recording his show. "We're what's happening, Babe. We're Murray the K and the Beatles, Babe on W.I.N.S". The Beatles admired his nerve and he became one of their regular escorts over the following few days, literally running their social life, taking them to various nightclubs and restaurants and introducing them to starlets such as Stella Stevens, Tuesday Weld and Jill Haworth.

Incidentally, Paul began a relationship with Haworth and visited her at her apartment. She said, "He wanted

a good cup of tea and he couldn't get it at the Plaza and he came to my apartment."

He next called her up and invited her to stay in Miami while the Beatles were there. Paul arranged for payment of her trip, although she was booked into another hotel while they

Carl Perkins

stayed at the Deauville. "A car would be sent for me to take me over there," she said. Paul wanted to keep the relationship out of the press, as Jane Asher was still his girlfriend.

On the Saturday evening Capitol Records hosted a special dinner party for the Beatles at the prestigious 21

Club. George Harrison was absent due to his throat infection and Ringo quipped to one of the waiters, "Do you have any vintage coke?" When asked at a press conference if they had enjoyed their dinner at the club, a journalist added, "Did they feed you on pheasant and stuff?"

"Pheasant, you're joking! I had chops and chips" was the reply.

A report in the New York Herald Tribune read: "The Beatles are all short, slight kids from Liverpool who wear four-button coats, stovepipe pants, ankle-high black boots with Cuban heels and droll looks on their faces. The Plaza, one of the most sedate hotels in New York was petrified. The reservations were accepted months ago before the Plaza knew it was for a rock and roll group."

The Beatles had to become members of the AFRA trade union before they could start rehearsals at the CBS Studios. They were located at 50 Broadway and West 53rd Street on the premises of the former Maxine Elliott Theatre. The theatre provided seating for the audience of 728 people and there was an unprecedented demand of over 60,000 ticket requests.

The group began their rehearsals without George who was still suffering with his throat and had remained behind at the Plaza Hotel. Neil Aspinall stood in for him at the rehearsals and a concerned Sullivan was assured that George would be present on the actual show itself.

"He'd better be or I'm putting on a wig myself," Sullivan said.

On February 9th there was a dress rehearsal and the taping of another *Ed Sullivan Show* to be broadcast on Sunday February 23rd, after the Beatles had returned to London. They performed *Twist And Shout*, *Please Please Me* and *I Want To Hold Your Hand*.

Ed Sullivan made an announcement, "All of us on the show are so darned sorry, and sincerely sorry, that this is the third and thus our last current show with the Beatles, because these youngsters from Liverpool, England, and their conduct over here, not only as fine professional singers but as a group of fine youngsters, will leave an imprint on everyone over here who's met them."

That evening Murray the K took them to the Playboy Club (Paul said 'The bunnies are even more adorable than we are' and it is alleged he took one of the bunnies to another hotel to spend the night with her) and then John, Paul and Ringo accompanied him to the famous Peppermint Lounge. Others in the party included John's wife Cynthia and press agent Brian Sommerville. The group declined to participate in the club's 'Twist Revue'. But Ringo took to the dance floor to 'do the Twist' with Peppermint Lounge captain Marlene Klaire, who was to comment

later, "It was that exhausting that it felt like a Beatle was on me, and I had to shake it off".

During the evening a group called the Seven Fabulous Epics – featuring the Four Younger Brothers, alias the American Beatles – played Beatle numbers, while wearing Beatle wigs!

The show itself drew the biggest audience for an entertainment programme in the history of television. An estimated 73,000,000 viewers saw the programme and it was reported that the crime rate amongst teenagers throughout America dropped to virtually zero that night.

Conductor Leonard Bernstein had requested tickets for his two daughters and Wendy Hanson, Epstein's personal assistant, arranged seats for them in the front row. She escorted Bernstein to the Beatles' dressing room. After he had left, John Lennon told her, "Look, luv, could you keep Sidney Bernstein's family out of this room".

Brian Epstein approached Sullivan with the request, "I would like to know the exact wording of your introduction".

Sullivan replied, "I would like you to get lost".

The show went on the air at 8pm and Sullivan opened with the words, "Now, yesterday and today, our theatre's been jammed with newspapermen and hundreds of photographers from all over the nation, and these veterans agree with me that the city never has witnessed the excitement stirred up by these youngsters from Liverpool, who call themselves the Beatles. Now, tonight, you'll twice be entertained by them – right now and in the second half of the show."

Sullivan also read out a congratulatory telegram from Elvis Presley (it had actually been sent by Colonel Parker), which stated, "Congratulations on your appearance on the Ed Sullivan Show and your first visit to America. We hope your engagement will be a successful one and your visit pleasant. Give our best

Elvis Presley

to Mr Sullivan. Sincerely, Elvis & the Colonel".

The Beatles then opened with Paul singing *All My Loving*. This was followed by *Till There Was You*, also sung by Paul. During this number their Christian names were flashed on the screen and when it was John's turn, there was also the comment, 'Sorry girls, he's married!' They ended the first part of the show with *She Loves You'*

Sullivan then announced that they would be back in the second half of the show and that the three numbers they had played had been dedicated to Randy Parr (daughter of the TV host Jack Parr). When the Beatles returned they performed *I Saw Her Standing There* and *I Want To Hold Your Hand*. During the last number, one of the mikes went dead. (For more details see: 'The Beatles On Ed Sullivan).

The show's producer was Bob Precht and the musical director was Ray Bloch.

The Neilson ratings indicated that it was Sullivan's highest rating show with 45.3 per cent of all TV sets in America tuned to the programme.

The performance was widely reported in the American press the next day and the Herald Tribune was to comment that the Beatles were: "75% publicity, 20% haircut and 5% lilting lament', while Newsweek reported: 'Visually they are a nightmare: tight, dandified Edwardian beatnik suits and great pudding bowls of hair. Musically they are a near disaster, guitars and drums slamming out a merciless beat that does away with secondary

rhythms, harmony and melody."

The New York Times reported, "The Beatles bounce erupted in Manhattan yesterday as the young men with heads like unmade beds made their first public appearance here at the CBS Studio at 53rd Street and Broadway. The bounce was introduced by 800 frenzied fans on the edge of hysteria and their seats who shrieked out their love for the bundles from Britain."

"From the moment the Beatles began blasting out *All My Loving* the kids bounced like dervishes in their seats to the driving beat. With the Beatle Bounce, performed best by wild-eyed girls aged between ten and fifteen, but likely to infect adults, goes a wild screaming as if Dracula had just appeared on stage. The screams reached a pitch dangerous to the eardrums at times when the Beatles shook their shaggy locks".

Evangelist Billy Graham had decided to watch television on the Sabbath to see what all the fuss was about, and later commented: "They're a passing phase. All are symptoms of the uncertainty of the times and the confusion about us."

Monday February 10th saw them conducting more press interviews during the day and Alan Livingston presented them with gold discs for a million sales of *I Want To Hold Your Hand* and a million dollars worth of sales for 'Meet The Beatles'. They also spent another night clubbing and returned to the Plaza at 4 am.

On Tuesday February 11th the Beatles performed their first live outdoor American concert appearance at

the Washington Coliseum in Washington D.C.

The group were due to fly down to Washington from New York but there was a snowstorm. The Beatles refused to fly in a blizzard, remembering what had happened to Buddy Holly a few years earlier, so arrangements were made for them to travel down in a private train coach from Pennsylvania Station in New York to Union Station in Washington. When they arrived there were 3,000 fans at the station, but they were prevented from approaching the Beatles by the twenty-foot high platform gates.

The group were rushed to the Shoreham Hotel. The entire seventh floor had been booked for them and their entourage, but one family had refused to move out of their room. While the Beatles were at the Coliseum the assistant manager cut off the family's light, heat and water and told them there had been a power failure on the seventh floor. They agreed to be relocated to the ninth floor.

That day the Beatles met up with Carroll James, the Washington disc jockey who had first begun playing their record in the States. He was the person who was to introduce them on stage that evening and he also recorded a ten-minute interview with them earlier in the day at the WWDC studio using, as his theme, the various questions that listeners had sent to him. For example, "what would Paul have been when he grew up if he hadn't joined the Beatles?" Paul said he might have become a teacher, but felt it was a good thing he had become a Beatle because "I think

I would have been a bad teacher". James asked John whether he liked tea or coffee. John told him he preferred tea. "How about tea bags?" asked James. "I don't like them, " John answered, "They get stuck in me teeth."

When he asked them what their influences were, he was told "Small Blind Johnny". When he asked who Small Blind Johnny was, the reply was,"Oh yes, he played with Big Deaf Arthur."

Carroll turned to John and said, "John, they call you the chief Beatle...".

John replied, "Carroll, I don't call *you* names!"

He asked "Excluding America and England, what are your favourite countries you've visited?"

"Excluding American and England, what's left?" asked John.

"Does anyone in the group speak a foreign language?" he asked.

"We all speak fluent shoe," said Paul.

The most perplexing part of the interview came from the conversation with George. When James asked him what he would have become without the Beatles, George said, "I wanna be a baggy sweeger". James asked, "A baggy sweeger?" "Oh, yeah" said George, "you know, in every town there's twenty-five baggy sweegers and every morning they get up and go to the airport and baggy sweeger all around."

The Beatles also held a press reception while they were in Washington:

Q: "Do any of you have any formal musical training?"
John; "You're joking."
Q: "What do you think of President Johnson?"
Paul: "Does he buy our records?"
Q: "What do you think of American girls and American audiences?"
John: "Marvellous."
Q: "Here I am, surrounded by the Beatles and I don't feel a thing. Fellas, how does it feel to be in the United States?"
John; "It's great."
Q: "What do you like best about our country?"
John: "You!"
Q: "I'll take that under advisement. Do you have any plans to meet the Johnson girls?"
John: "No. We heard they didn't like our concerts."
Q: "Are they coming to your performance tonight?"
Paul: "If they do, we'd really like to meet them"
Q: "You and the snow came to Washington today. Which do you think will have the greater impact?"
John: "The snow will probably last longer."
Q: "One final question. Have you heard of Walter Cronkite?"
Paul: "Nope."
John: "NBC News, is he? Yeah, we know him."
Q: "Thanks, fellas. By the way, it's CBS News."
John: "I know, but I didn't want to say it as we're now on ABC"
Q: "This is NBC, believe it or not"
John: "And you're Walter?"
Q: "No, I'm Ed"

John: "What's going on around here?"
Q: "What do you think of your reception in America so far?"
John: "It's been great"
Q: "What struck you the most?"
John: "You!"
Q: "We already did that joke when we first came in."
John: "Well, we're doing it again, squire!"
Q: "Why do you think you're so popular?"
John: "It must be the weather."
Q: "Do you think it's your singing?"
Paul: "I doubt it. We don't know which it could be."
Q: "Where'd you get the idea for the haircuts?"
John: "Where'd you get the idea for yours?"
Paul: "We enjoyed wearing our hair like this so it's developed this way."
Q: "Well, you save on haircutting at least."
Paul; "Roar…"
John: "I think it costs more to keep it short than long, don't you?"
Paul: "Yeah, we're saving our money."
Q: "Are you still number one in Europe?"
George: "We're number one in America."
Q: "Where else are you number one then?"
John: "Hong Kong and Sweden…"
Paul: "Australia, Denmark and Finland."
Q: "And you haven't any idea why?"
Ringo: "We just lay down and do it."
John: "In Hong Kong and these other places, suddenly you're number one

years after putting out your records. Even here, we've got records we've probably forgotten about"

Q: "You call your records 'funny records'?"

John: "'Funny', yeah, the ones we've forgotten."

George: "It's unusual because they've been out in England for over a year. Like 'Please Please Me' is a big hit over here now but it's over a year old."

Q: "Do you think they're musical?"

John: "Obviously they're musical because its music, isn't it! We make music. Instruments play music. It's a record."

Q: "What do you call it, rock and roll?"

Paul: "We try not to define our music because we get so many wrong classifications off it. We call it music even if you don't."

Q: "With a question mark?"

George; "Pardon?"

John: "We leave that to the critics"

Q: "Okay, that's it. Have a good time in America."

John: "Thank you. Keep buying them records and look after yourself."

The Beatles took to the stage at 8.31pm, following acts such as Tommy Roe and the Chiffons.

Roe had had his first hit 'Sheila' in 1962. The Beatles had liked the number so much they included it in their own repertoire, with George Harrison as lead vocalist. The Beatles also embarked on a month-long tour of Britain with Roe and Chris Montez in March 1963.

The Chiffons were a female vocal group comprising Patricia Bennett, Barbara Lee, Sylvia Peterson and Judy Craig, who had enjoyed their biggest hit, *He's So Fine*, the previous year. It was a number penned by their manager Ronnie Mack and ironically, almost ten years later, George was to be sued for allegedly plagiarising the number with *My Sweet Lord*.

They performed from a rotating stage before an audience of more than eight thousand fans and the noise was so deafening that they could not even hear themselves perform. They were

pelted by jellybeans for the first time. Unlike the soft British jelly babies, the beans were covered by a hard shell and rained down on them like bullets.

Jelly babies had proved something of a problem for the Beatles. During their British tour with Roy Orbison, fans began throwing jelly babies on stage because they had heard that George liked them. This soon became a standard procedure at concerts and increased to an extent where it became dangerous with literally thousands of the sweets being hurled at the group during their shows.

This was obviously worse in America because of the hard coated jellybean.

George was to comment: "They hurt. Some newspaper had dug out the old joke, which we'd forgotten about, when John once said I'd eaten all his jelly babies. Everywhere we went I got them thrown at me. They don't have soft jelly babies in America but hard jellybeans like bullets."

After the Coliseum appearance, Ringo commented, "Some of them even threw jelly beans in bags and they hurt like hailstones."

The group performed *Roll Over Beethoven*, *From Me To You*, *I Saw Her Standing There*, *This Boy*, *All My Loving*, *I Wanna Be Your Man*, *Please Please Me*, *Till There Was You*, *She Loves You*, *I Want to Hold Your Hand*, *Twist And Shout* and *Long Tall Sally*. Immediately after they finished their act they rushed to their dressing rooms surrounded by a phalanx of twelve policemen. A happy Ringo exclaimed, "They could have ripped me apart and I couldn't have cared less. What an audience! I could have played for them all night".

After the show, Paul said, "The atmosphere was electric. We came onstage to the most tremendous reception I have ever heard in my life. Our publicist, Brian Sommerville, who is normally a hardheaded businessman, had tears in his eyes as he was rearranging Ringo's drum kit. I told him to go dry up, but the reaction was so overwhelming that even I was on the point of tears".

Brian Epstein

A camera team from CBS was present filming the concert for a special closed circuit presentation to be screened at cinemas on March 14th and 15th. The film, entitled *Live At The Washington Coliseum* featured *Roll Over Beethoven*, *From Me To You*, *I Saw Her Standing There*, *This Boy*, *All My Loving'* and *I Wanna Be Your Man'*. The ending came part way through a version of *Twist And Shout* because the cameraman had run out of film!

This was not the only filming that took place during this first American visit. Two American filmmakers Albert and David Maysles filmed the Beatles during this trip for a documentary released that year in Britain by Granada Television called *Yeah Yeah Yeah – the Beatles In New York*.

They also used their footage to assemble another documentary of the trip called 'What's Happening; The Beatles In The USA' which was not released until 1967. This followed the Beatles on that February 1964 trip, covering their stay in New York,

their train journey to Washington D.C., their appearance on *The Ed Sullivan Show* and included several interviews.

Reporting on their Washington concert, Leroy Aarons wrote in the Washington Post: "An eight thousand voice choir performed last night at Washington Coliseum, accompanied incidentally by four young British artists who call themselves the Beatles. The effect is like being downwind from a jet during take-off. Interesting possibilities, what with the trend toward electronic music and all. One was impressed by the versatility of the choral group. Their range invites comparison with Yma Sumac, their intensity of emotion with the victim in a Hitchcock film, and Caruso would enjoy their volume".

Brian Epstein had arranged for the Beatles to attend an event at the British Embassy following the Washington Coliseum appearance. Sir David Ormsby-Gore was the British Ambassador at the time and the event was a formal staff dance to raise money for the National Association for the Prevention of Cruelty to Children. Ormsby-Gore had requested that the Beatles present the raffle prizes at the Gala.

News of their appearance had circulated by word of mouth and a cordon of police had to circle the embassy. The Beatles, together with Brian, had a private meeting with Sir David and Lady Ormsby-Gore.

Sir David asked John if he was John, but John said, "No, I'm Fred, he's John" and pointed to George. When Sir David referred to George

as John, George pointed to Ringo and said, "No, I'm Charlie, he's John."

Lady Ormsby-Gore then escorted them into the embassy rotunda, announcing, "Attention! Beatles are now approaching the area".

No one in their party was prepared for the behaviour from guests and staff, many of who had had more than their fair share of punch that evening. They were jostled and pushed around. There were condescending remarks such as 'those darling little baby boys' and one woman put her arm around Paul and asked, "Which one are you?" "Roger" he told her. "Roger what?" she asked. "Roger McClusky the fifth," he said.

John Lennon was furious at the treatment and wanted to leave. When an embassy official told him, "Come on now, go do your stuff," he said, "I'm getting out of here," but Ringo took hold of his arm and suggested that they get it over with.

When reports of the rude behaviour filtered out, the British press was incensed and Conservative MP Joan Quennell asked the foreign secretary, R. A. Butler, to look into the affair.

However, the real diplomat turned out to be Brian Epstein who, not wishing to make a fuss out of the situation, sent a thank-you note to Lady Ormsby-Gore.

Incidentally, it was the first and last time the Beatles ever accepted an invitation to attend a British Embassy. Lady Dixon, wife of the British Ambassador to Paris had invited them to their Embassy, but they had declined. Of the Washington affair, George commented, "We always tried to get out of those crap things. But that time we got caught. They were always full of snobby people who really loathe our type, but want to see us because we're rich and famous. It's all hypocrisy. They were just trying to get publicity for the Embassy."

The Beatles returned to New York by train on Wednesday February 12th ready to become the first rock 'n' roll act to appear on Carnegie Hall concerts. They travelled the two hours from Washington and arrived at New York's Penn Station where 10,000 fans were waiting for them and took taxis to their hotel where they showered, changed, and refreshed themselves before moving onto Carnegie Hall for the two thirty-four-minute shows, which took place at 7.45pm and 11.15pm.

Of their return to New York the Daily News reported, "In the shrieking pandemonium, one girl was knocked down and trampled, another fainted and a police sergeant was kicked by a horse. At times the cops could not control the mobs and the Beatle-lovers broke through barricades in wild assaults in the station and the hotel". "The fans surged forwards towards Track Four in the belief that the singers were arriving there. Some of the 30 patrolmen, who had to be reinforced by 20 more, went down to the ground and were trampled. Screams of 'Beatles Forever' and 'I Love Ringo' rang through the station."

"But the British idols were spirited away from the lower level into a taxi at the Seventh Avenue entrance. Discovering they had been cheated, the fans ran out of the station shouting 'On to the Plaza'."

There were 20,000 people milling about outside the hall, trying to get a glimpse of the 'phenomenon'. All 2,870 seats at each show had been sold out in advance and promoter Sid Bernstein had to obtain permission to place one hundred and fifty chairs on the stage.

Incidentally, John Lennon was upset when he saw all the people in the chairs on the stage and said, "It wasn't a rock show, it was a circus where we were in cages being pawed and talked at, touched backstage and onstage. We were just like animals."

Among the VIPs who shared the additional seats on stage were Lauren Bacall and Mrs Happy Rockefeller with her ten-year-old daughter Wendy, although other celebrities were unable to be accommodated.

Bernstein was to say; "It's a status symbol for the kids to be here, just as it's a status symbol for the 300 adults here tonight. I had to turn down David Niven, William Zeckendorf and Shirley MacLaine for tickets, I just didn't have one left."

Among the other acts on the bill were a folk group called the Briarwoods. One of the Beatles' backstage visitors was British singer Shirley Bassey, who was appearing at Carnegie Hall the following week. While backstage they were also presented with a Gold Disc from Swan Records for one million sales of *She Loves You*.

Murray the K was hired to compere their two concerts at Carnegie Hall, during which he announced, "This is your fifth Beatle talking, I'm what's happening, and for one or two of

you who want to leave your seats or throw things, we have people to take care of you."

There were 362 policemen handling security around the hall and Bernstein himself took to the stage to ask the audience to comport themselves in the presence of the foreign press. Disc jockey Murray the K also joked and told the audience not to leave their seats or throw things at the stage. "We have people especially to deal with things like that – but I'm sure you won't let it happen," he said.

Capitol Records had wanted to record the two shows but their attempts to do so have been blocked by the American Federation of Musicians.

For both shows, the Beatles grossed $9,335.78.

Reporting on the concerts, The Daily News commented, "Twenty-nine hundred Beatlemaniacs gave a concert early last evening at Carnegie Hall, accompanied by the thumping, twanging rhythms of the Beatles, an English rock 'n' roll quartet."

"The Beatles enthusiasts, who paid from $3 to $5.50 for the privilege of outshrieking their idols, might have been 99 percent female if one judged by the level of voices that they raised. Physical evidence, however, showed that there were a considerable number of males present, many of whom bounced in their seats but were no less vocal."

"The audience participation lasted for 34 minutes, from the moment the first Beatle mop head could be discerned at 7.45 o'clock moving through the 150 listeners who were seated onstage until all four Beatles fled amid a hail of jelly beans at 8.19 o' clock. During this time the Beatles appeared to be singing and playing 12 songs, each of which was covered almost totally by the enraptured adulations of their devotees".

After the second show, Bernstein walked with Epstein across to the 17,000-seater Madison Square Garden and told him that the huge venue wanted to present the Beatles and he could have the tickets printed up and on sale within twenty-four hours. He offered Epstein $25,000 for the booking and said he would pay an additional $5,000 to the British Cancer Fund. Brian pondered for a moment, then said, "Sid, let's leave it for the next time".

As it turned out, 'the next time' became an even bigger event – the largest-ever-live entertainment presentation up to that time. The box office manager of Carnegie Hall had told Sid that they could have sold 250,000 tickets if they had them. Bernstein then lost interest in Madison Square Garden and began to think in terms of the biggest venue in New York, Shea Stadium, the 55,600-seater baseball park.

He phoned Brian Epstein with the proposal. Epstein demurred. Bernstein told him he was so convinced it would be a success that he'd pay Brian for every empty seat. "Let's do it, Sid," said Epstein.

The spectacular Shea Stadium concert took place in August of the following year.

In the meantime, the Beatles left the Plaza Hotel at 1.30 am for another night out, beginning at the Headliner Club and following with a visit to the Improvisation, a coffee house in Greenwich Village.

The Beatles flew to Miami Beach, Florida on Thursday February 13th to film their second live appearance on the *Ed Sullivan Show*.

They arrived in Miami on National Airlines Flight 11, with a pilot who wore a Beatles wig. When the plane touched down at Miami International Airport at 4pm there were over 7,000 fans waiting, together with four beauty queens and a chimpanzee! The group's arrival caused a riot in which twenty-three glass windows within the airport terminal were smashed and chairs were torn to pieces, resulting in over $2,000 worth of damage.

They arrived at their hotel, the Deauville Hotel, which had been nicknamed 'Beatle Central'. The suite had three bedrooms and John and Cynthia had one room and Paul and Ringo another. George was disgruntled to find he had to share a room with disc jockey Murray the K.

Local police sergeant Buddy Bresner was in charge of their safety and supervised a Beatle patrol of two-dozen officers. Bresner acted as their personal bodyguard, advisor and friend. He had been chosen for the job because he had previously looked after celebrities in the district.

That evening the Beatles accepted the offer of having dinner at his home, where they met his wife Dottie and his children Barry, Andy and Jeri. Dezo Hoffmann, who was also present, was struck by Paul and how he seemed so completely at home with the children. "The unbelievable patience he had with those kids was incredible," Dezo said. "They didn't let him alone for a moment. He sat there reading to them, in a way that was obviously not an inconvenience to him at all – he was completely at home."

Buddy then took them back to the Deauville Hotel, which had a couple of nightclubs. They went in to see comedian Don Rickles who gagged, "Look at this, a police sergeant guarding four Zulus when all over the city there's fighting and burglary going on". After the show John was tired and went to bed, but the others went to the second nightclub to see comedian Myron Cohen and singer/dancer Carol Lawrence. Comedian Cohen liked the Beatles and later commented, "So long as they are still only TRYING to stamp out the Beatles in thirty years' time, who cares?"

Part of Bresner's duties consisted of conducting bed checks every night to make sure there were no girls in their rooms, and no drugs.

Murray the K took them to the Peppermint Lounge to see Hank Ballard and they also watched the Coasters perform in the Mau Mau Lounge of the hotel.

George was not the only one annoyed at Murray the K's presence. A reporter asked, "What the fuck is Murray the K doing here?" George replied, "Murray's the fifth Beatle".

Kaufman then had the audacity to continually refer to himself as 'the fifth Beatle'; a liberty that infuriated Brian Epstein so much that he threatened legal action.

On Saturday February 15th they rehearsed before a live audience dressed in their grey suits with velvet collars, and later, after a trip to the swimming pool, rehearsed without an audience and dressed in their swimming trunks in the Napoleon Room of the hotel.

George Martin arrived at the Deauville and was able to tell them that the recordings he had made at the Carnegie Hall concert had come out fine, although the album was never to be released.

Then, on Sunday February 16th the group performed their television show before a live audience of 3,200 people. Their numbers were 'She Loves You', 'This Boy', 'All My Loving', I Saw Her Standing There, From Me To You and I Want To Hold Your Hand.

The bill topper on this edition of The Ed Sullivan Show was not the Beatles, it was film actress Mitzi Gaynor. Nevertheless, due to the Beatles appearance the show had an estimated audience of 70,000,000.

The Beatles loved Miami so much they decided to remain at the Deauville for a week during which they took in more shows, and Buddy Bresner took them to see Elvis Presley's 'Fun In Acapulco' at a drive-in. They also visited Cassius Clay's (Muhammad Ali) training camp on Tuesday 18th February.

Harold Conrad, who was promoting the World Heavyweight Championship bout between Sonny Liston and Clay, had asked Brian Epstein if the Beatles would like to visit Clay's camp, but the offer was rejected. Following their televised show at the Mau Mau Lounge, Conrad asked Ed Sullivan if he could meet the Beatles and Sullivan took him to their room and introduced him. Paul said, "I think Clay is going to win". Conrad mentioned that the visit to Clay's

Back in England

camp had been turned down, but they said they'd go and John commented, "Don't worry about Brian, we'll handle him."

The boxer and the Beatles clowned it up for the assembled photographers, with shots of Clay standing over a supine group of Beatles on the canvas. The 'Louisville Lip' told the press that although the Beatles were the greatest, he was the prettiest. He made up a poem: "When Liston reads about the Beatles visiting me,

he'll get so mad, I'll knock him out in three". He also commented, "They were regular, friendly, everyday fellows. Success hasn't gone to their heads". A few days later he won the Heavyweight title for the first time.

Clay was to change his name to Muhammad Ali and he won the World Heavyweight Champion title three times.

On hearing Ringo play drums, he joked, "My dog plays better drums".

A local millionaire, Bernie Castro, also lent them his luxurious houseboat in his absence. It had a full staff, including butler and chef, and they were able to enjoy barbequed steaks on board.

At one time Brian Epstein and his temporary personal assistant Wendy Hanson and George Martin and his secretary Judy Lockhart-Smith joined them. Martin remembers that the millionaire benefactor had also left an armed guard to watch over them and he barbequed their steaks with his shoulder holster clearly visible. He says, "Brian was complaining about all the bootleg records that were coming out. Suddenly, this tough-looking guy who was barbequing our steaks leaned forward and said, 'You want we should take care of them for you, Mr Epstein?'".

During their time off John and Paul were also able to write Can't Buy Me Love.

Bresner also arranged some other outings, including a visit to Star Island.

The group finally flew out of Miami at 5.18pm on February 21st.

Another person who was part of the entourage during that first amazing American trip was the syndicated columnist and radio journalist Ed Rudy. Rudy had originally met up with Brian Epstein in New York late in 1963 through a friend, Bud Helliwell, who was promoting the non-Capitol Beatles material in America for Epstein.

He arranged to cover the Beatles' arrival and was at John F. Kennedy Airport, attending the famous press conference. He also travelled with them to Washington and Miami.

Some years later he was to relate in Beatlefan magazine, ""It was great fun. It was a happy time, magic time. We'd drive in my car, I had a station wagon and could get a lot of people in it, and there were reporters and Beatles and we'd tune in to WYNZ."

"Sometimes they tried to run away from the press, but it was nearly impossible. There was no place they could go that someone wouldn't tell us where they were. And sometimes they let some of us go along."

The Beatles flew back to London via Miami, with a short stopover in New York and arrived at Heathrow Airport on Saturday February 22nd, having conquered America and launched the British Invasion. The cumulative effect of the two *Ed Sullivan Shows*, the Carnegie Hall and Washington Coliseum Concerts and the chart-topping *I Want To Hold Your Hand* had a spectacular effect on the American music industry and opened the door to a flood of British artists in the American charts.

The Beatles had pioneered the way for them, just as they had done in Britain for all the groups from the provinces, changing the British music industry for the better.

The phenomenon created by the Beatles was to continue with an incredible record of charts hits, the biggest concert tours ever held in America, including the groundbreaking Shea Stadium concerts.

Another never-to-be repeated achievement occurred on March 31st 1964 when the Beatles occupied the first five places in the American charts:

1. *Twist And Shout*. The Beatles.
2. *Can't Buy Me Love*. The Beatles.
3. '*She Loves You*. The Beatles.
4. *I Want To Hold Your Hand*. The Beatles.
5. '*Please Please Me*' The Beatles.

Although the British Invasion was an incredible turning point in the history of 20th century popular music, the impact of the Beatles was felt throughout the world, particularly in Australia where the Beatles received the biggest on-street receptions of their career when they toured there.

On March 27th 1964 the Australian charts saw the Beatles occupying the first six places:

1. *I Saw Her Standing There*. The Beatles.
2. *Love Me Do*. The Beatles.
3. *Roll Over Beethoven*. The Beatles.
4. *All My Loving*. The Beatles.
5. *She Loves You*. The Beatles.
6. *I Want To Hold Your Hand*. The Beatles.

Following their triumphant American debut, the Beatles returned to Britain on February 22nd 1964 and continued with their recording and television commitments and on March 2nd began filming their debut movie *A Hard Day's Night*. May saw them embark on a World Tour, initially without Ringo due to him collapsing from acute tonsillitis and Jimmy Nicol replaced him for a short time. Ring rejoined the tour in Australia. On their return they attended the premiers of *A Hard Day's Night* in London and Liverpool and during their Liverpool visit were given a Civic Reception.

A Hard Day's Night opened simultaneously in five hundred American cinemas on August 12th. American critics said that it was a triumph and they were compared to the Marx Brothers. The four then set off on their twenty-five-date American tour on August 18th, beginning with an appearance at the Cow Palace, San Francisco the next day. During appearances in the Southern states they emphasised that they refused to appear before segregated audiences and their concert at the Gator Bowl in Jacksonville, Florida took place shortly after Hurricane Dora had passed over the state.

NOW OVER 250,000 READERS EVERY ISSUE — PRICE 6d.

MERSEY BEAT

Vol. 3 No. 86.   JULY 30, 1964   BRITAIN'S LEADING BEAT PAPER

John Lennon: The Literary Beatle

Ringo's Book   Next Beatles Film   Paul's House

September 17th was due to be a rest day but a local promoter in Kansas City offered Brian Epstein US $100,000 for the Beatles to appear at the Municipal Stadium there – and it was an offer too good to refuse. To honour the event they included a version of *Kansas City'/'Hey-Hey-Hey* during their performance. Their final concert took place at the Paramount Theater, New York and was in aid of the United Cerebral Palsy Fund Of New York.

Soon after their return to London they filmed a live appearance before an audience of Beatles Fan Club members at the Granville Theatre, Fulham for the American TV show *Shindig*. More recordings, another British tour and their second Christmas Show, brought them to the end of the year.

Filming of their second feature film *Help!* began in February 1965 and they began a European Tour on June 20th.

Help! opened in America on August 11th and the group arrived at John F Kennedy Airport in New York two days later to begin their second American tour. On August 14th they appeared at the Shea Stadium. This was the biggest concert for a popular music ever held and there was an audience of 55,600. It was an unprecedented event, the brainchild of Sid Bernstein, who had first promoted them at Carnegie Hall the previous year. Other American concerts also provided the Beatles with massive audiences of 22,000, 25,000, even 35,000 fans. During the trip they also became the guests of Elvis Presley, with an invitation to visit 'the King' at his Hollywood home on August 27th. They ended their tour at the Cow Palace and flew back to London on September 1st. On October 26 their received their MBE awards from Queen Elizabeth 11 at Buckingham Palace and continued with their recording and television commitments and also embarked on another British tour.

1966 proved to be their most controversial year and on March 25th they posed for a photograph for their American album *Yesterday and Today*, dressed in what looked like butchers smocks and holding broken dolls and pieces of meat. There was uproar in America and *Capitol Records* had to

withdraw the album and re-release it with a different cover. The original became known as 'the Butcher cover.'

The group began another major tour in Germany on June 24th, and then flew to Japan for their first appearances there. They arrived in Manila in the Philippines for concerts, but despite two successful concerts at the Rizal Memorial Football Stadium they later received extremely hostile receptions when it was found they had failed to attend a reception by Imelda Marcos, wife of the dictator President Ferdinand Marcos. Their money was frozen, demands for excessive tax were made, and they were harried on their way to the airport and greeted by hostile crowds as they tried to get away, with members of their party suffering physical attacks. It was an incident that made them begin to consider ending touring following their August tour of America.

Worse was to come. Comments John had made to an English journalist that "we are bigger than Jesus now" had raised no comment in Britain, but created a furore in America. Radio stations, particularly in the

Bible Belt and the Deep South, urged youngsters to burn all Beatles records – and there were even death threats. Brian Epstein considered cancelling the tour, but it was decided to continue after John Lennon was persuaded, reluctantly, to make a humiliating apology at a press reception in Chicago. George Harrison, commenting on the bonfires of Beatles records, said "They've got to buy them before they can burn them." Their appearance at Candlestick Park, San Francisco was the last time the group ever appeared before a paying audience and following the concert, a relieved Harrison, who always hated touring, commented, "I'm not a Beatle anymore!"

1967 also had its ups and downs. Following the end of their days as concert performers, they began what was to be called their 'studio years' and spent months working on what was to become the most eagerly awaited popular music album of all time – *Sgt Pepper's Lonely Hearts Club Band*. It was a time of psychedelia and the Beatles appearances changed, with brightly coloured clothes and moustaches, beards and shoulder-length hair,

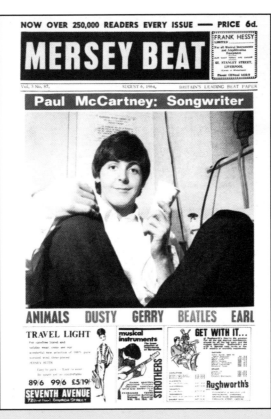

with American photographer Richard Avedon taking his famous set of four psychedelic portraits of John, Paul, George and Ringo.

George visited Los Angeles but wasn't impressed by the hippies in San Francisco and Paul, who had flown to America for Jane Asher's 21st birthday (she was touring with a theatre group), conceived 'Magical Mystery Tour.' The major tragedy occurred on August 27th when their manager Brian Epstein was found dead at his London home, said to be due to an accidental overdose. The Beatles who had confessed to taking the drug LSD earlier that year had just discovered transcendental meditation and a guru the Maharishi Mahesh Yogi and were attending his seminar in Bangor, Wales when the news of Brian's death was conveyed to them.

They began filming *Magical Mystery Tour* in September, but it was so critically mauled when it was screened on BBC 2 in December that the American networks who were offering up to a million dollars for the right to show it in America, withdrew their offers.

1968 was the year of travelling to India to study with the Maharishi, of *Apple*, of John meeting Yoko Ono and of their continuing success in the album field with the double album *The Beatles*, which came to be known as *the White Album* due to its plain white cover. Disharmony was beginning to set in and at one point Ringo left the group, John's wife Cynthia instigated divorce proceedings and there was trouble brewing in the *Apple* Empire, with the group deciding to close down the retail side of the business.

The last year of the decade saw them recording at Twickenham Studios for what was originally called the *Get Back* sessions. Yoko Ono was omnipresent and the other members of the group resented it. George left the group for a while, dissatisfied with John and Paul's attitude towards him. Further dissention was to come when John voiced his opinions of *Apple*'s financial state which resulted in American entrepreneur Allan Klein rushing to London for a meeting with John and Yoko, who hired him as their manager. Ringo and George also agreed to Klein rep-

resenting them, but Paul was having none of it. He had met and fallen in love with an American photographer Linda Eastman and wanted her father, a reputable show business lawyer in New York, to represent him.

In the meantime, the *Yellow Submarine* animated feature had been released to critical praise and the film project for *Get Back* was to reach its climax with a rooftop concert on the *Apple* building on January 30th 1970.

The *Get Back* session had proved to be extremely messy and Klein brought in American producer Phil Spector to turn the tapes into an acceptable album. The result was *Let It Be*. Paul was so incensed with how Spector had imposed his *Wall of Sound* onto the album, particularly on the number *The Long and Winding Road*, that he was informed that he had no choice but to instigate proceeding to dissolve the group.

The greatest group in popular music history had lasted until the beginning of the new decade.

Brian Epstein's press officer once stated that Epstein was "usually reluctant to use the bargaining power of his Beatles as a tool in his dealings on behalf of other NEMS artists."

Of course, he would say that, wouldn't he? But is it true? Brian did not like Lennon or McCartney giving their songs to artists outside his own stable and he bestowed their compositions to acts he had signed such as Cilla Black, Tommy Quickly, Billy J. Kramer, the Fourmost, Cliff Bennett & The Rebel Rousers and the Silkie.

Paul McCartney personally produced Cliff Bennett & the Rebel Rousers' version of the Lennon & McCartney number *Got To Get You Into My Life*, which reached No. 6 in the British charts. John Lennon produced the Silkie performing the Lennon & McCartney number *You've Got To Hide Your Love Away*, with Paul playing piano and George Harrison on tambourine.

Artists on the Beatles' first Christmas Show at Finsbury Park Astoria were Cilla Black, Billy J. Kramer, the Fourmost and Tommy Quickly. Another Epstein signing, Michael Haslam was on the Beatles Christmas Show the following year. Another of his signings, Sounds Incorporated was placed on the Beatles American

Brian Epstein

Tour of 1965 and Cliff Bennett & the Rebel Rousers supported the Beatles on their final tour of Germany and Japan in 1966.

Epstein was obviously keen on his other acts finding success in America and seems to have used the Beatles as

a lever, certainly in the case of Cilla Black.

Colonel Tom Parker could never understand why Epstein, managing the world's most successful group, had to sign up so many acts. He considered that looking after the Beatles was a full-time occupation for any manager. Yet Epstein also managed Cilla Black, Billy J. Kramer & the Dakotas, Tommy Quickly, Michael Haslam, the Rustiks, the Fourmost, Gerry & the Pacemakers, the Silkie, Sounds Incorporated, the Moody Blues – even a bullfighter, Henry Higgins! When Marianne Faithfull's mother approached Epstein to manage her daughter, Brian turned her down saying that he had one female artist and wanted to concentrate on her. Why did he not apply the same rule to the Beatles, rather than continue signing up groups?

Brian was desperate to establish Cilla Black in America, although she was only to have a single chart hit there. He instructed the Beatles' New York agents to set up a cabaret season for Cilla at a major Manhattan showplace, using the association with the Beatles as a tool.

The Nemperor's Stable

She initially appeared on the *Ed Sullivan Show* performing *Dancing In The Street* and *You're My World* and also appeared on the pop TV show *Shindig* performing *I've Been Wrong Before*.

The twenty-two-year-old singer was also to guest on *The Johnny Carson Show*. Carson said "Don't think I'm being rude, but I've never heard of you."

Quick as a whippet, Cilla replied, "Don't worry, chuck, because I've never heard of you either."

Obeying Brian's instructions his agents booked Cilla into the prestigious Persian Room of the 5-star Plaza Hotel.

Discussing her first night, she said, "The room was full of millionaires, it scared me just to think how much it cost to eat there."

Journal America was to report, "So infectious is her personality and so loud and clear her voice, she could easily become another Gracie Fields given the proper handling."

A report in Britain pointed out, "there were almost as many waiters as there were customers" and "instead of *You're My World*, she sings numbers like *Summertime*, *Bye Bye Blackbird* and, believe it or not, a medley from *My Fair Lady*.

When the season was over, Cilla said, "These have been the toughest and most terrifying weeks of my life. I never thought American audiences could be so hard to please."

Sadly, that was the end of Brian's attempts to launch her in America and she simply became another one-hit wonder over there with *You're My*

World reaching No. 26 on the Billboard chart on July 25 1964.

Gerry & the Pacemakers, who had come No. 2 to the Beatles' No. 1 in the Mersey Beat poll were the next group Epstein signed. Despite the fact that they were a completely different style of group to the Beatles, he virtually copied the steps he had used to promote the Beatles. He dressed them in mohair suits, placing them with EMI Records, having their

Cilla Black

photographs taken by Dezo Hoffmann, getting 'The Beatles Monthly' publishers to publish a 'Gerry & the Pacemakers Monthly', having them present their own Christmas show *Gerry's Christmas Cracker*, arranging for them to star in a film, *Ferry Cross the Mersey* and launching them in America on the *Ed Sullivan Show*.

On the eve of their first American

tour Gerry & the Pacemakers' fifth British single *Don't Let The Sun Catch You Crying* became their first American hit reaching No. 4 on the Billboard chart on June 6th 1964. In May 1964 they appeared on the *Ed Sullivan Show* where they performed *I'm The One* and *Don't Let the Sun Catch You Crying* and the appearance was so successful they were booked to return the following week.

During the American tour they appeared on TV shows such as *Shindig* and the following year they appeared at the *Murray The K Easter Show* at the Fox Theater in Brooklyn. They were top of the bill and the other acts were Marvin Gaye, Smokey Robinson & the Miracles, Martha & the Vandellas, the Temptations, the Four Tops, the Marvelettes, the Righteous Brothers, Little Anthony & the Imperials, the Rag Dolls, the Del Satins and Cannibal & the Headhunters.

The TV appearances, tours and success of *Don't Let The Sun Catch You Crying*, resulted in a two-year appearance in the American charts for Gerry & the Pacemakers records.

How Do You Do It? reached No. 9 on August 8th 1964, *I Like It* reached No. 17 on October 17th 1964, *I'll Be There* reached No. 14 on September 1st 1965, *Ferry Cross the Mersey* reached No. 6 on February 13th 1965, *It's Gonna Be Alright* reached No. 23 on April 24th 1965 and *Girl On a Swing* reached No. 28 on October 8th 1966.

In his autobiography *I'll Never Walk Alone*, Gerry related what happened when he returned from America.

"We were amazed to find that, far from making a profit, we owed people there a total of three thousand dollars. We'd been given the red carpet treatment – limousines, fancy hotel suites – and taken people on the trip who were not necessary, plus the press party. And there were lavish restaurant trips."

"When we asked Brian Epstein when the money from the U.S. tour would come in, he said we 'didn't make that much money because…' and then he produced this list of staff who'd travelled, car rental charges, people he had paid to entertain over there – but

Gerry & the Pacemakers

about whom he knew nothing. I hit the roof."

"This is bleeding stupid", I said to him in the language he often described as 'salty'. "Never again", I

said. "Next time we go to the States it's me and the band and you if you want to come – and they can supply the cars. We don't need a limousine each!"

Following Gerry's trip to America I interviewed him for Mersey Beat in a piece that I published on May 22nd 1964:

After ten hectic days in America and Canada, being mobbed wherever he went, Gerry Marsden relaxed in an armchair at his Dingle home and said: "It was fab - I still can't get over the reception which the kids gave us."

WENDY HANSON

When Brian Epstein arrived at the Plaza Hotel with the Beatles in February 1964 he immediately contacted *Capitol Records* and asked them to provide him with a temporary secretary during the trip.

They sent him Wendy Hanson, born in Huddersfield, Yorkshire and cousin to the financier Lord Hanson.

She had originally moved to New York when she was eighteen and became secretary to the classical conductor Leopold Stokowski for two and a half years. She was also temporary secretary to President John F. Kennedy.

Brian was so impressed by her efficiency that he offered her the position of his personal assistant and she returned to England with him.

She worked for him for three years but left his employ due to his moods and tantrums, although she was later asked to help gain permission to use the images of famous people on the *Sergeant Pepper* album.

Wendy died in Italy on January 27th 1991 after an accident in which she fell down some stairs and never recovered consciousness. She was fifty-six years old.

Gerry spent a few quiet days at home last week with his family before leaving for Blackpool last Saturday for a week's appearances at the North Pier.

He said, "America, especially New York, is great, but it's always good to get home - and we missed our Liverpool fans."

Talking about his trip, Gerry said that he had been a little worried before the group's first live appearance in Toronto. "But I needn't have bothered", he added, "the audience were great and set the mood for our whole stay over there."

The boys did three live shows, two in Canada in Montreal and Toronto, and one in Massachusetts, and also did a live Ed Sullivan TV show. Gerry added, "Ed was so pleased with the way we went down that he asked us to record another show before we left, which we did."

During their stay in New York, the group had quite a lot of spare time and they spent their leisure hours seeing the sights.

Gerry said, "We visited Harlem and the Bowery, and shopped along Fifth Avenue and Broadway." But he remarked that everything was so expensive in the States – "It cost about two pounds and five shillings for a bucket of ice at our hotel.", he said.

"I was disappointed in the American clothes, too", said Gerry. "I didn't think they were as good as our English ones, so I didn't buy any suits or clothes of any kind. Anyway, most good American clothes are now settled like English suits so there wasn't any point in buying anything."

But he did buy an automatic shoe polisher, an automatic carving knife for his mother, souvenir dolls and baseball gloves and bats.

Brian Epstein and Billy J. Kramer

During the day the boys gave press conferences, and evenings were often spent visiting the nightspots. Gerry said, "We went to see Sammy Davis Jr, Peggy Lee, Gene Krupa and Dizzy Gillespie at various clubs, and had a chat with them afterwards. It was great meeting so many people I've always admired", Gerry added.

Another highlight of their trip was the visit of the Liverpool football team to New York whilst they were there. Said Gerry: "We invited the team to see the *Ed Sullivan Show*, and it was nice to have a chat with them about our home town - though most of the players seem to hail from Scotland!"

But it was the fans that Gerry remembers best. "They were fantastic", he said.

"We had a chauffeur driven Cadillac to take us round New York, complete with telephone, and the kids found out the number and kept ringing up whilst we were in the car!"

Wherever they went, the boys had a bodyguard of 12 hefty men, "but we still got mobbed", laughed Gerry. "We had police guarding the hotel, the lift and our room, and there were fans crawling up drainpipes and in through the cellars to get to see us".

Two shirts that Gerry sent to the laundry were returned with letters from fans inside. Said Gerry: "I didn't discover one of the letters until after I returned home - quite a surprise!"

Frequently all the hotel's telephone lines were jammed with calls for Gerry & the Pacemakers, and their road manager had a full-time job answering them all.

Gerry's latest disc *Don't Let The Sun Catch You Crying* was released whilst he was over there. He said: "It's too early yet to see what it will do, but it jumped from nowhere to No. 5 in the New York charts whilst we were there."

Speaking of future plans, Gerry said he was looking forward to filming in Liverpool shortly, and after that he hoped to take a holiday. "I shall probably be going to the Canary Islands", he said.

There are also possibilities that he may go back to America for a tour later this year or early next year, Gerry said.

The Pacemakers were Epstein's second most successful British Invasion import following the Beatles, but their success was short-lived.

The group's American hits were not covers of old American rock 'n' roll standards but a combination of Mitch Murray compositions and original songs by Gerry Marsden, in contrast to a number of British Invasion groups who covered numbers which had already been released in America by American artists.

Billy J. Kramer also had limited success in America with all four of his hits being confined to a period of less than six months in 1964.

Billy, whose real name is William Howard Ashton was born in Bootle, Liverpool on August 19th 1943. His original band in 1960 was the Sandstormers, who became Billy Forde & the Phantoms, then Billy Kramer & the Coasters. The line-up was Billy on guitar and vocals, Arthur Ashton on lead, Ray Dougherty on rhythm, Tony Sanders on drums and George Braithwaite on bass.

A Liverpool pensioner Ten Knibbs managed Billy Kramer & the Coasters. When the Liverpool scene began to take off in Britain, Knibbs approached me asking if I would co-manager Billy with him. I suggested that he approach Brian Epstein, particularly as Billy had been voted into the No. 3 spot in the *Mersey Beat* poll and Epstein had already signed the groups who were Nos 1 and 2.

As Billy's group the Coasters refused to turn professional, Brian had to find another backing group for Billy. The Remo Four turned him down, so he made an offer to the Manchester band the Dakotas, who were backing singer Pete MacLaine at the time. They initially refused, but finally agreed when Epstein arranged for them to make records in their own right.

Considering that Billy only teamed up with the Dakotas in 1963, their American press release in 1964 read:

"Billy and the Dakotas chose their name when they were called to audition in England four years ago. They were told to return dressed as Indians.

Unable to afford the US $100 apiece for buckskins, the group skipped the audition but kept the name."

Billy recalled the time he was called into Epstein's office when John Lennon was present. He said, Brian said to me: "John's come up with an idea. He thinks your name would sound much better if we added the initial 'J' to it. How does Billy J. Kramer sound?"

"I said: 'That's okay by me, but what do I say to the press if they ask me what the 'J' stands for?"

John said "You can tell them it stands for Julian."

"To tell you the truth, I thought Julian sounded like a puff's name and I refused to use it. I didn't know at the time that John had a son and had named him Julian in memory of his mother."

Billy topped the British charts with his first release, the Lennon & McCartney number *Do You Want To Know A Secret?* His other Lennon & McCartney hits included *Bad To Me, I'll Keep You Satisfied* and *From A Window*.

It was Kramer himself who found the number *Little Children* and had to talk Brian Epstein into letting him record it. The song became his biggest hit and his first American chart entry.

Billy J. Kramer and the Dakotas

Little Children reached No. 7 in the American charts on May 2nd 1964. This was followed by *Bad To Me*, which reached No 9 on June 13th 1964 and *I'll Keep You Satisfied*, which reached No 30 on August 15th 1964. His final American chart entry was *From A Window* which reached No. 23 on September 19th 1964.

After Epstein's death, Billy embarked on a solo career in 1967.

He eventually left England in 1984 to make his home in America. His marriage had broken up, he had a drink problem and he felt he needed a fresh start.

Billy conquered his addiction, worked as an alcohol counsellor and remarried. He now holds dual nationality.

An Epstein artist who failed completely in the United States was Tommy Quickly.

His real name was Quigley and he appeared with his sister Pat in a group called the Challengers. Epstein first spotted him performing at the Queen's Hall, Widnes in January 1963, but did not sign him until the following year, changing his name to Quickly and dispensing with his backing group.

The Remo Four had not been successful on their own, so Epstein appointed them as Quickly's backing group and then he launched one of his biggest promotional campaigns.

He included Tommy on three Beatles tours, a Beatles Christmas show, a Gerry & the Pacemakers Christmas Show, a Gerry & the Pacemakers tour and a Billy J. Kramer tour.

On the recording front, since George Martin now had enough artists to contend with, Epstein placed him with Pye Records and gave him a Lennon & McCartney number, *No Reply* to record.

Slightly drunk, Tommy found it almost impossible to record the song and after 17 takes it was abandoned. This frustrated the Remo Four, who believed that a proper interpretation of the number would have brought them a major hit and possibly a British chart-topper.

Tommy made his recording debut with another Lennon & McCartney song, *Tip Of My Tongue*, which was not as strong as *No Reply*.

Brian Epstein then spent US $30,000 on a promotional trip to America, but was unable to break his new artists. Despite the major exposure he received, Quickly failed to have success with five singles and he left Epstein's organisation in February 1966.

Epstein did not really have any further success with his acts in America, apart from the Beatles, even though he placed groups such as sounds incorporated on Beatles U.S. tours.

As if he did not have enough work with the Beatles and all the other acts he had signed up, Brian then formed another company Nemperor Artists to co-manage acts in America in partnership with his American attorney Nat Weiss. Weiss brought a group from Pennsylvania called the Rondells to his attention. Epstein told Weiss to sign them up and suggested that they change their name to the Circle. John Lennon then suggested that the spelling by altered to Cyrkle.

Brian picked out a number penned by Paul Simon and Bruce Woodley as their debut disc and their record of *Red Rubber Ball* reached No. 2 in the American charts. They had their second and final hit, *Turn Down Day* a few months later, which reached No. 16 in the charts. As with his usual practice, he booked them on the Beatles final US tour in August 1966.

Tommy Quickly

Beatles manager Brian Epstein was born in Rodney Street, Liverpool on September 19th 1934.

Brian discovered the group when he began contributing record reviews to the local music paper *Mersey Beat*, which he stocked in his family music store NEMS (North End Music Stores).

He signed the Beatles, created NEMS Enterprises and also went on to manage a host of other artists including Gerry & the Pacemakers, Cilla Black, Billy J. Kramer & the Dakotas, the Fourmost, the Big Three and Tommy Quickly and the Remo Four. In addition NEMS Enterprises also acted as agents for numerous other acts such as Freddie Starr and the Midnighters.

Many people, including Elvis Presley's manager Colonel Tom Parker, believed he should have stuck to managing the Beatles alone, and he was to be unsuccessful with a number of the acts he personally signed such as the Rusticks, the Silkie and Michael Haslam. He also suffered financial losses when he bought the Saville Theatre in London's West End to promote rock shows.

Following Ed Sullivan's interest in the Beatles, Epstein flew to New York with Billy J. Kramer on November 5th 1963 and met Sullivan a few days later to arrange for the Beatles to appear on three Sullivan shows and for Gerry & the Pacemakers to appear on one. He also gave CBS TV

Young Brian Epstein

a year's exclusive rights to the Beatles' American television appearances. During the trip he also met Capitol executives to discuss the release of Beatles product in America.

During his February 1964 trip to America with the Beatles he met Jack Good to discuss the production of a Beatles television special. He made several other visits to America over the next three years, accompanying the Beatles on their tours, and also travelling with Gerry & the Pacemakers, Cilla Black and Tommy Quickly. In 1965 he told the New York Daily News, "Ten years from now the Beatles will, be popular. The Beatles tend to move with the times. At present they're just a bit ahead of their generation."

Epstein's autobiography, *A Cellarful Of Noise*, ghosted by Derek Taylor, who became his personal assistant, was published in 1964.

He also desired a high profile for himself and appeared on numerous UK television and radio shows ranging from *Juke Box Jury* to *Desert Island Discs*. At one time he even hosted a section of the American television show, *Hullabaloo*, although he recorded his segments in London.

Epstein was troubled by his homosexuality and became increasingly addicted to drugs, resulting in his death from an accidental overdose on August 25th 1967. He was thirty-two years old.

The landing of the Beatles in New York in February 1964 was, strictly speaking, the only 'British Invasion'.

What people might consider the first 'British Invasion' in 1774 wasn't actually an invasion at all, was never referred to as an 'invasion' and was actually called the War Of Independence.

The majority of the American colonies were basically inhabited by people who regarded themselves as Britons. Benjamin Franklin was to say "I am a Briton" and Francis Hopkinson, who was to become a revolutionary, had also said "We in America, are in all respects Englishmen."

The political, social, economic and cultural order in the American colonies was British.

The uprising was to come due to various laws and taxes levied on the colonies, but it was the longest American war outside the Vietnam conflict, lasting for eight-and-a-half years. It was also close to a civil war.

America was divided over whether the colonies should leave the British Empire or remain a part of it. 40% of colonists were neutral, 40% was revolutionaries and 20% fought alongside the British. American fought against American, even families fought against each other.

The original Paul Revere

Not only did it become a civil war, it developed into a world war.

The French had been secretly supplying the patriots with economic aid, weapons and foods right from the start and entered the war officially on the side of the revolutionaries in 1778 as a way to avenge their defeat by the British in 1763 at the end of the Seven Year Way. Both Holland and Spain also allied themselves with the revolutionaries hoping that their actions would help to destroy British worldwide trade.

Ships from the three Continental countries began to attack British possessions in the West Indies, Africa and India.

Although many people believe that the war ended in Yorktown when General Cornwallis was besieged and the French navy prevented British ships from rescuing Cornwallis' army, the British were still in a position to continue the war. They still had 10,000 troops in New York and could have sent thousands more from England. Instead, for political and economic reasons, they decided to grant the colonies their Independence, ending two centuries of British rule and leading to the drafting and ratification of the Constitution of the United States of America.

The war had bankrupted Louis XVI and led to the French Revolution and it also saw the demise of Spanish power.

Paul Revere and the Raiders

It was Paul Revere who warned 'The British are coming' in 1775, when the first British Invasion took place. On that occasion the citizens took up arms to repel the invaders.

The second British Invasion took place in the 20th Century and this time the citizens of America welcomed it with open arms. Appropriately an American group appeared on the scene called Paul Revere & the Raiders and, dressed in 18th century uniforms, they had a series of chart hits.

Almost two-dozen British artists found success in the American charts during the 1960s, and the impact they made was to change the landscape of popular music scene internationally, irrevocably, and for the good. There was a commonly held perception that the Beatles and the British bands virtually killed American solo artists and dominated the charts to the extent that they affected the homegrown artists.

Murray Wilson, the Beach Boys father-manager said, "The Beatles have swamped out the market with huge sales in such a short time. Ed Sullivan and all the other big US TV shows won't book American groups now – they're only interested in what's happening in England".

This was not the case, although many people believed it. The American Musicians' Union soon came into action and limited the number of British acts who could appear on tour and on American television. Who knows, The British Invasion might have become even bigger but for this action. This perception that the emergence of the Beatles and The British Invasion, together with the appearance of American groups, killed off the careers of the young solo singers *was* untrue. Some stars had already faded prior to the Beatles debut – Fabian, for instance, enjoyed his last hit in 1960 and Frankie Avalon's last chart entry had been in 1962, as had Pat Boone's.

However, following the Beatles' success Bobby Vee had his single *Come Back When You Grow Up*

reach No. 3 in the US charts in 1967, followed by *Beautiful People* and he also had a hit the following year with *My Girl/My Guy*. Dion reached No. 4 in the charts in 1968 with *Abraham, Martin and John*. Ricky Nelson charted with *The Very Thought Of You* in September 1964 and entered the charts with *She Belongs To Me* in January 1970 followed by a 1972 No. 6 with *Garden Party*. Paul Anka had a total of thirty-two chart hits, nine of them between 1969 and 1983 and solo singers such as Len Barry, Jim Reeves, Marty Robbins, Neil Sedaka, Roger Miller, Bobby Vinton and many others flourished with hits on both sides of the Atlantic.

American groups also continued to outnumber British acts the American charts. For example, the Beach Boys had their biggest successes from February 1964 with twenty-two further hits including classics such as *I Get Around, Help Me, Rhonda, California Girls, Sloop John B* and *Would Not It Be Nice*.

Scores of new American bands, some inspired by the Beatles, began to appear in the U.S. charts throughout the 1960s. These included the Amboy Dukes, the Beau Brummels (said to have chosen their name because they would be placed next to the Beatles in the record racks – BEA), Buffalo Springfield, Canned Heat, the Doors, the Electric Prunes and Mitch Ryder & the Detroit Wheels. The 'Swinging London' scene was one of the inspirations for the West Coast scene which spawned the San Francisco boom with artists such as Janis Joplin, Big Brother &

the Holding Company, Jefferson Airplane, the Grateful Dead and various psychedelic bands.

Of course there was the great success throughout the decade of the Motown artists, who were given a boost by the Beatles, who then produced an astonishing range of hit records internationally.

There is no denying that the impact of the Beatles and the other British bands and artists did have a profound effect on the American music scene and here are the main artists credited with being part of The British Invasion.

The Animals

In 1962 the Alan Price Combo, comprising Alan Price (organ), Chas Chandler (bass), Hilton Valentine (guitar) and John Steel (drums) were joined by singer Eric Burdon. Playing in their home area of Tyneside, the quintet soon adopted the name Animals, a term which had been attached to them because of their 'wild' performances of R&B and rock 'n' roll numbers during the group's residency at the Downbeat Club. Their local reputation was enhanced when they gained a residency at the larger Club A-Go-Go in Newcastle City centre.

During 1963 the Beatles and the 'Mersey Sound' had emerged and completely revolutionised the British music industry and opened the eyes of record company executives to the talent in the provinces.

Henry Henriod saw the Animals playing at the Cavern club in Liverpool and tipped off record producer Mickie Most, who signed the group.

He arranged for EMI to release their discs and in April 1964 their debut single *Baby Let Me Take You Home* was released, reaching No. 19 in the British charts. The number was taken from Bob Dylan's eponymous debut album, as was their second single *House Of The Rising Sun*, a traditional number which Alan Price re-arranged.

EMI were concerned as the track was 4 ½ minutes long, suggesting that disc jockeys would not play such a lengthy number. Mickie Most insisted that the song stayed as it was and it went on to top the British charts. *MGM Records* issued a shortened version in America, which also reached No. 1 and this then revived sales of their previous release, *Baby Let Me Take You Home*.

Their next single, *I'm Crying*, was the only number the group wrote themselves.

The gritty sound, the working class image, the haunting re-arrangements of R&B classics, the rough voice of Burdon, all contributed to the immense success of the band on both sides of the Atlantic and their debut album *The Animals* entered the Top 20 charts in both Britain and America.

The group continued to recycle American numbers and had hits with their versions of John Lee Hooker's *Boom Boom*, Nina Simone's *Don't Let Me Be Misunderstood* and Sam Cooke's *Bring It On Home To Me*. In 1965 they recorded an original number by Barry Mann and Cynthia Weill, *We've Gotta Get Out Of This Place*, followed by *In My Life*.

Despite their success on record and with live tours of Britain and America, there was dissention in the group, particularly between Alan Price and Eric Burdon, resulting in Price leaving the Animals to launch a solo career. Dave Rowberry replaced him. Price commented, "I hated flying and was a nervous wreck and drinking too heavily. The other guys could not believe their luck with all the booze, all the parties and all the women. They'd stopped rehearsing and killed everything the Animals stood for. I could not stand it".

Burdon then refused to re-sign with Mickie Most and EMI, with the group then moving to Decca Records and issuing 'Looking Out'. John Steel had also become disenchanted by this time and he left, to be replaced by Barry Jenkins from the Nashville Teens.

Their next hit in 1966 was *Don't Bring Me Down*, but there was increasing disharmony in the group and following their American tour that year, both Chas Chandler and Hilton Valentine left. Burdon and Jenkins formed the nucleus of Eric Burdon & the Animals, which relocated to America, with the addition of Vic Briggs and Danny McCulloch. There were various personnel changes, the name was altered to Eric Burdon & the New Animals with Zoot Money replacing Briggs and McCulloch and the group officially disbanded after a farewell concert in Newcastle at Christmas 1968.

By 1970 Burdon had teamed up with an American band called Night Shift who changed their name to

War and several further hits followed under the name Eric Burdon & War. Burdon continued to perform over the years with various different bands and line-ups. His autobiography, *I Used To Be An Animal, But I'm Alright Now* was published in 1986.

Alan Price had considerable solo success over a twenty year period with British hits such as *I Put A Spell On You*, *Hi Lili Hi Lo*, *Simon Smith & His Amazing Dancing Bear*, *Honey I Need*, *Cry To Me*, *Midnight To Six Man*, *Come See Me*; and *A House In The Country*. He also starred in a sequel to *Alfie*, *Alfie Darling*, with Joan Collins.

Chas Chandler also found success in his new career as a manager, discovering acts such as Jimi Hendrix and Slade.

The Animals single *The House Of The Rising Sun* was reissued in 1972 and became a chart hit for the second time. When it was reissued again in 1982 and charted for the third time, the original group decided to reform for a limited period and began to tour again in 1983.

They split up once again. Hilton Valentine had been working with a band called the Alligators, with singer Robert Kane. In 1993 he approached John Steel to form Animals II with Kane, plus Steve Hutchinson on keyboards, Steve Dawson on guitar and Martin Bland on bass. In 1997 they released an album on which they performed a number of the original Animals' hits, and they also toured Europe, Australia and America.

Sadly, Chas Chandler died in 1996.

The Bee Gees

Barry Gibb and his twin brothers Robin and Maurice were all born in Douglas on the Isle of Man and raised in Chorlton-cum-Hardy in Lancashire. Barry Alan Crompton was born on September 1st 1946 and Robin Hugh and Maurice Ernest were born on December 22nd 1949.

Their mother Barbara was a singer, their father Hugh the leader of an orchestra. Six months after their younger brother Andy was born in 1958, the family immigrated to Australia.

The three elder Gibb boys had already been performing as a trio in Manchester, with their first professional performance taking place in 1955 appearing in the Rattlesnakes and Wee Johnny Hays & the Bluecats.

Once in Australia, in Brisbane, Bill Good introduced them to disc jockey Bill Gates, who began playing their tapes on his radio show. Good named the group the B.G's, after the initials of himself and Gates. By 1962 they had moved to Sydney and changed their name to the Bee Gees.

After several chart entries in Australia, the group moved to London in 1967. They approached Brian

Epstein's office to see if he would manage them and met up with Robert Stigwood, who worked for Epstein at the time. Young Australian actor Colin Peterson joined them on drums. They were signed to Nems Enterprises and their hit streak began. When Epstein died, a deal was made with NEMS which resulted in Stigwood taking acts such as the Bee Gees and Cream with him.

The Bee Gees' recording success has been phenomenal and their hit singles have included *New York Mining Disaster*, *To Love Somebody*, *Massachusetts*, *World*, *Words*, *Jumbo*, *I've Gotta Get A Message To You*, *First Of May*, *Tomorrow Tomorrow*, *Don't Forget To Remember*, *I.O.I.O.*, *Lonely Days*, *My World*, *Run To Me*, *Jive Talkin'*, *You Should Be Dancing*, *Love Is So Right*, *How Deep Is Your Love*, *Stayin' Alive*, *Night Fever*, *Too Much Heaven*, *Tragedy*, *Love You Inside Out*, *Spirits (Having Flown)*, *Someone Belonging To Someone*, *You Win Again*, *E.S.P. One*, *Ordinary Lives*, *Secret Love* and *Paying The Price Of Love*.

Album successes have included *Bee Gees First*, *Horizontal*, *Idea*, *Odessa*, *Best Of The Bee Gees*, *Spirits Having Flown*, *Bee Gees Greatest* and *Living Eyes*.

1969 proved an eventful year, with Peterson being sacked and Robin embarking on a solo career, which resulted in Stigwood suing him. Maurice married Lulu but they were separated in 1973 and later divorced. Maurice then married Yvonne Spencely in 1975 and they had two children, Adam and Samantha.

Barry was also to prove very successful as a songwriter and producer, penning and producing Barbra Streisand's *Woman In Love* and her album *Guilty*. He was to write many hits for other artists such as Dionne Warwick and Diana Ross and also had a solo hit with *Shine Shine*. He and his wife Linda were married in 1970 and their children are Stephen, Ashley, Travis, Michael and Alexandra.

The Bee Gees

The brothers were reunited as the Bee Gees in 1971 and continued as a trio.

Their younger brother Andy was also to embark on a singing career and he had several hits. Sadly, he became a drug addict and died from heart failure in 1988 in a hospital in Oxfordshire.

As a solo artist Robin had a No. 2 chart hit in Britain with *Saved By the Bell* in 1970 while Barry and Maurice went on to record the album *Cucumber Castle* as a duo. Robin also issued a maxi CD single in Britain in January 2003 called *Please*. He

and his wife Dwina were married in 1985 and their children are Spencer, Melissa and Robin John.

On March 2nd 1997 the UK television programme *The South Bank Show* was dedicated to the group.

Sadly, Maurice died on Sunday, January 12th 2003. Just months later, on February 23rd 2003 Barry and Robin were presented with a Grammy 'The Legend Award' and on October 22nd 2003 Robin accepted 'The World Award' in Hamburg, Germany on behalf of the Bee Gees.

Chad & Jeremy

Chad Stuart and Jeremy Clyde were two former public schoolboys who teamed up as a duo. The singer-songwriters recorded for the Ember Record label between 1973 and 1965 and had one minor hit in Britain with *Yesterday's Gone*. However, in 1964 in the wake of the Beatles and the British Invasion in America, they enjoyed a series of hits in the American charts with *Yesterday's Gone*, *A Summer Song*, *Willow Weep For Me*, *If I Loved You*, *Before And After*, *I Don't Wanna Lose You Baby* and *Distant Shores*.

The two had decided to base themselves in California and began to appear in a number of television shows including *Hullaballoo*, *The Hollywood Palace*, *The Dick Van Dyke Show*, and *The Patty Duke Show* and even appeared in an episode of the *Batman* series.

Their psychedelic album *Cabbages And Kings* released in 1967 did not fare well. Neither did their follow-up, *The Ark*, so the two decided to disband.

For a time Chad acted as musical director of *The Smothers Brothers Comedy Hour* and made some singles with his wife Jill, later becoming a radio presenter in addition to concentrating on compositions, mainly for stage musicals.

Jeremy Clyde has pursued an acting career in films, television and stage and played the lead role in the British television series *Sexton Blake* in 1978.

The couple recorded a one-off reunion album in 1983 and also teamed up once again for 'the British Reinvasion Tour' of 1986.

In 2003 the duo decided to get together again and Chad travelled from his home in Idaho to London to meet Jeremy for the first time in more than a decade and they went off to France for new promotional photographs taken by Gered Mancowitz. Back in the States they began recording their first new album in 20 years. Chad commented, "The album will follow the wedding analogy – something old, something new, something borrowed, and something blue".

Cream

A trio that was hailed as one of the world's top bands, Cream comprised Eric Clapton (guitar), Jack Bruce (bass) and Ginger Baker (drums).

Their hits included *Wrapping Paper, I Feel Free, Strange Brew, Anyone For Tennis, Sunshine Of Your Love, White Room and Badge*. Their hit albums were *Fresh Cream, Disraeli Gears, Wheels Of Fire, Goodbye, Best Of Cream, Live Cream* and *Live Cream Vol 2*.

Despite their huge following and success on record, in 1968 Cream announced that they would be disbanding as they felt they had taken their music as far as it would go. Their farewell concert took place at the Royal Albert Hall in November of that year and was filmed by Tony Palmer for a television documentary. Clapton and Baker then went on to

Cream

form Blind Faith, while Bruce embarked on a solo career.

Eric Clapton remains an international star whose albums are bought en masse almost out of habit. He has carved a second career with psychiatrist-couch discussions to the media about his life, his soul and his torment. Tragedy seemed to dog him for a number of years. His five-year-old son Conor, the result of an affair with Italian model Lori del Santo, fell to his death from a fifty-third floor apartment window in New York. Clapton was to express his grief in the song *Tears In Heaven*.

In 1990 a helicopter crash claimed the life of his close friend Stevie Ray Vaughan who had just performed on stage with him. Other victims of the crash included Clapton's agent, his tour manager and his bodyguard.

His former girlfriend Alice Ormsby-Gore became hooked on drugs and he helped her enter rehab, but she died from an overdose. Clapton himself was hooked on drugs for twenty years and sex and drugs featured prominently in his life. He married Patti Boyd, ex-wife of his best friend George Harrison, and his lovers and girlfriends have included a variety of models, film stars and singers, including Michelle Pfeiffer, Paula Hamilton, Sheryl Crow, Stephanie Beacham and Susannah Doyle.

Clapton's grief for Conor came with some consolation when he rediscovered his daughter Ruth, born from a liason in 1984.

His own childhood was rather strange. He was reared by his grandparents in Sussex, and believed that his mother was his elder sister. He never knew his father, a Canadian soldier who returned home to his wife. His mother Pat later married another Canadian soldier and went to live abroad.

By 1998 the then fifty-three-year-old superstar was spending most of his days working with counsellors to help drug addicts and alcoholics in a London centre. He also established a thirty-six-bed clinic in Antigua, where he has a home.

He continues to hold regular concert seasons at the Royal Albert Hall, London.

The recorded output of Jack Bruce and Ginger Baker is more intermittent, although both of them joined up with guitarist Gary Moore in 1994 for a global tour with a set centered on Cream numbers.

In 2003 Universal Records reissued Bruce's solo albums as CDs with bonus material including previously unissued tracks and alternative versions. They were *Songs For A Tailor*, *Things We Like*, *Harmony Row*, *Out Of The Storm*, *How's Tricks*, *Jet Set Jewell* and *Jack Bruce And Friends Live At The Free Trade Hall, Manchester*. In the summer of 2003 Jack was diagnosed with liver cancer but underwent a successful liver transplant on September 19th. On September 15th Sanctuary released his latest album *More Jack Than God*, which was issued in America on September 23rd.

Ginger Baker, who was born Peter Edward Baker in Lewisham on August 19th 1939 originally joined the Bob Wallis jazz band. He appeared in several other jazz outfits before becoming a member of Alexis Korner's Blues Incorporated, taking over from Charlie Watts who had left to join the Rolling Stones. Later, together with Jack Bruce and Graham Bond, they left Blues Incorporated to form the Graham Bond Organisation. Bruce and Baker often did not get on and Bruce once destroyed Baker's drums on stage.

In 1966 impresario Robert Stigwood wanted to form a Supergroup around Baker and Eric Clapton and Clapton insisted on Bruce being the third member.

After Cream folded, Baker formed various other groups, at one time opening a studio in Lagos, Nigeria and then moving to America. His other bands included Ginger Baker's Airforce and Ginger Baker's African Force.

Petula Clark

Petula Clark was one of Britain's most successful female singers. Born on November 15th 1932 in Epsom, Surrey, she had her stage debut at the age of seven and as a child she enjoyed a career in radio and films, appearing in more than twenty movies.

During the 1950s her British hits included *The Little Shoemaker*, *Majorca*, *Suddenly There's A Valley*, *With All My Heart*, *Alone* and *Baby Lover*.

In 1959 Petula married Claude Wolff, press agent for the French label Vogue Records, and the couple were to have three children, Barra, Kate and Patrick.

Her most successful decade was the 60s when her major hits included *Sailor*, *Something Missing*, *Romeo*, *My Friend The Sea*, *I'm Counting On You*, *Ya Ya Twist*, *Casanova*, *Downtown*, *I Know A Place*, *You Better Come Home*, *Round Every Corner*, *You're The One*, *My Love*, *A Sign Of The Times*, *I Could not Live Without Your Love*, *This Is My Song*, *Don't Sleep In The Subway*, *The Other Man's Grass* and *Kiss Me Goodbye*.

She received three Grammy awards, the first for *Downtown*, voted 'Best Rock 'n' Roll Record of 1964', the second for *I Know A Place* which brought her the 'Best Female Performance of The Year' award in 1964. Many years later, in 2003, 'Downtown' was inducted into the Grammy Hall of Fame. Altogether she was to have fifteen top four hits in America.

Petula appeared in two major musical movies *Finian's Rainbow* with Fred Astaire and *Goodbye Mr Chips* with Peter O' Toole. She also had her own television shows on both sides of the Atlantic.

Her hits in the seventies were *The Song Of My Life* and *I Don't Know How To Love Him*. Her re-mix *Downtown '88'* hit the charts in 1988.

In addition to concerts, Petula set her sights on the West End stage and featured as Maria in *The Sound Of Music* in 1981/2. In 1990 she wrote her own West End musical, *Someone Like You* in which she starred. In 1990 she also made her Broadway debut in *Blood Brothers* and toured America in the play, penned by Liverpool playwright Willie Russell.

In 1998 Queen Elizabeth II presented Petula with a CBE (Commander of the Order of the British Empire) and 2000 she also proved successful in her appearances as Norma Desmond in the hit Andrew Lloyd Webber musical *Sunset Boulevard*, and in 2002 she toured California and Europe.

The Dave Clark Five

Following the impact of the Beatles, the next group to benefit from the huge publicity in America surrounding the Fab Four was the Dave Clark Five.

In Britain, London basically controlled not only the entire music industry but also the media. BBC Radio and television and all the national newspapers were based in London and there was, not unnaturally, a London bias. At the time there actually existed a North-South divide, with people in the North of England feeling that all the power and wealth in the country rested in the South and they resented it. Southerners seemed to have a feeling that the only things north of Watford were back alleys, slums, clog-wearing people and a sort of *Coronation Street* image existed.

The Beatles took the South by surprise and London naturally wanted to hit back. The agents, managers, recording studios, music publishers were all in London and when the Mersey sound began to dominate the charts, the status quo had been seriously upset.

Do You Love Me was a number originally recorded by the Detroit vocal group the Contours. A Liverpool

Petula Clark

group Faron's Flamingos adapted the song to their beat group style and recorded it. Oriole, their London record company were impressed, predicted it could be a number one hit, then placed it on the 'B' side of the record. Two London groups, Brian Poole & the Tremeloes and the Dave Clarke Five immediately copied Faron's version and both entered the charts with it, with the Tremeloes reaching the No. 1 position. The Flamingos were naturally dejected and split up.

The Dave Clark Five comprised Dave Clark (drums), Mike Smith (keyboards/ vocals), Rick Huxley (bass guitar), Denis Payton (tenor sax/guitars) and Lenny Davidson (guitar).

They had originally formed as an instrumental group and made their debut with *Chaquita* on the small Ember Records label. They next moved to Pye Records, but were unsuccessful with their releases. In 1963 they signed with Columbia and their first single, *Mulberry Bush* was also a miss. They actually recorded Mitch Murray's 'How Do You Like It?' but

never released it. It was the number George Martin wanted the Beatles to record and it became a chart topper for Gerry & the Pacemakers.

Then the Dave Clark Five recorded *Do You Love Me* and never looked back. Being a London group there was media saturation when their next single *Glad All Over* topped the charts, The press had a field day: 'Tottenham Sound Has Crushed The Beatles' was the headline in the Daily Express while the London Evening Standard now dismissed the Beatles as old fashioned. However, the attempt to promote the Dave Clark Five as a bigger group than the Beatles was unsuccessful.

The group did become a major band particularly in American where the publicity drive was the opposite of what it had been in Britain. Rather than being pushed as London's answer to Liverpool, the group were promoted as if they were exponents of the Mersey sound.

Since *Glad All Over* had replaced *I Want to Hold Your Hand* at the top of the British charts, the Americans be-

Dave Clark Five

lieved that The Dave Clark Five were the next big group from Liverpool. Nothing was done to dispel this impression and Epic Records exploited this belief by advertising them in Billboard as having 'the Mersey sound with the Liverpool beat'. Even today, the Motown Museum in Detroit sports a framed photograph of the Dave Clark Five with the Supremes under the caption 'Liverpool Meets Detroit'.

The DC5 (as they were sometimes known) were the first English group to tour the US. They had twenty-two hit records in Britain and twenty-four in America (fifteen top twenty hits in first three years in the U.S), six sell out tours of the U.S., thirteen appearances on the *Ed Sullivan Show* and sold out the Carnegie Hall in three days.

It is claimed that the group made eighteen appearances on the *Ed Sullivan Show*, this is because there were five repeats of shows they appeared in. Their Sullivan appearances and songs performed were: *Glad All Over* on March 8th 1964, *Do You Love Me*, *Bits And Pieces* and *Glad All Over* on March 15th 1964, *Can't You See That She's Mine* and *Do You Love Me* on May 31st 1964, *Anyway You Want It* on November 1st 1964, *Everybody Knows*, *Because* and *Anyway You Want It* on February 14th 1965, *Glad All Over*, *Come Home* and *I Like It Like That* on June 20th 1965, *Over And Over* and *At The Scene* on February 20th 1965, *Catch Us If You Can* on December 12th 1965, *Over And Over* and *At The Scene* on February 20th 1966, *Catch Us If You Can* and *Try Too Hard* on April 24th 1966, *Look Before You Leap* and *Please Tell Me Why* on June 12th 1966, *Sittin' Here Baby* (a live performance) and *19 Days* a promo video on March 20th 1966, and, finally, *I've Got To Have A Reason* and *You Got What It Takes* on March 26th 1967.

In1964 they made the film *Catch Us If You Can*, directed by John Boorman, who was to become a major director of films such as *Point Blank*.

Drummer Dave Clark, a former movie stunt man, proved to have an astute business sense and did much to steer the group to success, while the main musical asset was vocalist Mike Smith, who wrote most of the group's material.

The Dave Clark Five finally disbanded in August 1970, but Clarke then teamed up with Mike Smith in Dave Clark And Friends. The other members were Eric Ford, Alan Parker and Madeline Bell. The group disbanded and Clark attended drama school and spent six years writing the musical *Time*. It opened at the Dominion Theatre, London in 1986 with Cliff Richard starring and had a lengthy run, with David Cassidy taking over from Cliff.

His business sense led Clark to the ownership of all the group's songs and in 1993 he issued a 25-track compilation *Glad All Over Again*! He also bought the rights to all the original *Ready, Steady, Go!* shows, which have proved to be a very lucrative investment.

Lenny Davidson is now a guitar tutor in Hertfordshire and also runs a

business servicing organs in churches. Rick Huxley went to work for Vox in 1972 and then opened Musical Equipment Ltd in Camberwell, which he ran until 1987 before returning to electrical wholesaling. Denny Peyton is a real estate salesman who also plays in a quartet, Formula One.

Mike Smith has continued in the music business writing commercial jingles. At one time he teamed up with Mike D'Abo, former singer with Manfred Mann in Smith & D'Abo. They made one album and then disbanded. Mike also records artists such as Shirley Bassey and Michael Ball and has also formed a new five-piece band Mike Smith's Rock Engine, which toured America in 2003.

Mike Smith suffered an accident at his home in Spain, which affected his spinal chord and was taken by ambulance to London where he was placed in an intensive care unit on October 15th 2003. He is paralysed from the waist down and there is no movement in his right arm and limited movement in his left. His wife Charlie has been at his bedside night and day. Steve Van Zandt of the E Street Band and Paul Shaffer of *The Late Night Show* with Dave Letterman are organsing a benefit concert in New York on Mike's behalf.

Deep Purple

This progressive British heavy metal band made their recording debut with *Hush* in 1968. The record sold a million and reached No. 4 in the American charts. In 1969 they performed 'Concerto For Group And Orchestra' at the Royal Albert Hall with the London Philharmonic Orchestra and in America at the Hollywood Bowl with the Los Angeles Philharmonic.

Edinburgh-born Rod Evans was the group's lead singer and composed original music for the band with Jon Lord, who played organ. Other members were Nicky Simper (bass), Ritchie Blackmore (lead guitar) and Ian Paice (drums). Roger Glover and Ian Gillan were to replace Evans and

Simper in 1969.

Deep Purple made their first inroads in America, having three singles in the chart that were not even released in Britain. Following *Hush*, their first album *Shades Of Deep Purple* charted in America, followed by hit singles such as *Kentucky Woman* and *River Deep Mountain High*, and further albums such as *The Book Of Taliesyn* and *Deep Purple In Concert*.

Their hit singles in Britain over two decades included: *Black Night*, *Strange Kind Of Woman*, *Fireball*, *Never Before*, *Smoke On The Water*, *New Live And Rare*, *Perfect Strangers*, *Knocking At Your Back Door*, *Strangers* and a re-recorded version of *Hush*, which hit the U.K. chart in 1980.

Gillan and Glover left the group in 1973 to be replaced by Dave Coverdale and Glenn Hughes. Blackmore quit in 1975 to form Rainbow and American musician Tommy Bolin replaced him.

Deep Purple disbanded in 1976, with Coverdale forming Whitesnake,

Lord and Paice forming Paice Ashton & Lord with Tony Ashton, Hughes rejoining his former band Trapeze and Bolin returning to the States to form the Tommy Bolin Band.

Blackmore, Gillan, Glover, Lord and Paice reformed in 1984 and began to record and tour again. Gillan quit once again in 1989 to go solo. The group reunited again in 1992 with Blackmore, Lord, Paice, Glover and Gillan, releasing a new album, *The Battle Rages On* in 1993.

A new Deep Purple album, *Purpendicular* was released in 1996. It featured original members Jon Lord, Ian Gillan, Ian Paice and Roger Glover. The group which began a British tour that year included Gillan, Glover, Lord, Paice and an American musician, Steve Morse.

An entry in the Classic Album series was *Machine Head*, and in August 2003 their album *Bananas* was released in Britain to coincide with their *Bananas* world tour. Their Bananas European tour which took place in October, November and December of 2003 was one of the most

extensive European tours by a British group and took in Spain, France, Austria, Germany, the Czech Republic, Switzerland, Hungary, Finland, Estonia, Sweden, Norway, Denmark, Poland, Slovenia, Croatia, Serbia and Montenegro. The Deep Purple lineup of the *Bananas* tour was Don Airey, Ian Gillan, Roger Glover, Steve Morse and Ian Paice.

Donovan

This folk singer was born Donovan Phillip Leitch in Glasgow on May 10th 1946 and as a child his family moved to St Albans in Hertfordshire.

When he became resident on the British television programme *Ready, Steady, Go!* he was touted as the U.K.'s answer to Bob Dylan. The legendary Woody Guthrie, who had a guitar with the slogan 'This guitar kills fascists', also inspired him. In turn, Donovan's guitar sported the slogan 'This guitar kills.'

His singles between 1963 and 1968 included *Catch The Wind*, *Colours*, *Sunshine Superman*, *Mellow Yellow*, *There Is A Mountain*, *Jennifer Juni-*

Deep Purple

Marianne Faithful

per and *Hurdy Gurdy Man*. He had a dozen singles in the American charts, which he topped in 1966 with *Sunshine Superman*.

His album releases included *What's Bin Did And What's Bin Hid*, *Fairy Tale*, *Sunshine Superman*, *Universal Soldier*, *A Gift From A Flower To A Garden*, *Open Road* and *Cosmic Wheels*.

Rediffusion screened a documentary of him, *A Boy Called Donovan* and he is seen in *Don't Look Back*, the film of Bob Dylan's British tour, singing *To Sing for You* to Dylan. He also appeared on numerous American television shows including *Shindig* and *The Smothers Brothers Comedy Hour*.

His girlfriend during the 1960s was Enid Stulberger and the couple had two children, Donovan Leitch Jr and Iona Skye. They parted, however, and Donovan fell in love with Linda Lawrence, girlfriend of Brian Jones of the Rolling Stones.

Due to his immense success on record on both sides of the Atlantic, he became a tax exile. Following a Japanese tour in 1970, however, he decided to give up being a tax exile and retuned to Britain where he met up again with Linda Lawrence. They renewed their romance and married that same year. Linda had had a son Julian, by the late Brian Jones of the Rolling Stones, and she and Donovan were to have two daughters, Oriole and Astrella.

Donovan had composed a film score for *Poor Cow* in the late 1960s and in the early 1970s composed further ones for *If It's Tuesday, It Must Be Belgium* (he is seen performing *Lord of the Reedy River* in a hotel), *The Pied Piper* and *Brother Sun, Sister Moon*. He then decided to retire from music and he and Linda went to live a simple life in a place in California called Joshua Tree. After a gap of six years he decided to enter the recording studio once more and the couple returned to Britain to raise their children. He cut three further albums but then suffered a period of ill health and they moved back to the desert at the end of the 1980s.

In 1990 they moved to Ireland and Donovan began presenting a series of seminars and workshops called *Music and the Myth*, he also revived his recording career during the 1990s and his albums include *Donovan Rising* in 1990, *Troubadour* in 1992, *One Night In Time* in 1993 and *Sutras* in 1996. In 2002 he issued a CD for children called *Pied Piper* and in 2003 toured America and Spain.

Marianne Faithfull

Marianne Faithfull was the daughter of Austrian Baroness Eva Sacher Masoch and University lecturer Glynn Faithfull. With her angelic looks and virginal image, she became one of the major female pop figures of the 60s.

Marianne, born in Hampstead, London on December 29th 1946, was still attending St Joseph's convent school in Reading when her boyfriend John Dunbar took her to a party in London where she met the Rolling Stones and their manager Andrew Oldham.

Oldham was impressed by the seventeen-year-old girl's beauty and visual innocence and signed her up, issuing her recording of a Jagger/ Richards song *As Tears Go By*, which reached No. 9 in the British charts. Her follow-up, *Come And Stay With Me* reached No. 4. In 1965 she married Dunbar and later in the year gave birth to a son, Nicholas.

Her other record successes of the 60s included *This Little Bird* and *Summer Nights*.

The reputation and image of the convent-educated girl began to change from February 1967 when she was among the guests at Keith Richards' house Redlands when the

Georgie Fame

police raided the premises for drugs. Although Marianne was not charged, there were stories that she'd been caught with a rug draped over her naked body.

Marianne also left her husband to live with Mick Jagger, having been determined to become part of the Rolling Stones' world, commenting, "I slept with three and then decided the lead singer was the best bet."

The English rose image received another hammering when she co-starred in *The Girl On The Motorcycle*, a film with Alain Delon in which she did some steamy sex scenes. She

also appeared in the films *I'll Never Forget What's His Name* and *Don't Look Back*.

It seemed, however, that she did have talent as an actress and she appeared in Chekhov's *Three Sisters* at the Royal Court Theatre and was to star as Ophelia opposite Nicol Williamson in a film version of *Hamlet*.

In 1968 she became pregnant by Mick Jagger, but miscarried.

What really wrecked her career was her increasing dependence on drugs and both Marianne and Jagger were arrested for possession of marijuana in May 1969. The same year she travelled to Australia to co-star in the film *Ned Kelly* with Mick, but went into a coma after an overdose and was hospitalised and treated for heroin addiction.

Her divorce from Dunbar came through and her ex-husband was awarded custody of their son. Mick Jagger dropped her and she had no further record success apart from a minor hit in 1979, the year in which she married Ben Brierly, a member of the punk band the Vibrators. She continued to suffer from the drug habit and was again arrested for possession.

In subsequent years she has made a number of albums, which have received critical acclaim, such as *Broken English* in 1979 and *Dangerous Acquaintances*.

Her autobiography *Faithfull* was published in 1994.

These days she is busier than ever and recent albums have included *Blazing Away*, *Twentieth Century Blues* and *Vagabond Ways*. Of partic-

ular interest is *Kissin' Time* an album that featured Marianne recording with several guest artists including Blue, Beck, Jarvis Cocker and Billy Corgan.

Georgie Fame

Georgie was born Clive Powell in Leigh, Lancashire on June 26th 1943. On leaving school he became an apprentice cotton weaver and in his spare time began playing piano with a local group the Dominoes. Whilst at Butlin's holiday camp he was spotted by Rory Blackwell, leader of Rory Blackwell & the Blackjacks, who offered him a job.

Clive left his work in the cotton mill to move down to London with the Blackjacks and was spotted by London impresario Larry Parnes who signed him to a management contract and re-named him Georgie Fame. Initially, together with four other musicians, he joined a backing band for Billy Fury, but after a dispute the group left Fury and became known as Georgie Fame & the Blue Flames. In March 1962 they began a three-year residency at the Flamingo Club in London's Soho.

He topped the charts with his first record *Yeh Yeh* in December 1964 and the single went on to chart in America. Georgie had a dozen British hits between December 1964 and December 1969, including a second No. 1, *The Ballad Of Bonnie & Clyde*, which also charted in America.

In the early 1970s he teamed up with former Animals member Alan Price and they even had their own television series *The Price Of Fame*.

In 1974 Georgie reformed his Blue Flames and was to appear with a number of jazz artists ranging from Count Basie to Annie Ross. He also recorded and performed with various other artists such as Van Morrison.

Still performing as a professional after forty years in show business Georgie has recorded twenty albums and has had fourteen chart hits.

In 1990 his *Cool Cat Blues* album, recorded in New York featured several guest artists including Van Morrison, Boz Scaggs and John Hendricks. The following year his *The Blues And Me* album featured guest artists such as Dr John and Phil Woods. He recorded an album *Endangered Species* with the Danish Big Band, issued in 1992 and the following year another album *City Life* on which he was accompanied by Madeline Bell and the *BBC Big Band* was released. In his 1994 album *Three Line Whip* his sons Tristan and James supported him and in 1997 he teamed up with Bill Wyman in the Rhythm Kings.

The same year he released another Three Line Whip album *Name Droppin'*. 2000 saw the release of his *Poet In New York* CD and the following year saw another Three Line Whip album *Relationships* and a compilation album of his recordings *Funny How Time Slips By: The Pye Anthology*.

The Fortunes

The group formed in Birmingham in 1963 and comprised Glen Dale and Barry Pritchard (guitar and vocals), David Carr (keyboards), Rod Allen (bass and vocals) and Andy

Brown (drums). They made their recording debut with *Summertime, Summertime*, and their follow-up *Caroline* was adopted by the pirate radio station Radio Caroline as its signature tune.

Five of the group's singles were chart entries in Britain and their American hits were *You've Got Your Troubles*, *Here It Comes Again* and *Here Comes That Rainy Day Feeling Again*. They are also the voices behind the American Coca Cola commercials 'It's The Real Thing', which is still heard today.

In 1966 Dale left the band to turn solo and was replaced by Shel MacRae. Carr left the group in 1968 and they remained a quartet until George McAllister joined them in 1971.

David Carr now lives in America and is a record producer. Andy Brown works in a Worcester post office. Glen Dale resides in Tenerife in the Canary Islands and performs locally as a solo artist. Barry Pritchard has retired from the music business on health grounds. Rod Allen still

The Fortunes

leads the Fortunes on the 60s nostalgia circuit. The other members of his band are Mike Smitham, who joined in 1995 (guitar), Paul Hooker (drums) and Bob Jackson, a former member of Badfinger, (keyboards).

The group were still performing as part of the 'Call Up The Groups' British tour in January 2004.

The Foundations

The group originally formed in 1967 with members from Ceylon, Jamaica, Trinidad, Barbados and Dominica. This group comprised Alan Warner (guitar), Clem Curtis (vocals), Pat Bourke (sax), Eric Allendale (trombone), Peter MacBeth (bass), Tony Gomez (organ), Mike Elliott (tenor sax) and Tim Harris (drums).

Tony Macauley, who was their original manager, penned their debut hit *Baby, Now That I've Found You*.

Curtis, who had been born in Trinidad, moved to Britain when he was

15 and became a boxer. He was then asked to join the Foundations.

The group embarked on a world tour and appeared in 30 different American States. Whilst over there Sammy David Jr talked Curtis into going solo and he began appearing on the US club circuit and in Las Vegas. Colin Young replaced him. The group next had their biggest American hit *Build Me Up Buttercup*, followed by *In the Bad Bad Old Days*. Curtis returned to the U.K., deciding to lead a group called the Foundations and there are now two groups, one led by Curtis, the other by Young. In between his Foundation gigs, Curtis runs an antique business near Milton Keynes.

Freddie & the Dreamers

This group was originally formed in Manchester in October 1961. The members were Freddie Garrity (vocals), Derek Quinn (lead), Roy Crewsdon (rhythm), Pete Birrell

The Foundations

(bass) and Bernie Dwyer (drums).

Leader Freddie was born on November 14 1940 and was originally a member of the bands the Red Six and the Kingfishers before deciding to form his own group. They appeared at Liverpool's Cavern club and also performed in Hamburg, Germany.

The success of the Beatles led to record companies signing up numerous groups and the Dreamers were

contracted to Columbia, making their debut with *If You Gotta Make A Fool Of Somebody*. Freddie next co-wrote *I'm Telling You Now* with songwriter Mitch Murray.

The group had a comedy act in which Freddie pranced and danced around in a gawky fashion, creating a dance called *Do The Freddie*, which resulted in a single of the same name especially for the American market. Advance orders in America exceeded 200,000, the biggest order for a Mercury Records single at that time.

Freddie & the Dreamers found international fame and appeared in a number of films, including *What A Crazy World*, *Just For You* and *Every Day's A Holiday*.

Their other hit singles included *You Were Made For Me*, *Over You*, *I Love You Baby*, *Just For You*, *I Understand*, *A Little You* and *Thou Shalt Not Steal* – all between 1963 and 1965.

The original personnel changed in 1968 with Freddie finding a new backing band, which he also called the Dreamers, to appear on the cabaret circuit. Freddie and Birrell also appeared regularly on the weekly British children's television show *Little Big Time*. In 1988 Freddie was in a stage production of *The Tempest*.

He continued to work with different line-ups of the Dreamers. The other original members are no longer performing. Birrell became a taxi driver, Crewsden has his own bar in the Canary Isles, Quinn works for a soft drinks company and Dwyer has since died.

For a number of years Freddie has also been appearing in pantomimes (a British seasonal traditional theatre show) during the Christmas season in

roles such as Silly Billy in *Jack & the Beanstalk*. In 1996 he played a drug-pushing disc jockey in the hit British television series *Heartbeat*.

Sadly, he is now quite ill. Freddie collapsed following an American tour and had a mild heart attack. He finds it difficult to breath and has systemic sclerosis and spends much of his time in a wheelchair.

Gerry & the Pacemakers
Gerry Marsden was born in Liverpool on September 14th 1942. He led his first skiffle group at the age of fourteen and in 1959 transformed it into a rock 'n' roll band with his brother Freddie on drums, Les Chadwick on guitar and Les Maguire on piano.

Freddie & the Dreamers

Herman's Hermits

They were placed at No. 2 to the Beatles in the 1961 Mersey Beat poll and signed with Brian Epstein, who attempted to repeat his success with the Beatles by promoting them in the same way.

The group hit the No. 1 spot in Britain with a number the Beatles had turned down, *How Do You Do It*. They then topped the chart with their two subsequent releases, *I Like It* and *You'll Never Walk Alone*, making them the first artists ever to reach No. 1 in the U.K. with their first three records. As a result, Gerry's recording of *You'll Never Walk Alone* became a British football anthem.

Gerry & the Pacemakers had four further hits, *I'm The One*, *Don't Let The Sun Catch You Crying*, *Ferry 'Cross The Mersey* and *I'll Be There*.

The group disbanded and Gerry appeared in the stage musical *Charlie Girl* in London's West End. He then went on to working with children's television programmes.

In the 1970s he re-formed Gerry & the Pacemakers with different personnel and has been touring ever since. His brother Freddie launched a minicab company in Liverpool in 1996 called Pacemakers and Les Chadwick has been living in Australia since the early 1970s.

Following the Bradford City Football Club disaster in May 1985, in which 55 people were killed when a fire destroyed a stand, Gerry recorded *You'll Never Walk Alone* again as a charity disc to raise funds for the families of the victims. Under the name the Crowd he enrolled fifty artists to join him on the record, includ-

ing Paul McCartney and Zak Starkey. The record reached No. 1 – the first time an artist had topped the British charts with two different versions of the same number.

Gerry's autobiography *I'll Never Walk Alone* was published in 1993. He has been appearing on the Flying Music Solid Silver Sixties Tours almost annually and in 1996 featured in a stage musical based on his life, *Ferry 'Cross The Mersey*. In 2003

he was awarded an M.B.E. by Queen Elizabeth II and on September 3rd 2003 he had a triple heart-bypass operation.

Herman's Hermits

Herman's Hermits were originally known as the Heartbeats when they formed in Manchester in 1963. The group comprised Peter Noone (vocals), Karl Green (bass), Keith Hopwood (rhythm), Lek Leckenby (lead guitar) and Barry Whitwam (drums).

Although born in Manchester on November 5th 1947, Noone (whose full name was Peter Blair Dennis Bernard Noone) was raised in Huyton, Liverpool. Apart from fronting his group he was also appearing in the Granada Television soap *Coronation Street* and when leading British recording manager Mickie Most was watching the programme he thought that Noone looked like a young John F. Kennedy and got in touch with him. At the time Peter and his group had been appearing regularly at the Cavern in Liverpool.

Most had already signed the Animals and recorded Herman's Hermits performing the Goffin/King number *I'm Into Something Good*. Not only did their debut disc top the British charts, it established them in America.

Noone married a French girl Mireille Strasser in 1971, by which time he had a solo hit *Oh You Pretty Thing* under his own name. Although he'd gone solo in 1970 Noone reunited with Herman's Hermits for a British Invasion concert at Madison Square Garden in New York in 1973.

After appearing in cabaret for a number of years he settled in Los Angeles in 1980 and formed a group called the Tremblers, although they were not successful. In 1983 he returned to London to star in the musical *The Pirates Of Penzance* before returning to America where he found success once again, this time as a disc jockey and television presenter, running his own show *My Generation* for five years.

Following their initial split from Noone in 1970, Herman's Hermits remained in America appearing on the cabaret circuit. They then returned to Britain and have since continued to appear on nostalgia tours, although by 1997 there was only one original member of Herman's Hermits in the line-up- drummer Whitwam.

Noone once again teamed up with the group and has been touring regularly as Herman's Hermits With Peter Noone, completing another American tour in 2003.

Derek Leckenby died in Manchester in1996 of non-Hodgkins lymphona.

The Hollies

This Manchester group was noted for vocal harmonies. Allan Clarke and Graham Nash had already been performing as a duo and with the addition of Eric Haydock on bass and Don Rathbone on drums, they became the Fourtones.

The group changed their name to the Hollies in 1962 and were spotted performing at Liverpool's Cavern Club the following year by A&R man Ron Richards. With the addition of Tony Hicks on guitar, they made their recording debut with (*Ain't That*) *Just Like Me*. After this, Bobby Elliott replaced Rathbone on drums.

The Hollies had more than thirty singles in the British charts and have topped it twice, with *I'm Alive* in 1965 and *He Ain't Heavy, He's My Brother* in 1988. Among their other major hits were *Just One Look*, *Here I Go Again*, *On A Carousel*, *Carrie-Anne* and *The Air That I Breathe*. They also had a number of album successes.

Nash left the group at the end of 1968 because he had become dissatisfied with their musical direction and immediately teamed up with David Crosby and Stephen Stills in America. Terry Sylvester, a former member of Liverpool groups the Escorts and the Swinging Bluejeans, replaced him.

Clarke also decided to leave and was replaced by Mikael Rickfors, a singer from Sweden. Clarke's solo efforts proved unsuccessful and he rejoined the group in 1973.

During the 1980s there were various line-up changes, and the original

The Hollies

Mary Hopkin

members got together again with Graham Nash for a reunion recording of an album *What Goes Around*, in Los Angeles in 1983. Allan Clarke, Tony Hicks and Bobby Elliott continued during the decade, with the addition of Alan Coates and Ray Stiles.

A 3 CD boxed set, *Treasured Hits And Hidden Treasures* was released in 1993 and the Hollies got together again with Graham Nash for a recording at Abbey Road in late 1995, which resulted in the single *Peggy Sue Got Married*.

'The Hollies At Abbey Road '66-70' was issued in 1998. This CD featured a previously unreleased track *Schoolgirl*, written by Graham Gouldman. Extra guitars had been added by Tony Hicks and mixed down by his son, Abbey Road engineer Paul Hicks.

The Hollies are still recording and touring during the 21st Century and the current personnel comprised Carl Wayne, Tony Hicks, Bobby Elliot, Alan Coates, Ian Parker and Ray Stiles.

Their fortieth anniversary in 2003 saw them touring Britain, Germany and Denmark between January and November with plans for further tours of Britain and the U.S. in 2004. Their anniversary album *The Hollies Greatest Hits* also included a new track *How Do I Survive* by Carl Wayne and also released in 2002 was *The Hollies Special Edition*, a DVD EP containing four tracks, *Jennifer Eccles*, *Do The Best You Can*, *Listen To Me* and *Sorry Suzanne*. *The Long Road Home* was a 6 CD boxed set celebrating the forty-year career with five CDs of tracks from their EPs and albums, A and B sides and some previously unreleased tracks.

Former bass player Eric Haydock leads the Eric Haydock Band and Terry Sylvester lives in Canada.

Mary Hopkin

Born in Pontardawe, Wales on May 3rd 1950, this singer came to the attention of Paul McCartney after the fashion model Twiggy spotted her on the British television talent show 'Opportunity Knocks'.

McCartney signed her to *Apple Records* and picked and produced her first single, *Those Were The Days*, which sold five million copies after its release in 1968, reaching No 1 in the UK charts and No. 2 in America. Paul wrote and produced her second single *Goodbye*, which reached No. 2 in Britain and was also an American Top twenty entry.

McCartney produced Mary's album *Postcard* and next single, *Que Sera Sera*. She then chose her sister Carol to be her manager and within a year had left *Apple*.

Her next releases were produced initially by Mickie Most and then by Tony Visconti, whom she married. She gave birth to the first of her two children, a son Morgan and a daughter, Jessica.

After she left *Apple*, Mary's hits were *Temma Harbour*, *Knock Knock Who's There?*, *Think About Your Children*, *Let My Name Be Sorrow* and *If You Love Me*.

Having spent time raising her family, she appeared in a group called Sundance in the early 1980s and then another band called Oasis. Mary also appeared as a backing singer on various records including Thin Lizzie's *Dear Lord* and David Bowie's *Sound and Vision* and records by Tom Paxton and Ralph McTell.

Now divorced from Visconti (who went on to marry John Lennon's former girlfriend May Pang, although that marriage also ended), Mary Hopkin lives less than five miles upriver from the late George Harrison's Friar Park estate.

In 2001 she had a small part in the Welsh film, *Very Annie Mary* and the following year entered Strongbox Studios in Wales to re-record *Those Were The Days*, with a spoken word contribution from American actor/comedian Robin Williams. Later in 2002 she appeared in concerts with various different acts ranging from the Chieftains to Welsh band the

Crocketts.

Engelbert Humperdinck

Engelbert Humperdinck was born Arnold George Dorsey in Madras, India on May 2nd 1936 as his father was in the British army stationed there. The family returned to Leicester in England in the mid 1940s.

He began his singing career under the name Gerry Dorsey in 1958 appearing on shows such as *Oh Boy*, but did not have much success with releases such as *I'll Never Fall In Love Again*. Groups rather than solo singers seemed to be ruling the roost in the British charts in the mid 1960s and apart from his lack of success on record, he suffered a bout of tuberculosis and had to abandon singing for several months. Gordon Mills, Tom Jones' manager, decided to take him under his wing and changed his name to Engelbert Humperdinck, after the Austrian classical composer.

Engelbert had a stroke of luck when his single *Release Me* was issued. A cancellation by another artist meant he was put on the hit show *Sunday Night At The London Palladium* at the last minute. This was the biggest television show in Britain with an audience of twenty million and had launched many an artist into the big time. Following his appearance the record topped the British charts and was also his first American hit.

In Britain it kept the Beatles new single *Penny Lane/ Strawberry Fields Forever* from the top spot. However, it must be considered that George Martin issued the Beatles single as a double A side, which split the sales. He later said he regretted the decision because it cost them the No. 1 spot.

Other hits followed and Engelbert had nine charts singles in both the U.K. and the U.S. between 1967 and 1976. By that time he had left Britain to settle in America and became a regular attraction on the Las Vegas entertainment scene, not recording for a number of years. He finally made a comeback album in 1987 called *Remember I Love You*.

He still tours internationally, averaging one hundred and seventy-five concerts a year and in the year 2000 *The Ultimate Collection* CD was issued. To celebrate his 35th anniversary in show business he released a new album *Always Hear the Harmony: The Gospel Sessions*.

He followed his 2003 American tour with an Australian tour in December of that year.

Tom Jones

An artist who has sustained his American success over the decades. The Welsh singer was born Thomas Jones Woodward in Pontypridd, South Wales on June 7th 1940. A year after leaving school he married his sweetheart Melinda Trenchard and their son Mark was born the following year. In the meantime he worked at a variety of jobs; in a paper mill, as a door-to-door vacuum salesman and as a builder's labourer. He was asked to sing with the group Tommy Scott & the Senators when their lead singer suddenly left them.

The group was spotted by Gordon Mills, a Welsh impresario based in London who became their manager. He immediately named him Tom Jones, supposedly due to the popularity of the 1963 film *Tom Jones*. They

Engelbert Humperdinck

signed with *Decca* and their first release *Chills And Fever* was not a success. Then Tom was asked to make a demo for another artist of a song called *It's Not Unusual*, but decided to release the song himself. The BBC refused to play it but the pirate radio station Radio Caroline plugged the record, which then topped the British

Tom Jones

(*There Is Nothing*), *Daughter Of Darkness* and *She's A Lady*.

In 1970 he began to tour America extensively on a tax-avoidance scheme, beginning with a series of 34 one-nighters, which earned him two million pounds. He then settled there in 1974, obtaining a Green Card and buying Dean Martin's former estate in Bel Air. When Gordon Mills died in 1986, Tom's son Mark became his manager and, after a drought of ten years without a chart entry, Tom began to record numbers, which brought him into the chart arena again, such as the hit single *The Boy From Nowhere*. He had enjoyed other highlights, such as appearing on the popular animated series *The Simpsons* and in the film *Mars Attacks!*

In 2000 he received the Brit Award as Best Male Singer and the Spanish Amigo Award as Best International Male Singer. 1999 saw the release of his record *Reload*, a series of duets with hot new acts, which became his biggest selling album, going platinum six times in the U.K. and selling over four million copies worldwide.

In 2002 he recorded an album *Mr Jones* with hip-hop superstar Wyclef Jean and in October 2003 Universal released *Reloaded: The Greatest Hits* and Tom appeared on most of the major American television shows to promote it. Between October and December he appeared on *Larry King Live*, *Good Morning America*, *Regis & Kelly* and *The Tonight Show with Jay Leno*.

The Kinks

Formed in 1962, this group com-

prised Ray Davies and Dave Davies (vocals and guitar), Peter Quaife (bass) and Mick Avory (drums).

Since they topped the U.K. chart in 1964 with *You Really Got Me* they have continued to chart over three decades. Their hit singles have included *All Day And All Of The Night*, *Tired Of Waiting For You*, *Everybody's Gonna Be Happy*, *Set Me Free*, *See My Friend*, *Till The End Of The Day*, *Dedicated Follower Of Fashion*, *Sunny Afternoon*, *Dead End Street*, *Waterloo Sunset*, *Autumn Almanac*, *Wonderboy*, *Days*, *Plastic Man*, *Victoria*, *Lola*, *Apeman*, *Supersonic Rocket Ship*, *Better Things*, *Come Dancing* and *Don't Forget To Dance*.

They have also had numerous chart albums, including *Kinks*, *Kinda Kinks*, *Kinks Kontroversy*, *Well Respected Man*, *Face To Face*, *Something Else* and *Sunny Afternoon*.

It was rumoured that Ray's *Waterloo Sunset* was originally called *Liverpool Sunset* and the 'dirty old river' referred to the Mersey. However, when the Beatles came out with the single *Penny Lane/Strawberry Fields Forever*, Ray changed the title.

Raymond Douglas Davies was born in London on June 21ˢᵗ 1944 and is acknowledged as one of Britain's premier songwriters. For the group he also composed a number of rock operas: *Arthur*, *The Village Green Preservation Society* and *Soap Opera*. As an actor he played the lead in the television drama *The Long Distance Piano Player* and for Channel Four has directed *Return To Waterloo* in 1983 and in 1994 a docu-

charts. It also became his first American success.

Tom then had a formidable string of hits for almost two decades with such numbers as *What's New Pussycat?*, *Thunderball*, *The Green, Green Grass Of Home*, *Delilah*, *Love Me Tonight*, *Help Yourself*, *I'll Never Fall In Love Again*, *Without Love*

mentary of Charles Mingus, *Weird Nightmare*.

In recent years the leader of the Kinks has been touring with a very successful three hour one-man show, presenting an evening of music and anecdotes. The show is called *The Storyteller: An Evening With A Twentieth Century Man*. He plays acoustic versions of old Kinks hits and specially written new material, together with tracks from the Kinks CD *To The Bone and Animal*. His first solo album *The Story Teller* was released in March 1998.

Ray, whose 1995 autobiography is called *X-Ray*, has had an eventful life. He has suffered a couple of drugs overdoses, left his wife and children in 1973. He divorced his second wife Yvonne in 1981 when he began an affair with singer Chrissie Hynde, who gave birth to the couple's daughter, Natalie. Hynde left Ray in 1984 to take up with Jim Kerr of Simple Minds.

Ray Davies currently lives in London and in October 1997 published a book of his short stories, entitled *Waterloo Sunset*. Over the years he has also penned several stage musicals.

In 2003 he began recording a new album at Konk Studios and ITV is planning a documentary on him to be screened in Britain in 2004.

Dave Davies is based in California, where he writes screenplays and composes movie soundtracks. His autobiography was called 'Kink'. He has had several solo album releases

The Kinks

including *Rock Bottom: Live At The Bottom Line* and his most recent studio album, in May 2002, 'Bug'. He also released a new CD in 2003, *Transformation*.

Peter Quaife, now Peter Kinnes, emigrated to Canada. He is now a self-employed fine artist in Ontario whose exhibition in 1994 contained work of an autobiographical nature. He also teaches classical guitar.

Mick Avory left the group in 1984 and was replaced by Bob Henrit, but he met up again with Ray and Dave when the group was inducted into the Rock & Roll Hall Of Fame in 1990. He also appeared on a 1993 album for the Kinks called 'Phobia'. He is a mainstay of a group called Shut Up Frank, is a keen golfer and continues to work in an administrative capacity for Konk, the Kinks organisation. He also occasionally appears with an outfit called Kast Off Kinks, which includes John Dalton and various other members of the group from the 1970s.

Very occasionally Ray and Dave lead a reformed Kinks on limited appearances.

June 2003 saw the release of *The Kinks Ultimate Collection* and Sanctuary Records released 'Kinks BBC Sessions 1964-1977' and Ryko Records issued another Kinks album *This Is Where I Belong*.

Lulu

Lulu was born Marie McDonald McLaughlin Lawrie on November 3rd 1948 in Lennoxtown, Scotland. At the age of 15 she was singing with a band called the Gleneagles when Marion Massey signed her to a management deal and changed the group's name to Lulu & the Luvvers.

They entered the British top ten with their debut record *Shout* and other hits followed: *Here Comes The Night*, *Leave A Little Love* and *Try To Understand*.

Lulu went out on her own in 1966 and her solo hits included *The Boat That I Row*, *Let's Pretend*, *Love Loves To Love*, *Me The Peaceful Heart*, *Boy, I'm A Tiger*, *Boom Bang-A-Bang*, *Oh Me Oh My (I'm A Fool For You Baby)*, *The Man Who Sold The World*, *Take Your Mama For A Ride* and *I Could Never Miss You (More Than I Do)*.

Lulu

1966 was, in fact, a boom year for Lulu. Apart from three major chart hits she filmed her first BBC TV series *Three Of A Kind* and toured America, appearing on several top TV shows including *The Ed Sullivan Show*, *The Johnny Carson Show* and *the David Frost Show*. On her return to England she appeared on the *Royal Variety Show* at the London Palladium.

She appeared in the movie *To Sir With Love*, which was released in America in April 1967 and broke box office records. Producer/director James Clavell commented, "This girl has a naturalness, a straightforward quality coupled with a really exciting personality. A very important movie quality indeed".

Lulu also recorded the title song, which topped the American chart, remaining in the No. 1 position for five weeks, making her the only non-American female artists to remain at the top of the U.S. charts for that length of time. Strangely, the number was not released as an A side in Britain. Producer Mickie Most decided that *The Boat That I Row* was more commercial. It was the first time that an American No. 1 record by a British artist was not released in the U.K.

In 1986 she charted with another version of *Shout*, causing *Decca* to re-release the original Lulu & the Luvvers version and the combined sales took it into the Top ten.

Lulu's Eurovision Song Contest appearance in 1969 resulted in a win for her with *Boom Bang-A-Bang*, although she shared first place with the entries for France, Spain and the Netherlands. She had her own television series and David Bowie produced her when she recorded his composition *The Man Who Sold The World*.

1968 saw her appearing in several American venues, including the Coconut Grove in Hollywood and that year she was voted 'The Most Promising Female Vocalist of the Year'. The following year she appeared on several American television shows, had a season at the Flamingo, Las Vegas and in 1970 toured America with Engelbert Humperdinck and co-hosted *The Andy Williams Show*.

In 1972 she teamed up with comedian Dudley Moore for a television series *It's Lulu, Not to Mention Dudley Moore*. Over the years Lulu has

appeared in fourteen television series, including *Lulu's Back In Town*, *Happening to Lulu* and *It's Lulu*.

Lulu married Maurice Gibb of the Bee Gees in April 1969, but they separated in 1973 and she then married hairstylist John Frieda in 1976. They were also to split up.

In 1980 she appeared in the TV series *Oh, Boy!* and issued the album *The Very Best Of Lulu*.

Lulu – Her Autobiography was published in November 1986 and her second autobiography *Lulu. I Don't Want to Fight* was published in 2003.

In 1993 Barry Gibb produced Lulu's album *Independence* and the title track from it was issued as a single and reached No. 11 in the British charts. A second single from the album was *I'm Back For More*. She then recorded *Relight My Fire* with the popular Boy Band, *Take That*, which topped the British charts. She continued to have hits with *How 'Bout Us*, *Goodbye Baby And Amen* and *Every Woman Knows*.

The Queen presented Lulu with an O.B.E. in June 2000 and in December of that year she received the honour of a Doctorate of Music from the University of Westminster.

In March 2003 Taragon Records in America issued a nineteen-track compilation CD *The Best Of Lulu 1967-1968*.

Manfred Mann

This group were originally launched in London in 1962 as the Mann-Hugg Blues Brothers, but changed their name to Manfred Mann the following year. In 1964 they were asked to write a theme tune for the British television pop music series *Ready, Steady, Go*, it was '5-4-3-2-1' and it gave them their first hit.

The group featured Manfred Mann on keyboards. He was born Michael Lubowitz on October 21st 1940 in Johannesburg, South Africa. The vocalist was Paul Jones, born Paul Pond on February 24th 1942. Guitarist Mike Vickers was born on April 18th 1941, bass player Tom McGuinness on De-

Manfred Mann

cember 2nd 1941 and drummer Mike Hugg on August 11th 1942.

During the 1960s they had 17 hits, including *Hubble Bubble Toil And Trouble*, *Do Wah Diddy-Diddy*, *Sha La La*, *Come Tomorrow*, *Oh No, Not My Baby*, *If You Gotta Go Go Now*, *Pretty Flamingo*, *You Gave Me Somebody To Love*, *Just Like A Woman*, *Semi-Detached Suburban Mr James*, *Ha Ha Said The Clown*, *Sweet Pea*, *Mighty Quinn*, *My Name Is Jack*, *Fox On The Run* and *Ragamuffin Man*.

Vickers left in 1965 and was replaced by Jack Bruce. Bruce left the following year to join Cream at the same time as Jones quit to concentrate on a solo career. Mike D'Abo replaced Jones and Klaus Voormann joined on bass.

Jones reached the Top five with his first solo release, *High Time*, his other hits included *I've Been A Bad Bad Boy*, *Thinkin' Ain't For Me* and *Aquarius*. He appeared in the film

Privilege with model Jean Shrimpton and then quit the music scene for more than a decade to concentrate on acting work, mainly in the theatre.

Manfred Mann disbanded in June 1969 and Mann formed Emanon, which did not last for very long. He then began to compose advertising jingles with Mike Hugg.

McGuinness formed McGuinness Flint with drummer Hughie Flint, guitarists Benny Gallagher and Graham Lyle, and Dennis Coulson on keyboards, while Mann and Hugg formed Manfred Mann Chapter Three, but disbanded it after a few

months. McGuinness Flint had big hits with *When I'm Dead And Gone* and *Malt And Barley Blues*. They were to split up in 1975.

In 1972 Manfred Mann formed Manfred Mann's Earth Band with guitarist Mick Rogers, bassist Colin Pattenden and drummer Chris Slade. Their chart hits included *Joybringer*, *Blinded By The Light*, *Davy's On The Road Again*, *You Angel You*, and *Don't Kill It Carol*.

Paul Jones and Tom McGuinness reunited in 1979 to form the Blues Band.

Manfred Mann still leads Manfred Mann's Earth Band, working mostly in Europe. He says he rarely plays in the U.K. because the overheads of touring are too expensive. His band features original members Chris Slade and Mick Rogers.

Paul Jones, Mike d'Abo, Tom McGuinness, Mike Hugg, Mike Vickers, Benny Gallagher and Rob Townsend (a former member of Family) regrouped as the Manfreds in the late 1980s. They are an ongoing in-concert recreation of the group's most familiar moments. Each member, however, pursues other projects within the entertainment industry. D'Abo, for example, is a West Country radio presenter and Jones and McGuinness are mainstays of the Blues Band.

Manfred Mann records still sell well and at the close of 1996 EMI issued a twenty-six-track CD called *Groovin' With The Manfreds*. The multi-talented Manfreds produce a tremendous concert performance, with twenty-six numbers from the huge hit repertoire of the various members.

The Mindbenders

The Mindbenders were originally formed in Manchester in 1963 as the Jets. They signed with the Fontana label and changed their name to Wayne Fontana & the Mindbenders. Their initial recordings were the covers of American numbers, which were included in the basic repertoire of most groups in the north west of England at the time. They released

Hello Josephine' (with *Roadrunner*), *For You, For You* (with *Love Potion No. 9*)', *Little Darlin'* (with *Come Dance With Me*) and *Stop, Look & Listen* (with *Duke of Earl*). They finally hit the charts with their cover of Major Lance's *Um, Um, Um, Um, Um, Um* and followed with an even bigger hit, *The Game Of Love*, which also topped the American charts.

Wayne Fontana and the group went their separate ways in October 1965 and the Mindbenders who comprised Eric Stewart (guitar), Bob Lang (bass) and Ric Rothwell (drums) had

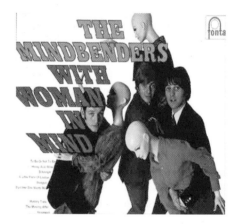

immediate success with *A Groovy Kind Of Love*, followed by *Ashes To Ashes*. They also appeared in the film *To Sir With Love* in 1968 before they disbanded.

Eric Stewart, who was born in Manchester on January 20th 1945, went on to form Inter City Studios in Stockport with Pete Tattersall, which they relocated to Manchester the following year, calling it Strawberry Studios. It became the first major recording studio outside London. Eric also teamed up with his former school

friends Kevin Godley, Lol Crème and Graham Gouldman to form Hotlegs, who had a hit with *Neanderthal Man*. They changed their name to 10cc and had a string of major hits.

Eric was later asked to perform as a musician singer on Paul McCartney's *Pipes Of Peace* and *Tug Of War* albums and then to collaborate with Paul on writing songs for the album *Press To Play*. He was also featured in the *Give My Regards To Broadway* film and played on the album.

10cc disbanded in 1983 but the members recorded a reunion album. There have been several further reunion concerts over the years.

The Moody Blues

Vocalist Denny Laine (real name Brian Hines), formerly of Denny Laine & the Diplomats, teamed up with Ray Thomas, Mike Pinder, Graeme Edge and Clint Warwick to form this group in Birmingham in 1964. Their debut single was *Lose Your Money*. Their second release, *Go Now* in 1965 topped the British charts.

Warwick left the group, and the music business, in 1966, and Rod Clarke replaced him. A few months later the group split up, with Laine embarking on a solo career. Within a matter of weeks Thomas, Pinder and Edge had re-formed with the addition of John Lodge and Justin Hayward.

1968 was an important year, open-

The Moody Blues

ing with the release of *Nights In White Satin*, penned by Hayward, plus the album *Days Of Future Passed*. The same year saw the release of a second album *In Search Of the Lost Chord*, plus the singles *Voices In The Sky*, *Tuesday Afternoon* and *Ride My See Saw*. In 1994 they released an 80-track boxed set, *Time Traveller*.

Singles hits over the years have included *Question*, *The Story In Your Eyes*, *Isn't Life Strange*, *Driftwood*, *Gemini Dream*, *I Know You're Out There Somewhere* and *Say It With Love*. The classic *Nights In White Satin* has entered the charts on several occasions.

The group have released twenty-six albums, some of the most recent being *Anthology* in 1998, *Strange Times* in 1999 and *Hall Of Fame* in 2000. Their first studio album in almost five years was *December*, their first seasonable album featuring several Christmas classics, plus some original Christmas numbers by the group. This also tied in with their 2003 American tour by the three mainstays of the group, Justin Hayward, Graeme Edge and John Lodge.

Denny Laine appeared on a nation-wide tour in 1996 and the following year, in partnership with business-man John Ashworth, opened a club called the Rhythm Station, near Manchester.

Peter & Gordon

Gordon Trueman Riviere Waller was born in Braemar, Scotland on June 4th 1945 and Peter Asher in London on June 22nd 1944. The two first met at Westminster School and teamed up as a folk duo, Gordon & Peter.

One of Peter's sisters was Jane Asher, who was Paul McCartney's girlfriend at the time. Peter asked him to provide them with a song and he gave them *World Without Love*, which became their debut disc and a British chart-topper. By that time they were billed as Peter & Gordon.

Paul then provided them with *Nobody I Know*, which was another million-seller. The duo then flew to America to appear on the *Ed Sullivan Show*.

Del Shannon gave their third disc, *I Go To Pieces* to them and although it did not make an impact in Britain, it reached No. 9 in the U.S. chart. Their next hits were *True Love Ways*, followed by *To Know You Is To Love You* and *Baby I'm Yours*.

Paul McCartney supplied the duo another number, *Woman* which was published under the pseudonym Bernard Webb and was again a trans-atlantic hit for them. They had one further British hit, *Lady Godiva* and two other singles *Sunday For Tea* and *The Jokers*.

Due to the ever-changing tastes in music, in 1967 Peter suggested to Gordon that they split.

Gordon Waller never had another chart placing. He went to New York to record a solo album '...and Gordon' and then released the solo singles *Rosecrans Boulevard* and *Weeping Analeah* and an album on Bell. In 1973 he appeared as Judas in *Joseph & the Amazing Technicolor Dreamcoat* at the Edinburgh Festival and also in London and Australia. It was while he was in Australia that he got married.

He later worked as a photocopier salesman before settling down in

Peter & Gordon

Northamptonshire and becoming a partner in a company making radio commercials. He also formed a music publishing company *Steele Wallet International Limited*.

Gordon now lives in California and has continued to perform in that State as a solo artist.

Peter Asher became head of A&R at *Apple Records* in 1968. In 1970 he moved to America where he became a manager and producer with artists such as James Taylor, Linda Ronstadt and 10,000 Maniacs. He was nominated for Grammy awards in 1975, 1977, 1978 and 1989 and received his 'Producer Of The Year' Grammy in 1977.

Procol Harum

This group had their biggest hit in 1967 with their debut single *A Whiter Shade Of Pale*, composed by Gary Brooker and lyricist Keith Reid. The other members of the band were Matthew Fisher (organ), Dave Knights (bass), Ray Royer (guitar) and Bobby Harrison (drums). The record was eventually to sell six million copies.

Robin Trower and B.J.Wilson replaced Harrison and Royer and the group's second hit was the single 'Homburg'.

Fisher and Knights left in 1969, to be replaced by Chris Copping on bass and keyboards. By this time the band consisted of all the members of a previous band called the Paramounts, who had had a minor hit with *Poison Ivy* in 1964. Trower left in 1971 to be replaced by Dave Bell, who in turn left the band in 1972, his replacement being Mick Grabham.

American songwriters Leiber & Stoller produced Procol Harum's ninth album. There were then more personnel changes before the group disbanded following a farewell tour in 1977, although they reunited briefly the same year to appear at the BPI Awards ceremony where *A Whiter Shade Of Pale* was voted 'Best British Hit Single 1952-1977'.

Gary Brooker pursued a solo career, his album *No More Fear Of Flying* being produced by George Martin, and he also collaborated with Eric Clapton. A keen angler, he became Europe's fly-fishing champion in 1987. Brooker had also bought himself a public house in Godalming, Surrey, and formed a pub band called No Stiletto Shoes.

At the end of 1990 he decided he wanted to record another Procol Harum album and contacted Keith

Procol Harum

Reid, who by then was living in New York. The group re-formed in 1992 with the Brooker, Trower, Fisher and Reid combination and issued a new album, *The Prodigal Stranger*, although it did not become a chart hit. In 1995 they recorded a CD of symphonic versions of their hits, *The Symphonic Procol Harum*, with a full orchestra and fifty-piece choir. The group carried on touring and in 1996 teamed up with the London Symphony Orchestra to perform in the Barbican Centre.

In November 1997 the fifty-two-track triple CD set *Procol Harum: 30th Anniversary Anthology* was released. This contained their four complete albums, A and B sides of singles, demo discs and the first-ever stereo release of *A Whiter Shade Of*

Cliff Richard & the Shadows

Pale. In 1998 the eponymous *Procol Harum* was issued, their debut album from the original master tapes, plus ten bonus tracks.

Albums continue to be released and Procol Harum still tour. The personnel of their sixty-three date concert tour in 2003 comprised Gary Brooker (guitar/vocals), Matthew Fisher (Hammond organ), Mark Brzezicki (percussion), Matt Pegg (bass) and Geoff Whitehorn (lead guitar).

In 2002 *Repertoire Records* issued *Broken Barricades*, *Live In Edmon-*

ton, *Liquorice John Death* and *Singles A&B* a three CD set of all fifty-six of their seven inch singles. *Metro Records* also issued *Classic Tracks & Rarities – An Anthology*.

Cliff Richard

Britain's biggest solo star and, together with his Shadows, the leading British group act immediately prior to the Beatles. Richard has remained a chart star through four decades in Britain, an incredible record, although he did not become a star in America, despite a degree of record

success and the release of his films.

However, it would be wrong to say that Cliff never found success in America, as some sources maintain, as he had eight chart entries between 1959 and 1982. They were *Livin' Doll*, *It's All In The Game*, *Devil Woman*, *We Don't Talk Anymore*, *Carrie*, *Dreaming*, *A Little In Love* and *Daddy's Home*.

However, the Shadows, who also found record success on their own in the British charts, never enjoyed an American hit.

Cliff Richard's recording career in Britain is unique. He is the only artist to have achieved No. 1 hits in all the decades that followed his first chart-topper and can boast more than one hundred chart entries.

Cliff formed his first band, the five-piece vocal outfit the Quintones while still attending Cheshunt Secondary Modern School. On leaving school in 1957, he worked as a credit control clerk and began playing in local pubs with the Dick Teague Skiffle Group. By the following year he had formed Harry Webb and the Drifters. After playing in the 2 I's coffee bar in Soho he met Ian Samwell, who joined the group as guitarist and they decided to rename the band Cliff Richard & the Drifters.

In August 1958 he left his job to become a full-time musician and signed a contract with EMI, making his record debut with *Schoolboy Crush*, which had *Move It* on the flip. A few weeks later he was appearing on Jack Good's popular TV show *Oh Boy* and performed *Move It*, which was now promoted as the A side and reached No. 2 in the charts.

Cliff's first million-selling record and first No. 1 hit was *Livin' Doll*, which had been written by Lionel Bart for Cliff's movie debut, *Serious Charge*. The number won the Ivor Novello Award.

It was the only chart-topper for Cliff Richard & the Drifters. To avoid confusion with the American band the Drifters, the group changed their name to the Shadows.

Cliff's next No. 1 was *Travellin' Light*, penned by Sid Tepper and Roy C. Bennett, which enjoyed a five week spell at the top of the charts.

In July 1960 *Please Don't Tease* hit the top spot. This was the only record personally selected as an A side by fans. Cliff and his recording manager decided to invite 80 youngsters to EMI's HQ in Manchester Square, London for tea and biscuits to listen to 24 tracks that had been recorded at Abbey Road.

Cliff and Norrie Paramour had preferred *Nine Times Out Of Ten* as the next release, but the group of young people, who included members of Cliff's fan club, youngsters from youth clubs and representatives of EMI's younger staff members, opted for 'Please Don't Tease', which received seven hundred and fifty eight points. This was followed by *Gee Whizz It's You*, with seven hundred and twenty four points and *Nine Times Out Of Ten* with seven hundred and eight points.

Please Don't Tease slipped from the No. 1 position and then reached No. 1 again a few weeks later, which also happened with *Summer Holiday*. It remained at the top of the charts for

five weeks and was knocked off its perch by the Shadows' first instrumental hit, *Apache*, on which Cliff played bongos.

Shadows rhythm guitarist Bruce Welch and Peter Chester, son of comedian Charlie Chester, wrote *Summer Holiday*.

Bruce Welch also wrote Cliff's next No. 1 *I Love You*, which was coupled with *D In Love* and became his 9th million-selling record and his first double-A side. At this time the group were usually booked into Abbey Road studios for three hours, during which they would cut three numbers. Apart from the double-A side, the session also produced *Catch Me, I Love You* (with *D In Love*)providing Cliff with his first Christmas No. 1.

D In Love was penned by Sid Tepper and Roy C. Bennett who were later to write *The Young Ones*.

By the end of 1960, EMI's managing director L.G. Wood was able to announce that Cliff had sold five and a half million records in Britain over the past two years, an unprecedented achievement. By that time he was undoubtedly the biggest male star in Britain and had been voted Top Male Singer in most music paper polls.

Although he found the American market hard to crack, he was a major star in most countries of the world, including, outside Europe: Australia, New Zealand and South Africa.

In June 1960, *A Girl Like You* provided his fifth No. 1 hit with a song composed by Jerry Lordan, who had penned the instrumental numbers *Apache* and *Wonderful Land'* for the

Shadows.

The Young Ones went straight to No. 1 during its first week of release in January 1962 and was only the fourth single in the history of the British charts to go straight to the top spot. It was also No. 1 in India, Australia, New Zealand, South Africa, Ireland, Belgium, the Netherlands and Japan and a big hit in Finland, Sweden, Norway, Germany, Austria, Spain, Israel, Venezuela and Chile.

The song was taken from his film *The Young Ones* and the soundtrack album also reached No.1 in a year when it was announced that Cliff was voted the top box office draw in British cinemas. He also received the award as Show Business Personality of the Year.

His next double A side, Bachelor Boy (with *The Next Time*) also reached No. 1 and was taken from his film *Summer Holiday*. When it was discovered that the film was a few minutes short in length, Cliff and Bruce penned *Bachelor Boy* within a matter of minutes for a sequence filmed in the studio.

In April 1965 his new chart topper was *The Minute You're Gone*, which had been recorded the previous year when Cliff had recorded in Nashville and New York. The number was written by Jimmy Gateley and produced in Nashville by Billy Sherrill and Bob Morgan and was Cliff's first No. 1 hit without the Shadows.

The Minute You're Gone hit the top of the charts just as Cliff and the Shadows were finishing a three month season in the pantomime *Aladdin* at the London Palladium, with Cliff in the title role and the Shadows as Wishee, Washee, Noshee and Toshee.

His twenty-seventh million-seller, *Congratulations* hit the top spot in April 1968. It was the British entry for the Eurovision Song Contest, which took place at the Royal Albert Hall, London as Britain had won the contest the previous year with Sandie Shaw's *Puppet On A String*. Bill Martin and Phil Coulter, who had also been responsible for Sandie's hit, had written *Congratulations*. It lost by one point to Spain's *La La La* but proved to be a massive hit throughout Europe, even toppling *La La La* from the No. I position in Spain.

Cliff ended the 60s an international star in most countries of the world, with the exception of America, although he had a larger number of hits in that country during the decade than several of the groups regarded as part of the British Invasion.

Like Paul McCartney and George Martin, Cliff has been knighted by the Queen and is now Sir Cliff Richard.

He has sold a staggering 250 million records – and still they come. The most recent being *My Songs*, an EMI compilation of the numbers which Cliff has penned himself and *Cliff At Christmas*, a new Christmas album issued on November 17th 2003.

Cliff continues to perform and begins a series of concerts at the Royal Albert Hall in April 2004.

The Rolling Stones

In rock circles they are second only to the Beatles. The Rolling Stones had their origins in 1960 when Mick Jagger and Keith Richards were together in R&B groups.

Brian Jones, from Cheltenham, arrived in London in 1962 and began playing guitar with Alexis Korner's Blues Incorporated. He then advertised that he was forming an R&B band and pianist Ian Stewart joined him. They later teamed up with Jagger, Richards and Dick Taylor and formed a band called the Rollin' Stones. They had a variety of drummers before settling on Charlie

Watts, who had been a member of Alexis Korner's Blues Incorporated. Bill Wyman joined them in 1962.

The Beatles saw them perform in Richmond and George Harrison mentioned them to Decca A&R man Dick Rowe, who immediately signed them up. Young Andrew Loog Oldham, who had recently handled publicity for the Beatles, signed them to a management deal and decided to build an image the reverse of the comparatively clean-cut Beatles.

This was interesting in the light of the background of the two groups. The Beatles from the tough seaport of Liverpool were playing wild rock 'n' roll and R&B in Hamburg's clubs, mixing with gangsters and prostitutes. John Lennon recalls that they were at their best when playing in Liverpool and Hamburg and they sold out musically when Brian Epstein came along. Despite the reluctance of John Lennon, Epstein made them dispose of their leather outfits, dressed them in mohair suits, taught them to bow to audiences, forbade them to smoke on stage and smoothed them out until they were the loveable moptops we now know best.

The Rolling Stones, on the other hand, came from middle class backgrounds with Jones from the spa town of Cheltenham and Jagger studying at the London School of Economics.

Oldham recalled the first time he had seen the Beatles on stage: "I sat there with a lump in my throat. In one night you knew they were going to be very big. It was just an instinctive thing. From that night on, it registered subconsciously that when they made it, another section of the public was going to want to opposite".

So Oldham created the 'bad boy' image of the Stones, which infuriated Lennon, who believed they had ripped off the image of the original Beatles, an image Epstein had not allowed them to keep.

All those fans who regarded the Stones as a rougher rock 'n' roll band than the Beatles had never seen the

The Rolling Stones

real, savage Beatles of Liverpool and Hamburg.

Oldham, during the image change, got rid of Ian Stewart and changed the first word of the name from Rollin' to Rolling. The line-up now comprised Jones, Jagger, Richard (having dropped the 's'), Wyman and Watts.

They made their recording debut with *Come On*, a minor hit, but scored a bigger impact with their second release, the Lennon & McCartney number *I Wanna Be Your Man*. Their hits have continued ever since, with the majority of their material penned by Jagger and Richard.

Loog Oldham's decision to bring Jagger and Richard to the forefront as songwriters in reality placed Brian Jones on the sidelines and he left the group disillusioned in June 1969. He was arrested on a drugs charge and was sent to prison, but his medical state was such that he was released and sent for treatment in a clinic.

On July 3rd 1969 he was found dead in the swimming pool of his home. He was 25 years old. The death has always been the subject of controversy and books have been published which allege that Jones had been murdered.

Among the Stones' numerous hits were *Not Fade Away, It's All Over Now, Little Red Rooster, The Last Time, (I Can't Get No) Satisfaction, Paint It Black, Let's Spend The Night Together* and *Jumpin' Jack Flash.* All these were released in the 60s, and despite all their singles being hits, this seemed to be their most successful singles decade, with seven reaching the No. 1 spot in Britain.

They were also incredibly successful in the album field, with over thirty-five albums stretching from their debut *Rolling Stones* in 1964 to their *The Bridges Of Babylon* album many years later.

When Andrew Loog Oldham took over the management of the group he demoted pianist Ian Stewart to being the group's roadie, because he considered he did not have the right image for the group. Ian remained with them throughout their career and he was often referred to as 'the sixth Stone'. He died as a result of a heart attack in a Harley Street clinic on December 12th 1985 at the age of forty-seven. The group dedicated their 1986 album *Dirty Work* to his memory.

The Rolling Stones' entire history has been littered with exposed skeletons – drug busts, romantic affairs and so on.

The Rolling Stones' tours continued to gross higher and higher figures and now earn hundreds of millions of dollars. Despite their continuing ability to dredge in the cash, however, Bill Wyman, himself

no stranger to scandal gossip, left the group in 1993 to run a chain of Sticky Fingers restaurants.

The Stone who has created most headlines over the years is, of course, Mick Jagger. Romances with Marianne Faithfull and others have provided numerous newspaper column inches. On December 9th 1997, Jagger's wife Jerry Hall gave birth to their fourth child, Gabriel Luke Beauregard Jagger. The couple had been living together for twenty-nine years and married for six. Jagger was not present at the birth as he was still in the States completing the Rolling Stones latest tour, which

coincided with the release of their album, *Bridges To Babylon.* The tour began in 1997 and ran through 1998, although the band caused further controversy by cancelling their British appearances in August due to changes in the tax laws.

They continue to tour and their 'Licks World Tour' lasted almost two years during 2001 and 2002. November 2002 saw the release of their four DVD set *Four Flicks.* The five-hour DVD contained more than twenty-five numbers plus two documentaries *Tip Of The Tongue* and *Links Around The World*, the latter being a film of their tour. In September 2003

Crispian St Peters

ABKCO issued a seven-track maxi single *Sympathy for The Devil Remix* with the original Stones version plus remix versions by the Neptunes, Fat Boy Slim and Full Phatt. A video *Sympathy for the Devil* was also released.

Crispian St Peters

This singer was born Robin Peter Smith in Swanley, Kent on April 5th 1943. He initially joined a skiffle outfit called the Hard Travellers, followed by the group Beat Formula Three. He was spotted by David Nicolson, who became his manager and christened him with the colourful name Crispian St. Peters. Crispian recorded *At This Moment* and *No No No* and then had charts hits with *You Were On My Mind*, *Pied Piper* and *Changes*, all in 1966.

St. Peters tended to blot his copybook with extravagant claims to the music press about his vocal and songwriting talents, although he was later to say that these were just flippant comments made to a single newspaper, which were then blown out of all proportion.

When the pop hits dried up he turned to a country style, even dubbing himself Country Smith for one release in 1968. He also issued a country-style album in 1967 called 'Simply – Crispian St. Peters'.

In 1970 he suffered the first of three breakdowns. He remained in the wilderness for years until a feature in the *Beat Goes On* magazine in 1996 attracted attention and he began to emerge as a performing artist again.

1997 saw the release of 'Crispian

St. Peters: The Anthology', a twenty-nine-track CD and in 2000 the CD *Songs From The Attic* was issued. The following year he announced his final retirement due to ill health. He was hospitalised on June 30th 2003 suffering from pneumonia and his recurring schizophrenia.

The singer still lives in his native Kent.

The Searchers

The Searchers were one of the best groups to emerge from the Mersey scene. Mike Prendergast and John McNally originally teamed up as an instrumental duo, naming themselves the Searchers after the John Wayne movie. Tony Jackson joined them on bass and vocals, and Norman McGarry on drums. The group began backing singer Johnny Sandon, who then went on to front another Liverpool band, the Remo Four. When McGarry left to replace Ringo Starr in Rory Storm & the Hurricanes, Christopher Crummy joined them. Mike adopted the surname Pender and Chris became known as Chris Curtis.

Their debut single *Sweets For My Sweet* topped the British hit parade in 1963 and a Star Club recording track *Sweet Nothins'* was rush released, entering the lower end of the chart. Their second Pye release *Sugar and Spice* proved to be another big hit, reaching No. 3 in the chart. The groups other British hits were *Needles And Pins*, which also topped the chart, plus *Don't Throw Your Love Away*, *Someday We're Gonna Love Again*, *When You Walk In The Room*, *What Have They Done To The Rain*, *Goodbye My Love*, *He's Got No Love*, *When I Get Home*, *Take Me For What I'm Worth*, *Take It Or Leave It* and *Have You Ever Loved Somebody*.

The Searchers toured the States in April 1964 during which time they appeared on the *Ed Sullivan Show*. After seeing them, noted jazz critic Nat Hentoff commented, "the initial impression was more favourable musically than had been the case with the Beatles and the Dave Clark Five".

In August 1964 Tony Jackson left for a solo career and Frank Allen, former member of Cliff Bennett & the Rebel Rousers, replaced him. Jackson formed a backing band called the Vibrations, but only had one hit, *Bye Bye Baby*.

Chris Curtis left the band in 1966 suffering from nervous exhaustion, and John Blunt replaced him. Later that year, Billy Anderson was to replace Blunt.

They almost cracked the chart again in 1981, following their signing with Sire Records and the release of two highly acclaimed albums. Unfortunately, due to some complicated legal problems, further copies of the albums were not pressed to cope with the demand and their potential return

to the chart was stifled.

Mike Pender split from the band at the end of 1985 and was to form a breakaway group, Mike Pender's Searchers. Spencer James, former lead singer with First Class, replaced him.

Both outfits now tour the world and the Searchers appear regularly on the Solid Silver Sixties Tour concerts organised by *Flying Music*.

Mike Pender's group became the first 1960s outfit to appear on the QE2 when they were booked to en-

The Seekers

tertain on the 25th anniversary cruise in 1994.

In 1964 Tony Jackson, the lead voice on *Sweets For My Sweet* and *Sugar and Spice* formed a band called Tony Jackson & the Vibrations and had one minor chart hit, *Bye Bye Baby*. On the proceeds of his previous recordings, Tony and his wife established a golf and leisure club.

In the 1990s Jackson returned to the music scene to appear on the 60s

nostalgia circuit, although he had now begun to suffer from ill health with arthritis, asthma and very poor eyesight. He lost his business, then his arthritis became so bad that he could no longer play guitar. In December 1996 Jackson was found guilty of possessing an imitation weapon after pretending to fire an air gun at a woman and was sent to prison for eighteen months, but was released in 1997 and decided to return to live performances.

Tony died from cirrhosis of the liver in a Nottingham hospital on August 18th 2003.

The Searchers went off to the Middle East in February 1997 while Mike Pender's Searchers appeared in Switzerland prior to a tour of South Africa.

Now retired from the civil service, Chris Curtis has resurfaced in Liverpool venues as half of a duo called Jimmy.

John Lennon once said that the Searchers' *Sweet For My Sweet* was the best record to come out of Liverpool and Brian Epstein regretted not signing them up. Their jangly guitar style was to influence the Byrds.

Although one of the best of the Mersey groups, they did not write their own material, which is probably one of the reasons why their chart life was limited.

The Seekers

This Australian group, formed in 1963, comprised Athol Guy (vocals and double bass), Keith Potger (vocals, guitar), Bruce Woodley (vocals, guitar) and Ken Ray (lead guitar). The following year Judith Durham became their lead vocalist and the group travelled to London where they signed with the powerful Grade Agency, which had links with every field of British showbusiness. As a result they appeared on *Sunday Night At The London Palladium*, a television show with such a vast audience that it virtually created stars overnight.

Tom Springfield stepped in to offer his services as songwriter and producer, and the group's run of hits began. Their British chart singles included *I'll Never Find Another You*, *A World Of Our Own*, *The Carnival Is Over*, *Someday One Day*, *Walk With Me*, *Morningtown Ride*, *Georgy Girl*, *When Will The Good Apples Fall* and *Emerald City*.

The Seekers hits eventually seemed to dry up and the group made a farewell appearance on a television show. Judith became a solo artist, but only had one further hit, *Olive Tree*, while Keith Potger formed the New Seekers.

Members of the original group re-formed in 1975 without Durham, adding Dutch singer Louisa Wisseling as lead vocalist. They had one final entry, a chart-topper in Australia, *The Sparrow Song*.

The original group re-formed once again in 1994 for an anniversary tour of Australia and a live album - it was twenty-five years since they originally disbanded. The four also performed two concerts at the Royal Albert Hall in London. In December, Judith and her husband Ron issued the album *The Hottest Band In Town Vol 1*, followed by *Vol 2*. Ron Edgeworth, her husband, was a fellow musician who, tragically, died of motor neurone disease on December 10th 1994.

In the year 2000 Judith, Athol, Keith and Bruce reunited for 'The Carnival Of Hits Tour 2000' and a double CD and cassette was issued called *The Seekers Night Of Nights... Live!*

In March 2002 Judith appeared at the Melbourne Concert Hall and an album of the event was issued in Australia that year called 'Melbourne Welsh Choir with Judith Durham'.

She was sixty in 2003 and toured Australia with fellow members of the Seekers on the 'Never Say Never Again Tour!' She also appeared on a solo world tour called 'Diamond Tour 2003' and Warner Music Australia released her album *Hold On To Your Dream*, which comprised thirteen inspirational songs. The year also saw the publication of her autobiography *Colours Of My Life: the Judith Durham Story* published by Virgin in June. Judith also wrote a children's book *Sylvia Slug And Billy The Bug*.

Dusty Springfield

Dusty Springfield had seven hits in America during the period of The British Invasion.

The Convent-educated girl, who became Britain's best female singer of the 60s, was born Mary Isabel Catherine Bernadette O'Brien on April 16 1939 in North Hampstead, London.

For a time she worked in a record

Dusty Springfield

store and a department store, and then began appearing in nightclubs with her brother Dion before becoming part of the vocal trio the Lana Sisters in 1958.

In 1960, under the name Dusty Springfield, she teamed up with her brother, who changed his name to Tom Springfield and, together with Tim Field, became the successful folk group the Springfields, who signed with Philips Records in 1961 and made their debut with *Breaka-*

way.

They followed with four further hits, *Bambino*, *Island Of Dreams*, *Say I Won't Be There* and *Come On Home* before disbanding in September 1963.

The next month Dusty launched her solo career and had a formidable string of hits in Britain throughout the 60s, including *I Only Want To Be With You*, *Stay Awhile*, *I Just Don't Know What To Do With Myself*, *Losing You*, *Your Hurtin' Kind Of Love*, *In The Middle Of Nowhere*, *Some Of Your Lovin'*, *Little By Little*, *You Don't Have To Say You Love Me*, *Goin' Back*, *All I See Is You*, *I'll Try Anything*, *Give Me Time*, *I Close My Eyes (And Count To Ten)'* and *Son Of A Preacher Man*.

Dusty had a distinctive visual appearance with her candyfloss bouffant styled blonde hair and heavy mascara make-up around her eyes. She had what was described as a wacky personality, which often led to her throwing cream cakes at people! She was also strong willed and campaigned against apartheid, which led to her being deported from South Africa in 1964.

Although she had a number of hits in America, it was in Britain where her main success lay. Her popularity began to wane when she moved to America in 1972 after declaring that she found Britain boring.

The girl who had been described as 'the white Aretha Franklin' had travelled to Memphis in 1968 to record the album *Dusty In Memphis*. This became her first album not to enter the British charts, although one of the tracks, *Son Of A Preacher Man*

became, arguably, her best single (although her biggest selling hit was *You Don't Have to Say You Love Me*).

Dusty decided to move to California because she said that she was being forced into a rut in Britain and driven into routines of summer shows and such. She had also fallen in love with the California sunshine and the lifestyle in Los Angeles.

Son Of A Preacher Man became her last major British hit and after her single *How Can I Be Sure?* only reached No. 27, she did not have another single released in the U.K. for nine years.

The Pet Shop Boys then encouraged her to join them on a duet *What Have I Done To Deserve This* which was a massive international hit and revived her career. She said, "I'm really grateful to the Pet Shop boys. They had the faith in me that I did not have. They saw something in me that I was about to lose".

Her album *Reputations* followed in 1990 and spawned the hits *Reputations*, *In Private* and *Nothing Has Been Proved*, the latter a number from the film *Scandal*, about the Christine Keeler affair.

Dusty discovered she had breast cancer in 1994 and when she was told, she recalled, "I shed about three years in the hallway and then said, 'Let's have lunch'. My brother came, the neighbours who brought me to town, my secretary, my accountant. I had a really good time".

She died on March 3rd 1999 at the age of fifty-nine, eleven days before she was to be inducted into the 'Rock 'N' Roll Hall Of Fame'.

The Tremeloes

The Tremeloes originally formed in 1959 as a quintet with Rick West (guitar), Alan Blaikley (rhythm), Alan Howard (bass) and Dave Munden (drums).

They auditioned for Decca on the same day as the Beatles – New Year's Day 1961 – with their lead singer Brian Poole. Decca rejected the Beatles and gave a three-year contract to the Tremeloes, who then had eight hits before parting company with front man Poole.

The decision to sign the Tremeloes over the Beatles led to Dick Rowe, Decca's head of A&R, being unfairly labelled 'the man who turned down the Beatles' for the rest of his life, when really he should have been acclaimed as 'the man who signed the Rolling Stones'. Mike Smith was the A&R man who held the recording audition for both groups that day. As he was new to the post Rowe told him that he could only sign up one of the groups and Smith chose Brian Poole & the Tremeloes. They were from nearby Aldershot while the

The Tremoles

Beatles, in the days before the motorway, were an eight-hour drive away from London. The decision may well have been a matter of convenience by selecting a group who were close to the recording studio.

Brian Poole later turned solo and the Tremeloes continued as a quartet and went on to score a further series of hits, including *Here Comes By Baby, Silence Is Golden, Even The Bad Times Are Good, Be Mine, Suddenly You Love Me, Helule Helule, My Little Lady, I Shall Be Released, Hello World, (Call Me) Number One, By The Way, Me And My Life* and *Hello Buddy*.

The Tremeloes also acted as producers and session band for Jeff Christie on a song called 'Yellow River', which sold over nine million copies. They then decided to cease live performances for a while.

Individual members began to work on solo projects, but they then drifted back together again. The current line-up features two of the original members of the band, Dave Munden and Rick West. Davy Freyer (bass, lead vocals) and John Gillingham (keyboards, vocals) joined them.

Former member Chip Hawkes, who had joined in 1966, was to see his son Chesney experience a brief but meteoric rise to fame when he starred in the pop film 'Buddy's Song' and topped the British charts with 'The One And Only'. A few years later, in 1997, Chesney was leading a London band called the Ebb. Alan Blakely lost a long battle against cancer in 1996.

The Troggs

This group was originally formed in Andover, Hampshire, in 1964 under the name the Troglodytes. By the following year their line-up comprised Reg Ball, who was born on June 12th 1943 in Andover (vocals), Chris Britton, who was born June 21st 1945 in Watford (guitar), Pete Staples, who was born May 3rd 1944 in Andover (bass) and Ronnie Bond, who was born on May 4th 1943 in Andover (drums).

In 1966, now managed by Larry Page, they truncated their name and

The Troggs

saw the release of their first single, *Lost Girl*, which was unsuccessful. They next recorded 'Wild Thing', which reached No 2 in Britain and became a chart-topper in the States. By this time Ball had changed his surname to Presley.

The Troggs other hit singles were *With A Girl Like You, I Can't Control Myself, Anyway That You Want Me, Give It To Me, Night Of The Long Grass, Hi Hi Hazel, Love Is All Around* and *Little Girl*.

Both *Wild Thing* and *Anyway That You Want Me* were penned by Chip Taylor, brother of American actor Jon Voight and uncle of actress Angelina Jolie.

The group split up in 1969 and Presley and Bond recorded solo singles, which did not have any chart success. Britton's solo album venture also failed to register.

In recent years Peter Lucas and Dave Maggs joined Presley and Britton, following the departure of an ailing Ronnie Bond. Britton rejoined in the 1970s after running a club in Portugal.

In 1995 Presley had a financial boost when Wet Wet Wet had an international chart-topper with his composition *Love Is All Around*. Reg is a known authority on crop circles and similar mysterious matters. He still lives in Andover, as does Chris Britton. Pete Staples has an electrical business in Basingstoke. Ronnie Bond, who was born Ronald Bullis, died at Winchester Hospital on November 13th 1992, the year that his former group recorded the *Athens To Andover* album with members of REM.

Vanity Fare

Vanity Fare were a vocal harmony group, originally formed in Kent under the name the Avengers and comprising Dick Allix (drums), Trevor Brice (vocals), Tony Goulden (guitar), Tony Jarrett (double bass/guitar) and Barry Landeman (keyboards). They decided to change their name and based it on William Makepeace Thackerey's novel 'Vanity Fair', slightly altering the spelling.

They signed with Page One Records and made their debut with *I Live For The Sun*, their first British hit. Their next two singles also hit the American charts, *Early In The Morning* and *Hitchin' A Ride*.

The group appeared in America but mainly at small venues on the East Coast. They felt that they should have been appearing at major venues in California, particularly since their singles had attained cult status with the West Coast groups. Disenchanted with their American experience, Tony Goulden left the group, later followed by Dick Allix. Over the years there were numerous changes in personnel, although the group continued and toured various countries around the world. Their current line up includes Eddie Wheeler, Mark Ellen and Bernie Hayley.

The Who

The Who were one of the major British rock groups. The line up of Pete Townshend, born in London on May 19th 1945 (guitar), Roger Daltrey, born in London on March 1st 1944 (vocals), John Entwistle, born in Chiswick, London on October 9th 1944 (bass) and Keith Moon born August 23rd 1947 (drums) was finalised in 1964, the year Peter Meadon took over their management and es-

tablished them as the leading group for the 'Mods'. Mods were a teenage tribal unit who were always at odds with Rockers – a relationship developed by the Who in their rock opera *Quadrophenia*.

They had originally been known as the Detours when Townshend, Entwistle and Daltrey joined forces in a group in 1962, with drummer Doug Sanders.

Meadon changed their name to the High Numbers, but when Kit Lam-

bert and Chris Stamp took over the management from Meadon late in 1964, Lambert changed the group's name to the Who.

Over the years their hit singles have included *I Can't Explain*, *Anyway Anyhow Anywhere*, *My Generation*, *Substitute*, *A Legal Matter*, *I'm A Boy*, *The Kids Are Alright*, *Happy Jack*, *Pictures Of Lily*, *The Last Time/Under My Thumb*, *I Can See For Miles*, *Dogs*, *Magic Bus*, *Pinball Wizard*, *The Seeker*, *Summertime Blues*, *Won't Get Fooled Again*, *Let's See Action*, *Join Together*, *Relay'*, *'5: 15*, *Squeeze Box*, *Who Are You*, *Long Live Rock*, *You Better You Bet*, *Don't Let Go The Coat*, *Athena* and *Ready Steady Who*.

Their hit albums have included *My Generation*, *A Quick One*, *The Who Sell Out*, *Tommy*, *Live At Leeds*, *Who's Next*, *Meaty, Beaty, Big & Bouncy*, *Quadrophenia*, *Odds And Sods*, *The Who By Numbers*, *The Story Of The Who*, *Who Are You*, *The Kids Are Alright*, *Face Dances*, *It's Hard*, *Who's Last* and *The Who Collection*.

They appeared at the Monterey Pop Festival in 1967 and were to consolidate their success in America in 1969 when their album

The Who

Tommy was released and they appeared at Woodstock.

Keith Moon was something of a legendary figure and once blew up his drum kit on 'The Smothers Brothers Show' causing Bette Davis to faint. He also accidentally killed his chauffeur when he ran him over. Moon was a prodigious drinker and collapsed on stage several times. He died from an overdose of chlormethiazole, prescribed to combat his alcoholism, on September 8th 1978.

Entwistle had nine albums, some solo, some with his groups Ox and John Entwistle's Band, the latter while still appearing with the Who. He was known as 'Ox' or 'Thunderfingers'. In the 1990s Entwistle (who joined Ringo Starr's All-Starr Band in 1995) and trout farmer Roger Daltrey were seen performing at Who Conventions. They were also involved with Pete Townshend in supervising latter-day presentations of the Who's rock operas *Tommy* and *Quadrophenia*.

They were touring America in June 2002 when Entwistle died at the Hard Rock Hotel & Casino in Las Vegas, Nevada. He was on medication for a heart complaint.

The Who were inducted into the Rock 'n' Roll Hall of Fame in 1990.

The Yardbirds

This group originally formed as the Metropolitan Blues Quartet at Kingston Art College in 1963. The members were Keith Relf, born March 22nd 1943 in Richmond (guitar, harmonica), Paul Samwell-Smith born May 8th 1943 in Richmond (bass),

Chris Dreja born November 11th 1945 in Surbiton (guitar), Jim McCarty born July 25th 1943 in Liverpool (drums) and Anthony Topham (guitar). By the end of the year Eric Clapton, who was born March 30th 1945 in Ripley, had replaced Topham, who had decided to stay on at college.

As the Yardbirds they enjoyed a string of hits, including *For Your Love*, *Heart Full Of Soul*, *Over Under Sideways Down* and *Happenings Ten Years Ago*.

Clapton left in March 1965, unhappy with recording numbers such as *For Your Love* and Jeff Beck replaced him. Later that same year Jimmy Page joined them on guitar, while Dreja switched to bass. A few months later, Beck left.

The group split in July 1968. Page then formed the New Yardbirds, who evolved into Led Zeppelin. Dreja became a photographer and Relf and McCarty appeared together in Renaissance. The two were actually planning a new band when Relf died in an accident on May 4th 1976, electrocuted by faulty wiring on his guitar.

For a time in the early 1980s Dreja, McCarty and Samwell-Smith teamed up once again under the name Band of Frogs.

The Yardbirds were inducted into the Rock 'n' Roll Hall of Fame in 1992.

In 2003, almost 30 years after the original split, two of the group's founder members, Chris Dreja and Jim McCarty, decided to re-form the Yardbirds with three new members; John Idan (vocals), Gypie Mayo (guitar) and Laurie Garman (harmonica).

The Yardbirds

They launched their new career with a six-week tour of the States in July and began to record a new studio album. This was the Yardbirds' first studio album since 1968. The April release featured guest appearances by Jeff Beck, Brian May, Steve Vai, Slash, Joe Satriani, Johnny Rzeznik, Steve Lukather and Jeff 'Skunk' Baxter. Warner Music Vision UK also issued a DVD *The Yardbirds* featuring the original group performing eight numbers and interviews with Jeff Beck, Eric Clapton, Peter Grant, Chris Dreja, Paul Samwell-Smith and Giorgio Gomelski.

The Zombies

This group was formed by keyboards player Rod Argent, who was born on June 14th 1945 in St Albans, while he was still at St Albans Grammar School in 1963. The other members were Hugh Grundy, who was

The Zombies

born on March 6th 1945 in Winchester (drums), Paul Atkinson who was born on March 19th 1946 in Cuffley (guitar), Colin Blunstone who was born on June 24th 1945 in Hatfield (drums), Paul Arnold (bass). Chris White, who was born on March 7th 1943, soon replaced Arnold.

In 1964 they were to win a local beat group competition, held by the London Evening News, which led to a Decca Records audition and a contract. On leaving school that year they recorded their debut single, *She's Not There*, a number penned by Argent.

The group's proposed tour of America was reduced to a series of gigs in New York due to the ban by immigration authorities, then worried about the number of British bands performing in the States.

Their second single, *Tell Her No*, was their final British hit, although it prevented them from being tagged 'one-hit-wonders'.

They were finally able to tour America in 1965, when they had two minor hits with *She's Coming Home* and *I Want You Back Again*. The following year they appeared in the film *Bunny Lake Is Missing* and toured Europe and the Far East. Due to their apparent lack of chart success at home, the group disbanded in 1967.

A previously unreleased track, 'Time Of The Season' was issued in America in 1969 where it became a million-seller, reaching No 3 in the charts. Due to its success, the record company wanted the group to reform, but they refused.

Atkinson and Grundy went on to work as A&R men at CBS Records, while Argent and White teamed up to become record producers and Blun-

stone continued with a solo career. Colin Blunstone now lives in Surrey and in 1997 he toured Britain to promote a new album. He has also sung with a re-formed Zombies that contains Hugh Grundy on drums and Chris White on bass.

Paul Atkinson and Rod Argent, a music equipment shop owner, put in guest appearances on a 1993 Zombies album *New World*, recorded after *Time Of The Season* had been included on the soundtrack of the movie *Awakenings*, reviving interest in the band. In October 1997 *Zombie Heaven* a 4 CD boxed set compiled by Alec Palao, was released in Britain on the Ace Records Big Beat label. It was a one hundred and nineteen track package with forty-two previously unissued cuts.

To mark the launch of the retrospective CD package, the 1964 line-up of the Zombies re-formed for a performance at the Jazz Café, London in December 1997.

In May 1998 Blunstone released a new album on *Mystic Records*, *The Light Inside* and embarked on a British concert tour. Mystic also issued *The Best Of Colin Blunstone*.

Cilla Black

The One Hit Wonders

A handful of British artists occasionally made a fleeting appearance in the American charts, but did not have the lasting power of some of the acts that succeeded in the wake of the Beatles.

Here is some background to some of the British acts that only managed a single chart entry in America during The British Invasion years.

Madeline Bell

She reached No. 26 in the American charts with *I'm Gonna Make You Love Me* on March 9th 1968. The following year, as lead singer with Blue Mink, she had a British chart hit with *Melting Pot*.

Although born Madeline Bell Bredus in Newark, New Jersey on June 23rd 1942, Madeline has based her career in England. She arrived in the U.K. as a member of the 'Black Nativity' gospel cast in 1962 and remained in the country, becoming one of the leading session singers providing vocal backing on most of Dusty Springfield's records and also on those by Cliff Richard, Tom Jones, Scott Walker, Long John Baldry, Joe Cocker, Elton John and many more.

I'm Gonna Make You Love Me had originally been recorded by Dee Dee Warwick. Madeline returned to promote it, together with the release of an album *Picture Me Gone*. In July 1999 she received an award for her services to music from 'The International Alliance for Women In Music'.

Cilla Black

Despite the power of Beatles manager Brian Epstein behind her, an appearance on the *Ed Sullivan Show* and a season at the exclusive Persian Room at the Plaza Hotel in New York, Cilla's only America hit was *You're My World*, which only reached No. 26 in the Billboard charts. Before Epstein died he arranged for Cilla to have her own television series.

She developed into one of the most popular and highest paid female television presenters in Britain when she hosted shows such as *Surprise, Surprise* and *Blind Date* and eventually decided to end her decades-long stint on *Blind Date* in 2003, the 40th anniversary of her show business career.

The Honeycombs

This group hit the American charts only once when their debut disc *Have I The Right* reached No. 5 on November 14th 1964.

British hit songwriters Ken Howard and Alan Blaikley had penned the number, which topped the British charts. Much of the group's publicity

Honeycombes

in Britain centred on the fact that they had a female drummer, Honey Lantree, who was the sister of the group's bass guitarist John Lantree.

Lead guitarist Martin Murray originally formed the group in 1963. The members were Dennis D'Ell (vocals, harmonica), Alan Ward (lead), John Lantree (bass), Honey Lantree (drums) and Martin Murray (rhythm).

The initial name for the band was the Sherabons, but they swiftly changed it to Honeycombs. Some say this was based on Honey's nickname, others that it was chosen by *Pye Records* MD Louis Benjamin after a track by Jimmie Rodgers.

The band received a great deal of press due to the novelty factor of having a girl drummer. Their debut single *Have I The Right'* topped the British charts in 1964. The group embarked on a U.K. concert tour and their single sold a million copies in the States, although their follow-up, *Is It Because?* only became a minor British hit and had no impact in America.

Murray was temporarily replaced in the group by Peter Pye following a fall in which he broke bones in his hand and leg. He left the group at the end of 1964, prior to their tour of Australasia, and formed a new band called the Lemmings.

The Honeycombs next release was *Something Better Beginning*, followed by *That's The Way*. During 1965 they toured Japan. In 1966 their singles failed to chart and D'Ell, Ward and Pye left. Colin Boyd, Rod Butler and Eddie Spence replaced them and the band changed their name to the New Honeycombs. Honey Lantree left the group in 1967, but her attempts to launch a solo career failed and she rejoined, although the group disbanded soon after.

In 1991 the Honeycombs reunited for a tribute concert in honour of their late recording manager Joe Meek.

Dennis D'Ell leads the present-day Honeycombs and the group included Honey and Peter Pye in the line-up at a special anniversary concert in 1995. Alan Ward is the owner of a musical equipment shop and manufactures his own make of speaker cabinets. John Lantree lives in London.

Shirley Bassey

A world-class singer, but her only American chart placing during the British Invasion period was *Goldfinger*, which reached No. 8 on March 27th 1965.

She was born in Tiger Bay, Cardiff on January 8th 1937, the youngest of seven children of a Nigerian seaman and his Yorkshire-born wife but they were divorced when Shirley was two years old.

She recorded her first hit. *The Banana Boat Song* in 1957. Her other British chart entries included *Fire Down Below*, *You You Romeo*, *As I Love You*, *Kiss Me Honey Honey Kiss Me*, *With These Hands*, *As Long As He Needs Me*, *You'll Never Know*, *Reach For The Stars/Climb Every Mountain*, *I'll Get By*, *Tonight*, *Ave Maria*, *Far Away*, *What Now My Love*, *What Kind Of Fool Am I?*, *I (Who Have Nothing)*, *My Special Dream*, *Gone*, *Goldfinger*, *No Regrets*, *Big Spender*, *Something*, *The Fool On The Hill*, *Love Story*, *For All We Know*, *Diamonds Are Forever* and *Never Never Never*.

She was also to record renditions of George Harrison's *Something* and Paul McCartney's *The Fool On The Hill*.

Following *Never Never Never* in 1971, fourteen years were to pass before *The Rhythm Divine* entered the chart in 1987. There was then another gap of several years before *Diso La Passione* in 1996.

Shirley's powerful voice, used to dramatic effect in the delivery of a number of her songs, her glamorous wardrobes and her sheer vocal passion have maintained a huge fan following over the years. She is also an icon of the gay community. Her

Shirley Bassey

success was international and she is best remembered for the James Bond movie theme songs *Goldfinger*, *Diamonds Are Forever* and *Moonraker*. She has had hits with numbers from several musicals, some of which she has made uniquely her own, including *Big Spender* from *Sweet Charity*. She received a Brittania Award in 1977 as the 'Best Female solo Singer in the Last Fifty Years'.

Shirley's first husband, film producer Kenneth Hulme, committed suicide soon after their divorce in 1965. Of her three children, tragically, her daughter Samatha drowned, reputedly after jumping off the Clifton Suspension Bridge in Bristol. Her surviving daughter, Sharon, has three children and Shirley also has an adopted son, Mark, who lives in Spain with his daughter Tatjana. Shirley's second marriage to Italian hotelier Sergio Novak also ended in divorce in 1981.

The Welsh diva announced her semi retirement in 1981, initially emerging only for television specials and a tour to celebrate her fortieth anniversary in the business in 1994. In January 1996, stars gathered for a television tribute, *An Evening With Shirley Bassey*, on her sixtieth birthday.

In December 1997 the television documentary *Shirley Bassey: This Is My Life* was screened. It covered her appearance at Carnegie Hall in 1996 and her appearances in Atlantic City, Antwerp and Hollywood in 1997. It also featured her recording session for *History Repeating*, the 1997 single that she made with the Propellerheads.

The Caravelles

Louis Wilkinson and Andrea Wilson, two former office girls, hit the No. 6 position in the British charts in August 1963 with their reworking of Tennessee Ernie Ford's *You Don't Have To Be A Baby To Cry*. They were to have even greater success in the American charts reaching No. 3. They also appeared with the Beatles on their first American concert at the Coliseum, Washington DC on Tuesday February 11th 1964.

You Don't Have To Be A Baby To Cry was their only hit. Wilkinson then embarked on a solo career under the name Lois Lane and Wilson continued using the Caravelles name for a number of years using various other female singers

David & Jonathan

This was the name of the vocal duo who took the Beatles composition *Michelle* to No. 18 in the U.S. charts on February 12th 1966. They were actually the successful song writing team of Roger Greenaway (Dave) and Roger Cook (Jonathan).

The two had originally been members of another vocal outfit, the Kestrels, before deciding to write songs together, having an immediate success in Britain with *You've Got Your Troubles* for the Fortunes.

David & Jonathan

They were to record another Lennon & McCartney composition, *She's Leaving Home*, but it failed to register in the charts. The pair had no further record success under that name, but they composed several songs that various artists took into the charts. They also collaborated with a number of session musicians in the band Blue Mink, with Cook and singer Madeline Bell fronting the group. The outfit had seven chart entries, including *Melting Pot* and *Stay With Me*.

Cook currently commutes between Nashville and London and has penned numbers for country artists such as Crystal Gale and Don Williams while Greenaway is an executive of the Performing Rights Society in Britain.

The two occasionally join forces for charity events.

The Equals

The Equals reached No. 32 in the American charts with *Baby, Come Back* on September 28th 1968. Eddie Grant, the lead guitarist was from Guyana, Derv and Lincoln Gordon were twins from Jamaica on vocals and rhythm guitar respectively, and Patrick Lloyd and John Hall were from London on rhythm and drums respectively. They began playing together as a group in 1965.

Their major hit, *Baby, Come Back*, recorded the following year, was originally issued as a B side in the U.K. Due to its success on the continent, it was re-issued as the A side and topped the British charts. Other hits which followed included *Viva Bobby Joe* and *Black Skinned Blue-Eyed Boys*.

Eddie Grant, who penned the songs, left the group in 1971 to embark on a solo career. The rest of the band began to appear regularly on the cabaret circuit, although there were numerous changes in personnel.

Grant, whose real name was Edward Montague, was born on March 5th 1948. He set up his own production company when he left the band and as a solo artist his hits included *Do You Feel My Love, Don't Wanna Dance, Electric Avenue* and *Gimme Hope Jo'Anna*.

Derv Gordon and Patrick Lloyd, still based in north London, are the only original members left in the current line-up, which performs on the 60s nostalgia circuit.

Eddie Grant returned to the West Indies where he has his own recording complex.

Jonathan King

Jonathan King reached No. 17 in the American charts with *Everyone's Gone To The Moon* on October 23rd 1965. He was born Kenneth King on December 6th 1944 and made his recording debut in 1965 with *Everyone's Gone To The Moon*, which became a Top 5 entry in Britain.

His other British hits were *Let It All Hang Out, Lazy Bones, Hooked On A Feeling, Flirt, Una Paloma Blanca, One For You One For Me, You're The Greatest Lover* and *Gloria*.

King then had a succession of hits under numerous different names, including Bubblerock, 53rd & 3rd, Sakkarin, Shag, 100 Ton & A Feather, Weathermen, Sound 9418, and Father Abraphart & the Smurfs.

He was also a record producer and launched his own label, U.K. records, was a columnist in the national press and hosted a popular television series *Entertainment USA*.

Jonathan King

In November 2001 he was given a seven year prison sentence after being found guilty of sexually abusing young boys throughout the 1980s.

Leapy Lee

This artist reached No. 16 in the American charts with *Little Arrows* on November 9th 1968. Lee was born Lee Graham in Eastbourne, East Sussex on July 2nd 1942. *Little Arrows* in 1968 was his only major hit. He followed with a minor chart entry, *Good Morning*, but his career was seriously compromised when he was jailed. Lee and Diana Dors' husband, Alan Lake, were involved in an altercation in a pub in Sunningdale in Berkshire, during which a flick knife slashed the publican's wrist. Following his jail term, Lee tried his hand at producing and then moved to Spain, where he currently runs a night club in Majorca.

The Magic Lanterns

A group from Manchester, The Magic Lanterns reached No. 29 in the American charts in November 1968 with *Shame, Shame*.

The group had originally formed as the Sabres and comprised Jimmy Bilsbury (vocals), Peter Shoesmith (guitar), Ian Moncur (bass) and Allan Wilson (drums). As the Magic Lanterns they issued several singles on the *CBS Records* label including *Excuse Me Baby*, *Rumpelstintskin*, *Knight In Rusty Armour* and *Auntie Grizelda*. Following their minor hit with '*Shame Shame*',

Moncur, Shoesmith and Wilson left the group.

The Nashville Teens

This R&B outfit was formed in Weybridge, Surrey in 1962 with members Arthur (Art) Sharp (vocals), and Pete Shannon (bass), John Hawkens (piano), Ray Phillips (vocals), Michael Dunford (guitar) and Roger Groom (drums). Dunford and Groom left in 1963 to be replaced by John Allen (guitar) and Barry Jenkins (drums). Phillips later switched to vocals and they toured with the unusual style of having two lead singers up front.

After a spell in Hamburg they backed Bo Diddley on a British tour and were spotted by Mickie Most,

The Nashville Teens

who produced their debut single, *Tobacco Road*. They followed with *Google Eye*, *Find My Way Back Home*, *This Little Bird* and *The Hard Way*.

The group backed artists such as Carl Perkins and Chuck Berry and continued recording until 1969 before disbanding. They were to reform many years later. With Ray Phillips the only remaining original member, the Nashville Teens were the toast of a Festival of the 60s at Butlin's in Bognor Regis in November 1997.

The New Vaudeville Band.

They had one American hit, *Winchester Cathedral* which topped the U.S. charts on December 3rd 1966.

Despite their No.1 hit, they never registered in the American charts again. Drummer Henry Harrison, a former member of Cops 'N' Robbers, originally formed the group in 1966. They developed a jazzy style based on sounds of the 1920s and 1930s and registered big with 'Winchester Catherdral'. Geoff Stephens wrote the song. They followed with 'Peek A Boo', 'Finchley Central' and a minor hit, 'Green Street Green'.

Allegedly, an American group calling themselves the New Vaudeville Band still operates.

Julie Rogers

Julie Rogers reached No. 10 in the American charts with *The Wedding* on December 5th 1964. Julie was born Julie Rolls in London on April 6th 1943. After a variety of jobs, she sang with a dance band led by Teddy Foster and made her recording debut in 1963 with *It's Magic*. Her next release, *The Wedding* became her biggest hit, reaching No 3 in the British charts, in addition to its American success. The number was a cover version of an Argentinean song, *La Novia*.

Julie commented, "My only regret was the use of the words 'Ave Maria' for I thought it might be too sickly and religious for the fans. My big problem is this, most of the hit discs are bought by girls, so it's extra important they should like me, not regard me as a sort of opponent."

The Small Faces

Julie's other British hits were *Like A Child* and *Hawaiian Wedding*. She also enjoyed a very successful career on the cabaret circuit and she continues to perform and appears on 60s nostalgia concerts.

During 1997 thieves seriously injured her husband when they raided her home.

The Small Faces
The Small Faces reached No. 16 in the American charts with *Itchycoo Park* on January 13th 1968. The group was formed in London in 1965 and comprised Steve Marriott (vocals, guitar), Ronnie 'Plonk' Lane (bass), Jimmy Wilson (organ) and Kenny Jones (drums). The same year they signed with *Decca Records* and made their debut with *Whatcha Gonna Do About It* and Ian McLagan replaced Winston. They were popular with the 'Mods' at the time and took their name from the fact that all the members were short in stature.

Their hit singles in Britain were: *Whatcha Gonna Do About It*, *Sha La La La Lee*, *Hey Girl*, *All Or Nothing*, *My Mind's Eye*, *I Can't Make It*, *Here Comes The Nice*, *'Itchycoo Park*, *The Soldier*, *Lazy Sunday*, *Universal* and *'Afterglow Of Your Love'*.

They also had three chart albums: *Small Faces*, *From The Beginning* and *Ogden's Nut Gone Flake*.

Marriott left the band to team up with Peter Frampton in Humble Pie in February 1969 and the Small Faces disbanded. Lane, Jones and McLagan brought in guitarist Ron Wood and vocalist Rod Stewart, and relaunched themselves as the Faces. They disbanded at the end of the year.

In 1977 Marriott re-formed the group with Jones and McLagan and began to tour the U.K., but the group split the following year. Jones was later to join the Who.

When the group re-formed Ronnie Lane refused to join them. He contracted multiple sclerosis and battled against the disease for twenty years, being confined to a wheelchair almost permanently for the latter part of his life. He moved to a Florida Hospital for treatment and died on June 4th 1997.

Marriott had formed a group called Steve Marriott & His Packet Of Three, but died in a fire at his cottage on April 20th 1991.

In 1996 Jones, McLagan and Wood received a Lifetime Achievement Award at the Ivor Novello Awards ceremony.

Ian McLagan is currently a highly paid international session musician. Kenny Jones is a businessman, horse owner and keen polo player.

Sounds Orchestral
Producer John Schroeder, who had originally written hits for Helen Shapiro and recorded the two *This Is Mersey Beat* albums, assembled this orchestra, led by pianist Johnny Pearson. Pearson had originally had a British hit with *Cast Your Fate To The Wind*, penned by Vincent Guaraldi, which reached No. 5 in the British charts. They then had a minor hit with their follow-up, *Spanish Harlem*.

Cast Your Fate To The Wind was an April 1965 hit for them, reaching no. 10 in the billboard chart.

The Swinging Bluejeans
A Liverpool group who formed in 1957 under the name the Swinging Bluegenes. They had a guest night at the Cavern and the Beatles made

their debut as guests of the Blue-genes. Leader Ray Ennis recalled, "I thought they were German. It was the old leather gear, which I'd never seen before. It wasn't till they actually spoke that I realised they were from Liverpool. I thought they were awful and only listened to two numbers and went to the White Star for a drink".

The group had hit singles in Britain between 1963 and 1996 and their personnel at the time were Ray Ennis (rhythm), Ralph Ellis (lead), Les Braid (bass) and Norman Kuhlke (drums).

They changed their name to the Swinging Bluejeans and signed with EMI's HMV label and their debut single *It's Too Late Now* was issued in June 1963, followed by *Do you know?* in September. It was their third disc *Hippy Hippy Shake* which launched them into the big time. It also became their only American hit.

Ennis was to recall, "We had to fight like hell with EMI to get *Hippy Hippy Shake* released. They said, "No, this will never make it." We felt so strongly about it, four little humble lads from Liverpool that we said, "If you don't release it, we won't make any more records." It was issued – and sold three million copies!

There have been one or two changes in personnel but Ellis and Braid are still performing with the band who continue to tour throughout the world.

Thunderclap Newman

This band reached No. 37 in the American charts with 'Something In The Air' on October 25th 1969. The group had only formed in 1969 and had a relatively short career. Former post office engineer, keyboard player Andy 'Thunderclap' Newman, had met Pete Townshend of the Who at Art College. The two became friends and it was Townshend who suggested the group to Newton after spotting lead guitarist Jimmy McCulloch. They were joined by drummer John 'Speedy' Keen, who also penned *Something In The Air*. The number became their debut single and topped the British charts. Unfortunately, their live appearances did not live up to expectations and they split up in 1970 following one further single, a minor hit called *Accident*, and an album, *Hollywood Dream*.

Andy Newman issued an album 'Rainbow' in 1971 before retiring from the record business. Jimmy McCulloch joined Blue, Stone the Crows and then Wings. He died in mysterious circumstances on September 28th 1979. Speedy Keene released some solo albums as a vocalist before concentrating on songwriting and record production.

Whistling Jack Smith

The only entry in the American charts was *I Was Kaiser Bill's Batman*, which reached No. 20 on June 3rd 1967.

There was no such person as Whistling Jack Smith. Songwriters Roger Greenaway and Roger Cook penned the number, which was recorded by the Mike Sammes Singers and released under the name Whistling Jack Smith.

In Britain, to promote the number,

Status Quo

Decca Records approached singer Billy Moeller and he was given the name Whistling Jack Smith to promote it on a U.K. tour.

Moeller who was born in Liverpool, had been recording under the name Coby Wells and never had a hit in his own right. He now lives in Hertfordshire.

Status Quo

Status Quo reached No. 12 in the American charts on August 3rd 1968 with *Pictures Of Matchstick Men*, their only hit during the British Invasion period. The group had originally formed in London in 1962 as the Spectre and comprised Francis Rossi (guitar, vocals), Alan Lancaster (bass, vocals), John Coghlan (drums) and Rick Parfitt (guitar, vocals).

They changed their name to Status Quo when they recorded *Pictures Of Matchstick Men* in 1967.

With a completely different style they became a major force in rock music, with an impressive list of British chart singles and albums. The group originally split in 1984 but have reformed, split and reformed again on a number of occasions, led by the two premier guitarists Francis Rossi and Rick Parfitt.

The Crazy World Of Arthur Brown

The British chart topper *Fire* reached No. 2 in America in October 1968. Brown, a former Oxbridge graduate, who had been born in Whitby, Yorkshire on June 24th 1942, had formed the group in 1967 with Sean Nicholas (bass), Vincent Crane (keyboards) and Drachen Theaker (drums). Brown was noted for wearing a flaming fire-helmet during the performance of the number and

Arthur Brown

screaming *I am the God of Hellfire*.

Pete Townshend produced their debut album *The Crazy World Of Arthur Brown*, but unfortunately Brown was sued for stealing the tune of *Fire*, which resulted in him losing most of his royalties. By this time Carl Palmer had replaced Theaker, but halfway through the band's first American tour he left to join Atomic Rooster.

Brown was to form a new band called Kingdom Come with guitarist Andy Dalby and keyboards player Mike Harris, but they were unsuccessful and folded in 1973, with Brown moving to Texas, where he set up a business as a carpenter.

He remains a full-time carpenter with his painting and decorating business in Texas, in partnership with Jimmy Carl Black, a former member of the Mothers of Invention. Drachen Theaker spent a number of years in Los Angeles as a session musician, but later returned to the U.K.

The Silkie

A folk group who reached No. 10 in the American charts on November 6th 1965 with *You've Got To Hide your Love Away*. They were a group of students from Hull University who were managed by Brian Epstein. They comprised Silvia Tatler, vocals; Mike Ramsden, guitar/vocals; Ivor Aylesbury, guitar/vocals and Kevin Cunningham, guitar/vocals. Their British debut record *Blood River* on the Fontana label was unsuccessful, so Brian Epstein decided to pull all the stops out and presented them with a Lennon & McCartney composition,

You've Got To Hide Your Love Away which was produced by John Lennon with Paul McCartney on piano and George Harrison on tambourine.

Their other releases, *Keys To My Soul* and *Leave Me To Cry* were unsuccessful.

Frank Ifield

A singer originally born in Coventry whose family immigrated to Australia when he was a young lad. He returned to Britain and made his debut on the Columbia label with *Little Devil*. His *I Remember You* became the first-ever single to sell more than one million copies in Britain and also brought him his sole American hit when it reached No. 5 in the charts on September 22nd 1962.

In 1962 Brian Epstein approached British promoter Arthur Howes trying to get him to place the Beatles on one of his Tours. Howes decided to give them a try out on a show with bill-topper Ifield at the Embassy Theatre, Peterborough on December 2nd 1962.

The group received a poor reception as the audience for Ifield were not the type of audience the Beatles appealed to. The report in the local newspaper praised Ifield, but commented, "The exciting Beatles' rock group quite frankly failed to excite me. The drummer apparently thought that his job was to lead, not to provide the rhythm. He made far too much noise and in their final number *Twist And Shout* it sounded as though everyone was trying to make more noise than the others. In a more mellow mood, their *Taste Of Honey* was much better and *Love Me Do* was tolerable."

Despite the unfortunate reaction, Howes decided to take a chance and booked them on his Helen Shapiro tour.

In 1964, Vee Jay records in America issued an album *Jolly What! The Beatles And Frank Ifield On Stage*. The title was misleading as all tracks by both artists were studio recordings and were not taken from the one and only night they appeared on the same stage at Peterborough.

Adam Faith

Adam Faith had one minor American hit in February 1965 with *It's Alright*.

Born Terence Nelhams in Acton, west London on June 23rd 1940, he topped the British charts with his debut disc *What Do You Want?* and followed with another chart-topper, *Poor Me*. By 1966 he had spent two hundred and sixty weeks in the British charts, with twenty-four hits over a seven-year period, including *Someone Else's Baby, When Johnny Comes Marching Home, How About That, Lonely Pup, This Is It, Easy Going Me, Don't You Know It, The Time Has Come, Lonesome, As You Like It, Don't That Beat All, Baby Take A Bow, What Now, Walkin' Tall, The First Time, If He Tells You, I Love Being In love With You, Message To Martha, Stop Feeling Sorry For Yourself, Someone's Taken Maria Away* and *Cheryl's Going Home*.

Faith's hit streak ended in 1966, but by 1970 he had married and begun a second career as a television actor,

Adam Faith

appearing in the successful U.K. series *Budgie*. He continued with film appearances, which have included roles in *Beat Girl, Never Let Go, What A Whopper. Mix Me A Person, Stardust, McVicar* and *Yesterday's Hero*.

Over the years Faith involved himself in various business enterprises, launching a celebrity financial management consultancy called Faith and contributing financial columns to the *Daily Mail* and *Mail On Sunday* newspapers. For a time he also managed Leo Sayer.

A fraudster caused Faith's businesses to crash, but he did not declare himself bankrupt, opting to pay off

his two million pound debts over a period of years – which he managed to do. His marriage also ended following a two-year affair with tennis star Chris Evert.

After another successful television series, *Love Heals*, Faith decided to return to the stage by taking the lead, as Zach The Choreographer, in a nine-month tour of the musical *A Chorus Line*.

Faith was one of the first British pop artists to have a book devoted to him, *Poor Me*, in 1962. In 1996 his autobiography, *Acts Of Faith* was published.

Faith had a history of heart problems and underwent open-heart

the Sorrows, followed by Don Faron and the Soul Machine. He then turned solo and recorded the John D. Loudermilk number *Indian Reservation*, which brought him his only major hit in America, although he had another British hit, *Belfast Boy* about soccer star George Best. Fardon recorded fourteen singles and a couple of albums, but then became a licensee of the Alhambra public house in Coventry. Later he owned his own pub the Plough Inn. He then became a business development manager for Mayfair Security and also co-runs a theatrical business, PrestigeArtiste Management.

Unit Four Plus Two

surgery in 1968 to relieve blocked arteries. He died of a heart attack on March 8 2003 at the age of 62. He was survived by his wife Jackie and daughter Katya.

Unit Four Plus Two

This group was originally formed in 1964 as a quartet under the name Unit Four, and changed their name when two other members were added.

They comprised Buster Meikle (vocals, guitar), Tommy Moeller (vocals, tambourine, piano, guitar), Peter Moules (vocals, autoharp, guitar, banjo), Rodney Garwood (bass) and Hugh Halliday (drums).

They made their chart debut with *Green Fields* in 1964 and topped the chart with their next release, *Concrete And Clay*, They had two further British chart singles, *You've Never Been In Love Like This Before* and *Baby Never Say Goodbye*.

They disbanded in 1969.

A Unit Four Plus Two re-emerged in 1992 when Tommy Moeller and other members of the 1960s edition were involved in the writing and production of a London musical play about Leonardo Da Vinci.

Don Fardon

Don Fardon reached No. 20 in the charts on September 21 1968 with *(The Lament Of The Cherokee) Indian Reservation*. He was born Don Maughn in Coventry in 1943 and originally appeared in a group called

Flying Machine

Flying Machine, a psychedelic British band reached No. 5 in the Billboard charts with *Smile A Little Smile For Me* on October 18th 1969. The number was penned by Geoff Stephens and Tony Macauley. The group comprised Stuart Coleman on bass, Steve James on lead guitar and vocals, Tony Newman on vocals and Paul Wilkinson on drums. The group released six singles and one album but disbanded in 1971. Coleman became a BBC Radio One and then a Capitol Radio disc jockey and now lives and works in Nashville.

The Beatles and the British bands inspired many an American youth resulting in more home-grown groups, rather than solo singers, beginning to emerge on the American music scene. A prime example is the Byrds, who were once tagged 'the American Beatles'.

Roger McGuinn had originally been a folk singer, but became inspired by the Fab Four when he saw the film *A Hard Day's Night* in August 1964.

During his performances at the folk club the Troubadour, he began to play Beatles songs in his set. Then, together with Gene Clark, another folk artist he knew who was also interested in the Beatles, they formed a duo, similar to Peter & Gordon. They then wanted to form a group and together with David Crosby and Chris Hillman recorded some demos under the name the Jet Set. Another friend, Mike Clarke was brought in as a drummer.

McGuinn recalled, "We each heard them, saw them in *A Hard Day's Night*, and I personally went out and got a Rickenbacker twelve-string guitar like George had and David got a Gretch and our drummer got Ludwig drums and we just patterned ourselves after the Beatles individually."

Later in 1964 they made a record for Elektra under the name the Beefeaters, but by the end of the year had changed their name again, this time to the Byrds, once again inspired by

the Beatles, they spelled birds with a 'y' just as beetles was with spelt with an 'a'.

McGuinn says that without the Beatles they would never have existed. He said, "We loved them. We revered them. After we made it, I went to parties with the Beatles and I was in awe at the time, a great feeling." He was also to comment, "The Beatles came out and changed the whole game for me."

When they came to England in August 1965 the Byrds were billed

The Byrds

as 'America's answer to the Beatles' and John Lennon, George Harrison, Brian Jones of the Rolling Stones and Denny Laine of the Moody Blues attended their first show.

The Byrds met the Beatles socially on several occasions and David Crosby has been credited with bringing Ravi Shankar's music to the attention of George Harrison.

The Beatles helped to popularise many American artists in the United

Kingdom and led to debut tours by artists such as Chuck Berry and Carl Perkins. Their admiration for Motown artists, which resulted in covers of three Motown hits on their debut album *Please Please Me*, also helped to promote the Motown acts. The Beatles added Mary Wells to one of their British tours and Brian Epstein booked artists such as the Four Tops to tour Britain. The British blues boom in the 1960s also led to the revival of interest in veteran blues artists and to U.K. tours for artists such as B.B.King and Muddy Waters.

The Beatles also lauded the Beach Boys and the lightweight California type surf numbers began to mature considerably with Brian Wilson finding the Beatles an ideal act to compete against in his creation of classic numbers such as *God Only Knows* and *Good Vibrations*.

One of the most obvious Beatles-inspired outfits was the Monkees; a band specially created for a television series by American producers Bob Rafelson and Bert Schneider. Impressed by the Beatles film *A Hard Day's Night*, they formed the Raybeat Company to develop a pilot sit-com for Screen Gems based on the Beatles movie.

Series director Schneider was even to comment, "The Beatles made it all happen, that's the reality. Richard Lester is where the credit begins for the Monkees and for Bob and me".

Initially, Rafelson and Schneider

considered using an existing group the Lovin' Spoonful for the series, then they decided that they would prefer actors and took out an advertisement in the entertainment magazine Variety. It read: MADNESS! Auditions – folk and rock 'n' roll musicians/singers. Running parts for four insane kids, ages seventeen to twenty-one, with courage to work".

Among the four hundred and thirty seven young hopefuls interviewed were Stephen Stills, Paul Williams, Danny Hutton (who became leader of Three Dog Night) and Charles Manson. One member of the group, however, had been pre-selected. He was David Thomas Jones, more familiarly known as Davy Jones, a Manchester born actor/singer who had appeared in the Broadway version of *Oliver* as the Artful Dodger. He had also appeared as a member of the *Oliver* cast on the Beatles debut appearance on the *Ed Sullivan Show* in February 1964.

The other members were Mike Nesmith, a Texas born guitarist who had moved to Los Angeles where he had appeared with various bands. Peter Thorkelson, more familiarly known as Peter Tork, a Washington born keyboardist and bass guitarist and Mickey Dolenz, a Los Angeles born actor who had appeared as Corky in the TV series *Circus Boy*.

The first name considered for the group was the Turtles, then the Inevitables and finally, the Monkees.

A month before the series made its debut on NBC on September 5th 1966, a single *Last Train to Clarksville* was released which went on to top the American charts.

Although the group had been formed especially for the series, it was decided to include music in all the shows and publisher Don Kirshner, who had been asked to find songs for the group's initial recordings, gathered songs for a number of songwriters including Neil Diamond, Leiber & Stoller, Neil Sedaka, Gerry Coffin, Carole King and Barry Mann.

Echoes of the Beatles' influence can be seen in *Last Train To Clarksville* when the group sang 'no no no' as a counterpoint to the Beatles 'yeah yeah yeah'.

There were fifty-eight episodes of the television series, which lasted until March 25th 1968. Brian Epstein's NEMS Enterprises also brought them over to England to appear at the Empire Pool, Wembley.

Apart from the TV series, the Monkees had nine albums and fourteen singles released between August 1966 and May 1970.

The surf music craze had begun in the early 1960s with artists such as the Beach Boys, the Surfaris and Jan & Dean, but after the Beatles appeared, the amount of American rock bands who began to feature in the charts increased. They included the Beau Brummels (who chose their name because they thought it would place their records next to those of the Beatles in the record bins), the McCoys, the Byrds, Sam the Sham & the Pharoahs, the Turtles, the Lovin' Spoonful, Paul Revere & the Raiders, the Outsiders, Cyrkle, the Young Rascals, ? & the Mysterians, the Gentrys, the Ramsey Lewis Trio, the Bobby Fuller Four, Shadows of Knight, Tommy James & the Shondells and many others.

The Monkees

Solo singers continued to have hit records in America, despite the impression that the Beatles had stifled their popularity. The Beatles had simply caused the influx of British and American groups into the charts, adding to the diversity of the listings.

Arguably, the Beach Boys were the American band who were closest to the Beatles in overall creativity, mainly due to the genius of Brian Wilson. While many of the other bands recorded songs provided to them by songwriters, the Beach Boys material, like that of the Beatles, was individual to them.

Later, inspired by the Beatles, many British and American bands began to record their own material and it is the songwriters more than the solo singers, who suffered most from the influence of the group.

The Beatles probably diverted the Beach Boys away from their surf sounds and, in fact, the Beach Boys were No. 5 in the American charts with *Fun Fun Fun* when the Beatles made their impact in February 1964. They also topped the charts later that year with 'I Get Around'.

The American band shared the same label as the Beatles, Capitol Records and were also bedfellows in the record bins due to the first three letters of their name. In 1965 the Beach Boys appeared in the film *The Girls On The Beach* in which kids at a school hop think they had booked the Beatles, but get the Beach Boys instead!

A fierce competitiveness was generated when the Beatles 'invaded' America, particularly in the mind of

The Beach Boys

Brian Wilson. Brian was the creative fire behind the group, which also comprised his brothers Carl and Dennis, his cousin Mike Love and friend Al Jardine. Brian's output following the appearance of the Beatles was so stimulated that the group had a huge string of hits and became the biggest selling band on Capitol Records next to the Beatles. Brian turned his concentration increasingly to production and songwriting and ceased touring.

After hearing the *Rubber Soul* album in 1965 he was so impressed he decided he would try to surpass it stating that he would produce the greatest rock 'n' roll album ever made and began to work on *Pet Sounds*. It was well received critically in Britain, but in America it did not fare so well, particularly as Capitol

rush-released *The Best Of the Beach Boys* compilation several weeks later which was far more successful and turned Gold.

He then began to work on another album which he called *Smile*, intending that work to surpass the Beatles. During the making of the album the Beatles came out with *Sgt Pepper's Lonely Hearts Club Band*, which was such a masterpiece that Brian became disillusioned, scrapped his project and just issued a few of the tracks on an album called *Smiley Smile*.

However, the Beatles had great admiration for the Beach Boys and became friends of theirs, with Paul McCartney saying at the time that he regarded *God Only Knows* as the best song ever written.

THE BOYS NEXT DOOR

AMERICAN SOLO SINGERS PRIOR TO THE BRITISH INVASION

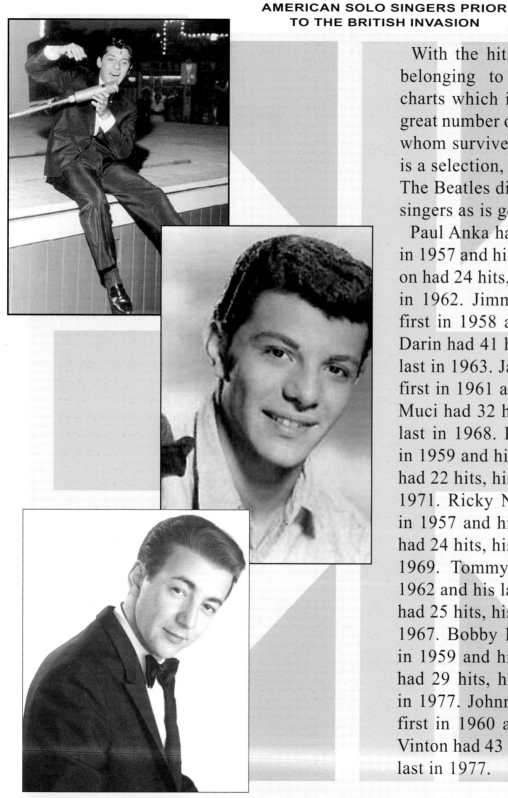

With the hits of the rock 'n' roll greats belonging to the 1950s, the American charts which immediately followed saw a great number of solo male singers, many of whom survived the British Invasion. Here is a selection, indicating that the advent of The Beatles didn't bury the American solo singers as is generally assumed.

Paul Anka had a total of 51 hits, his first in 1957 and his last in 1977. Frankie Avalon had 24 hits, his first in 1959 and his last in 1962. Jimmy Clanton had 12 hits, his first in 1958 and his last in 1969. Bobby Darin had 41 hits, his first in 1959 and his last in 1963. James Darren had 10 hits, his first in 1961 and his last in 1977. Dion Di Muci had 32 hits, his first in 1958 and his last in 1968. Fabian had 10 hits, his first in 1959 and his last in 1960. Brian Hyland had 22 hits, his first in 1960 and his last in 1971. Ricky Nelson had 53 hits, his first in 1957 and his last in 1973. Gene Pitney had 24 hits, his first in 1961 and his last in 1969. Tommy Roe had 22 hits, his first in 1962 and his last in 1973. Jimmie Rodgers had 25 hits, his first in 1957 and his last in 1967. Bobby Rydell had 29 hits, his first in 1959 and his last in 1965. Neil Sedaka had 29 hits, his first in 1960 and his last in 1977. Johnny Tillotson had 25 hits, his first in 1960 and his last in 1965. Bobby Vinton had 43 hits, his first in 1962 and his last in 1977.

From the top: Paul Anka, Frankie Avalon, Bobby Darin

The image of 'Swinging London' helped to glamorise The British Invasion years. Fashion, films and images of a city bursting with young talent and ideas added to the impact of the music of the British groups.

The leading fashion models of the decade included Twiggy, Jean Shrimpton and Celia Hammond. There were the photographers such as David Bailey (who inspired the leading character in Antonioni's 'Blow Up'), Terence Donovan and . The trendy clothes of teenage girls, particularly with the mini-skirts created a revolution in styles and places such as Carnaby Street, the Kings Road and shops such as Biba's and I Was Lord Kitchener's Valet added to the ambience.

There was a young and sexy image with the 'dolly birds' in their mini skirts and kinky boots, all appealing to American youth who were thrilling to the music of the Beatles. Jane Asher, Patti Boyd, Carol White, Charlotte Rampling, Sarah Miles, Jane Birkin, Anita Pallenberg, and British television series such as *Danger Man*, *The Prisoner* and *The Avengers* also began to make an impact on the American market.

In some ways, the creative young artists from the provinces and the East End of London were breaking down the class barriers which were once so strong and kept working class people in the low paid categories. An example is photographer David Bailey who was born the son of an East End tailor in 1938. He secured a contract with Vogue magazine where the photographs he took of his then girlfriend Jean Shrimpton,

Twiggy

known as 'the Shrimp', turned her into one of the leading models of the 1960s. Bailey's second wife was the French actress Catherine Deneuve and the best man at the wedding was Mick Jagger.

Jean Shrimpton was born in 1942 and helped to popularise the mini skirt. She created headlines when she appeared at Melbourne Cup Day in Australia in a mini skirt and was to say, "Surely people are more important than clothes". Following her affair with Bailey she lived with actor Terence Stamp for three years and appeared in the film 'Privilege' with Paul Jones. She was known as 'the face of the 1960s' and now runs a hotel in Penzance.

The other famous model was Lesley Hornby a working class girl from Kilburn, born in 1949 who was known as 'Twiggy' because she was so skinny it was said that her legs looked like twigs! She only had a 32-22-32 figure but became a sensation in the modelling world. Later in her career she was to turn to acting and now still lives in London with her second husband, actor Leigh Lawson.

Of course, the baby boom, known in Britain as 'the bulge', meant that there were more teenagers in Britain than ever before and they were now earning money and demanding their own styles of fashion. Mary Quant brought out the mini skirt, which began to creep up the leg as it became ever shorter, exposing flesh above the knee, which had never been seen in clothes in public places before. By 1968 it had developed into the microskirt, which was more like a pelmet. That was followed by the maxiskirt, which brought the hemlines right down again to the ankles!

Young men's fashions were also in evidence and the Kinks were to observe these trends in their hit *Dedicated Follower Of Fashion*. The Beatles in particular influenced British and American youth with their visual appearance, particularly in America where their 'mop-top' style was initially ridiculed, but then adopted by American youth, as were their style of clothes and Cuban heeled boots.

Mary Quant, born in London in 1934, was one of the British dress designers who changed the fashion landscape, not inventing the mini-skirt, but popularising it and opening her Bazaar boutiques in the Kings Road and Knightsbridge. She also launched the Ginger Group to export her fashions to America and Mary Quant cosmetics, jewellery, sunglasses and other leisure wear.

Boutiques began to spread all over London: Bazaar, Biba's and men's fashions in stores by John Stephens. Stephens, a grocer's son from Glasgow, opened ten shops in Carnaby Street, a street that became a major fashion centre during the decade.

Barbara Hulanicki, the daughter of a Polish diplomat, born in 1938, launched her successful boutique Biba's in 1963. By the time she moved to larger premises in Kensington High Street it was known as 'the dolly birds' department store'. Barbara also developed a range of cosmetics in colours not previously used for make-up and eventually sold her cosmetics empire to Dorothy Perkins when Biba's finally closed in 1975.

I Was Lord Kitchener's Valet was also a popular boutique, mainly specialising in vintage military style wear for men, with stars such as Jimi Hendrix and Mick Jagger popularising the trend.

Pop art also sprang up in Britain and the art revival placed artists such as David Hockey and Peter Blake in the forefront. Hockney, a grammar school boy from Bradford in Yorkshire had his first one-man show in 1963. He became so popular with an American audience that he began to teach art in the United States in the mid-sixties and then went to live in California, although he still maintains a London studio. Peter Blake, of course, went on to design the 'Sgt Pepper' sleeve, one of the most identifiable images of the 20th century.

For the first time British television series were screened in America, beginning with *Danger Man*, which featured actor Patrick McGoohan. McGoohan was to follow up with one of the most enigmatic television series ever made, *The Prisoner*.

It was basically the story of the former secret agent featured in *Danger Man* who is kidnapped and held in a mysterious village from which there seems to be no escape.

Known only as Number Six, McGoohan attempted to escape in each episode and although there were only seventeen episodes made, it still remains a television classic.

Another popular British series that successfully crossed the Atlantic was *The Avengers*. This starred Patrick McKnee as John Steed, a British secret agent who was assisted by a number of glamorous females, be-

ginning with Honor Blackman as Mrs Gale, a leather clad lass skilled in the martial arts. She left the series to become Pussy Galore in the James Bond film *Goldfinger* and was replaced by Diana Rigg, who was to become Steed's most popular assistant, Mrs Peel. American TV screens had been saturated by Western series but now, inspired by the British secret agent shows, home-grown American shows such as *The Man From Uncle* and *I Spy* appeared.

Other British television series were actually re-made specially for television audiences and included *Till Death Do Us Part*, which became *All In The Family*, *Steptoe And Son* which became *Sandford and Son* and *Man About the House* which became *Three's Company*. These three British series were screened in the Sixties, the America versions at the beginning of the Seventies.

British stage musicals also began their rise in the 1960s with Lionel Bart's *Oliver*. Bart was born in London in 1930 and his first musical was *Fings Ain't Wot They Used To Be*. *Oliver* was based on Charles Dickens' *Oliver Twist* and became the most popular musical of the decade and a sensation of Broadway (the Broadway cast appeared on the same *Ed Sullivan Show* in which the Beatles made their debut and a member of the cast was Davy Jones, who later became a Monkee). It was also turned into an Oscar winning film. Bart wrote other musicals, in addition to songs such as *Livin' Doll* for Cliff Richard and the title song for the James Bond movie *From Russia With Love*. He died in April 1999.

'Hammer'

The Swinging Screen

British films have never enjoyed such a boom as they did in the 60s. Hand in hand with the musical British Invasion international screens were filled with a stream of British movies and, for the first time, numerous British actors and actresses became international stars. Those who became well known included Peter O'Toole, Sean Connery, Michael Caine, Richard Burton, Albert Finney, Peter Sellers, Julie Christie, Vanessa Redgrave, Julie Andrews, Susannah York, Oliver Reed and Terence Stamp, along with directors such as David Lean, John Schlesinger, John Boorman and Ken Russell. At the same time American directors such as Stanley Kubrick, Joseph Losey and Richard Lester based themselves in Britain,

alongside Polish director Roman Polanski. Continental directors such as Jean Luc Goddard, Francois Truffaut and Michelangelo Antonioni also began to make films in Britain.

Apart from the revolution in music and fashion, the profound social and cultural revolution in the country between the years 1958 – 1963 also swept aside accepted conventions and traditions concerning sexual mores, all of which were reflected in some of the British movies of the decade.

Two major British genres were the James Bond movies and Hammer films, which all became popular in America, bringing for the first time, a true Invasion of British movies, albeit many of them financed by the Hollywood studios (but also garnering lots of Oscars). These included

Laurence Of Arabia (1962 Oscar as 'Best Film'), *Dr Strangelove*, *Zulu*, *Dr Zhivago*, *Tom Jones* (1963 Oscar as 'Best Film'), *The Ipcress File*, *The Knack*, *The Italian Job* (Cilla Black was originally offered the part of Michael Caine's girlfriend, but her agent asked for too much money), *Get Carter*, *A Man For All Seasons* (1966 Oscar as Best Film), *The Lion in Winter*. British movie musicals such as *Oliver* (recipient of five Oscars), *Chitty Chitty Bang Bang* and *My Fair Lady* (1964 Oscar as Best Film) also made an impact.

In addition there were a number of films, which specifically projected the 'Swinging London' image, including: *Blow-Up*, *Tonite Let's All Make Love In London*, *Alfie*, *A Swinging Time*, *Wonderwall* and *Modesty Blaise*.

It was initially the success of *Tom Jones* and the Bond films which convinced American movie companies that a bonanza awaited them in promoting 'Britishness' as the country had now become the music and fashion centre of the world. It is interesting to note that in the 21st Century Hollywood has been relocating a number of those British films to America in various remakes of *The Italian Job*, *Get Carter* and *Alfie*.

Here is a selection of a few of the many British actors and actresses who found fame in the 60s:

Michael Caine was born Maurice Micklewhite in 1933 and first gained attention in 1963's *Zulu*. He then appeared as Harry Palmer in the spy movies *The Ipcress File Funeral In Berlin* and *Billion Dollar Brain* and acclaimed films such as *Alfie*, *The Italian Job* and *Get Carter*.

He is still making movies and has received Oscars as Best Supporting actor.

Sean Connery was born in Edinburgh in 1930 and his first major lead was co-starring with Lana Turner in *Another Time, Another Place,* set in Liverpool. He only received five thousand pounds for starring in the first James Bond movie *Dr No*, but went on to become the definitive Bond, until he decided to retire from the role to star in what he considered more mature movies, examples of which are *The Hill, The Offence, The Man Who Would Be King* and *The Wind and the Lion.*

Julie Christie was born in India in 1941. She made her initial impact in *Billy Liar* and won an Oscar as best Actress for *Darling*. She appeared as Lara in *Doctor Zhivago* and Bathesheba in *Far From The Madding Crowd*. In the early 1970s she moved to America to appear in three films with her lover Warren Beatty, but then virtually retired from the screen and now rarely makes an appearance.

Terence Stamp was born in 1940 and his first major role was in *Billy Budd* in 1960, films such as *The Collector, Modesty Blaise* and *Poor Cow* followed. These days he remains an acknowledged actor starring in films such as *Priscilla, Queen of the Desert* and *The Limey.*

Vanessa Redgrave appeared in several 60s films including *Morgan: A Suitable Case For Treatment, Blow-Up, Isadora, A Man For All Seasons, Camelot* and *The Charge Of The Light Brigade*. She comes from a thespian family, the daughter of Sir Michael Redgrave.

Michael Caine in 'Alfie'

David Hemmings was a child actor, born in 1941 who appeared in a string of pop films at the beginning of the decade before making his impact in *Blow-Up*. These days he is a character actor appearing in movies such as *Gladiator.*

Sarah Miles was also born in 1941 and also appeared in *Blow-Up*. She had strong roles in *Term Of Trial* and *The Servant* and her husband, the late Robert Bolt, wrote *Ryan's Daughter* especially for her.

Susanna York, was born in 1941 as well and made her film debut in 1960. During the decade she appeared in various films including ones which portrayed a background of Swinging London such as *Kaleidoscope*

and *Sebastian*. In 1969 she gained acclaim for a dramatic appearance in the American film *They Shoot Horses Don't They*.

Rita Tushingham, a Liverpool girl, born in 1942, appeared in *A Taste Of Honey* (incidentally nothing to do with the Beatles track sung by Paul McCartney), *The Girl With Green Eyes, The Knack, Smashing Time, Dr Zhivago* and *The Bed Sitting Room*.

Here are some of the British films of the 60s which had an element of 'Swinging London' in the background:

Alfie was the tale of a Cockney Cassanova who had 'the birds' lining up. His various lovers in the film included Jane Asher, Shirley Anne

Field, Millicent Martin, Julia Foster, Eleanor Bron, Vivian Merchant and Shelley Winters, although a tragedy finally made him more mature. It was a dream part for an actor and Caine took every advantage of the role, which included him revealing his thoughts to the audience by speaking directly into the camera.

Georgy Girl was a 1966 film starring Lynn Redgrave, Charlotte Rampling and James Mason. This film reflected the changes brought about by the 'Swinging Sixties' and the relaxation of censorship restrictions in Britain. The film had four letter words and references to abortion and unmarried mothers in the tale of the adventures of a rather plain girl from the provinces on her arrival in 60s London. The Seekers topped the charts with the title song.

Smashing Time was directed by Desmond Davis and produced by Carlo Ponti and Roy Millichap. The comedy about two Northern girls who descend on 'Swinging London' starred Rita Tushingham with Lynn Redgrave and Michael York. The soundtrack was issued in Britain by Stateside and in America by ABC. The tracks were *Baby Don't Go*, *Carnaby Street*, *Day Out*, *It's Always Your Fault*, *New Clothes*, *Smashing Time*, *Trouble Waiting For My Friend*, *While I'm Still Young* by Keith West and *Tomorrow*.

In 1966 *Blow-Up* was an unusual interpretation of the 'Swinging London' scene by the Italian director Michelangelo Antonioni. It was a haunting evocation of a decade, which is also an exploration of both reality and illusion.

The film followed a series of events in which a fashion photographer (David Hemmings) takes some shots in a park for a projected book. In his studio he blows up the photographs to reveal the blurred image of a man hiding in the bushes, pointing a gun. He visits the park again and discovers the body of a man.

Jane (Vanessa Redgrave), a mysterious woman, visits him in the studio and steals his negatives and blow-ups. He returns to the park to find that the body had disappeared.

The story acted as a link to scenes which depicted Antonioni's vision of London: all rock shows, pot parties, free love and the seeming apathy of the main character to the events which surround him. The photographer watches, almost with disinterest as his wife (Sarah Miles) makes love to another man. He witnesses the hysteria at a rock club where the Yardbirds are performing and a frenetic Jeff Beck smashes his guitar

Terence Stamp

and is pursued by hysterical fans. The photographer creates a sexual atmosphere in the studio to arouse his model, Verushka, at a photographic session, then immediately loses interest as soon as the photos are taken.

Blow-Up gained some notoriety at the time because it was the first British film to present full-frontal nudity and receive a censor's certificate. The scene took place in the studio when Hemmings was involved in a nude romp with Jane Birkin and Gillian Hills. Birkin went on to star in *Wonderwall*, make a controversial record *Je T'aime* with her French lover Serge Gainsbourg and was a British 'dolly bird' who became a star in France.

The role of the photographer was said to have originally been offered to Sean Connery but he turned it down. Connery later commented that he regretted the decision. Terence Stamp was then signed for the role, but Antonioni changed his mind and opted for a new face, choosing Hemmings.

Tonite Let's All Make Love In London was a 70-minute documentary, produced and directed by Peter Whitehead. A portrayal of the Swinging London scene which included illustrator Alan Aldridge painting the nude body of a girl to the strains of 'Paint It Black' and interviews with Andrew Loog Oldham, Vanessa Redgrave, David Hockney, Edna O'Brien, Michael Caine, Julie Christie and Mick Jagger with music from Eric Burdon & the Animals, the Rolling Stones and Pink Floyd.

There had been a number of American monochrome 'B' movies about rock 'n' roll in the 1950s. Following the success of *The Blackboard Jungle* with Bill Haley's *Rock Around the Clock* on its soundtrack in 1955, a shoal of low-budget movies were released, including *Shake Rattle & Roll*, *Rock Around The Clock*, *Rock All Night*, *Rock Baby Rock*, *Rock Pretty Baby* and *Rock Rock Rock*. Cheaply made and in monochrome, the stories were superficial and generally about the generation clash – youngsters like rock 'n' roll, the elders object, but in the end they come to like it and they

begin dancing like teenagers!

Some were virtually remakes; you only have to look at the titles – *Don't Knock The Rock* and *Don't Knock The Twist*.

The 1950s was the decade when the word 'teenagers' was first coined and most of the early films featuring youngsters portrayed them as virtual juvenile delinquents. The rock 'n' roll movies changed that by showing that the music could unite the generations.

The 1960s were to see two main strands of musical movies in the States; the Elvis Presley's series of lightweight contenders and the formulaic Beach movies, in addition to some B films in which one or two British acts were to appear as guests.

There were also seen a few low budget black and white British films in the 1950s such as *The Gold Disc*, *The 6.5 Special* and *The Tommy Steele Story*, but apart from the quality of *A Hard Day's Night* the British pop films of the 60s were no improvement and were quite embarrassing, not only for the paucity of the plots, but also the fact that most of them did not even take advantage of the potentially strong musical content they had available to them with the range of top groups and chart hits on hand.

For some reason, instead of utilising the talents of acts such as the Moody Blues, Creation, the Escorts, Wayne Fontana, Tom Jones, the Kinks, the Mindbenders and others, British films were littered with forgettable artists and groups such as the Vacqueros, the Wackers, Louise

Cordet, the Cheynes, the Warriors, the Zephyrs, Ray Sone, the Aces and Ray Lewis & the Trekkers who were unknown and hitless.

There had also been a number of trite British films made shortly prior to The British Invasion. In 1963 they included *Live It Up* (called *Sing And Swing* in the U.S.), in which David Hemmings was one of a group of postal workers who want to get into show-business. Music was provided by Heinz Burt, Gene Vincent, Sounds Incorporated, Andy Cavett & the Saints, the Outlaws and Kim Roberts. *What A Crazy World* starred Joe Brown & the Bruvvers, Marty Wilde, Freddie & the Dreamers and Susan Maughan and *Just For Fun* with Dusty Springfield, Brian Poole & the Tremeloes, Jimmy Savile and others.

There were only one or two exceptions to the 'turkeys', such as the 1962 *Some People*, starring the ubiquitous David Hemmings, Kenneth Moore and Ray Brooks. With music by a British band called the Eagles, it was an interesting and likeable feature.

Beatles Movies

The Beatles made their film debut in *A Hard Day's Night* in 1964, a film that added to the consolidation of the Beatles success and which proved an inspiration to many young American musicians. It was the most important of the British Invasion movies.

Despite its low budget it was intelligent, witty and was described as 'the Citizen Kane of jukebox movies'.

The film was only budgeted at £200,000 because United Artists were primarily interested in obtaining rights to a Beatles soundtrack album. Walter Shenson, an American producer based in Britain engaged another London-based American, Richard Lester, to direct. Lester had made a film featuring the Goons (Peter Sellers, Harry Secombe, Spike Milligan), *The Running, Jumping And Standing Still Film* which impressed John Lennon. He had also directed *It's Trad, Jazz*, a movie with a host of British and American stars ranging from Gene Vincent, Chubby Checker and Del Shannon to Helen Shapiro, Craig Douglas and John Leyton. It was in this film that Lester introduced some of the innovative camera techniques, which he was to use in the Beatles debut movie.

Alun Owen received an Oscar nomination for his script, which captured the Beatles sense of humour and their banter, although John Lennon was to change his attitude about the film a few years later saying, "We were a bit infuriated by the glibness and silliness of the dialogue and we were always trying to get it more realistic, but they wouldn't have it. It ended up okay, but the next one was bullshit because it really had nothing to do with the Beatles."

Director Dick Lester commented, "The concept came from John's reply to a question I asked him about a trip they'd made to Sweden". When Lester asked him how did he like the trip, John replied, "Oh, it was a room and a car and a room and a room and a car."

Producer Walter Shenson was to say, "Now I've got the Beatles, do I need stars? Are they necessary, even playing bit parts? My guess is no. It would be all wrong to have say Kenny More or Dirk Bogarde appearing with the boys, though maybe not Margaret Rutherford. I have a hunch

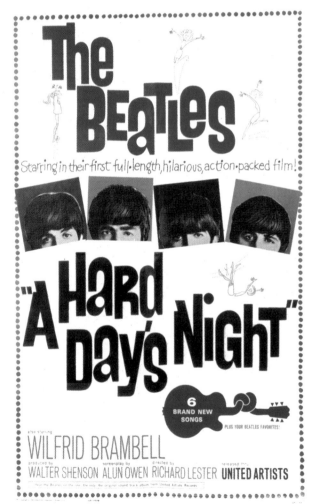

the fans would love her. But say, just say, it was Hayley Mills, will they feel resentful of her?"

Shenson had considered Hayley as a love interest for one of the Beatles, but fortunately was talked out of the idea. Yet a real-life romance did take place during the filming when George Harrison fell in love with Patti Boyd.

So, what was the story-line?

Once upon a time there were four happy Liverpool lads called Paul, John, George and Ringo, and they played their music all over the country. Now, when they finished playing in one place they had run to the nearest railway station and go on to a new place to play some more of their music, usually pursued by hundreds of young ladies.

On the day of our story, John, George and Ringo get to the station and fight their way into the railway compartment where they meet up with Paul, who has a little old man with him, a very dear little old man. Anyway, who is he? The little old man is 'mixing' John McCartney, Paul's grandfather (Wilfred Brambell). Grandfather is dedicated to the principle of divide and conquer. The mere sight of a nice friendly group of clean-cut lads like the Beatles brings him out in a rash of counterplots.

Norm (Norman Rossington), the boys' road manager, is conducting a war of nerves with John, the group's happy anarchist. He collects Grandfa-

 116

ther and together with Shake (John Junkin), the general dogsbody, he retreats to the restaurant car for coffee, leaving the boys to settle in for their journey to London and a live television show. However, a well-established first-class ticket holder (Richard Vernon) drives the boys out of their carriage by being pompously officious, so they go and join Norm, Shake and Grandfather in the restaurant car.

By this time Grandfather has managed to get Norm and Shake at each other's throats and Paul warns the others that this could be only the beginning. Sure enough, Grandfather has started a campaign of dissention that leads to frightening schoolgirls, a proposal of marriage to a chance acquaintance and general chaos culminating with Grandfather being locked in the luggage van where he and the boys complete their journey making music.

When the boys arrive in London, they go to their hotel where Norm leaves them to sort out their fan mail. However, Grandfather has noticed that a certain amount of good-humoured banter is directed at Ringo. Here, thinks Grandfather, is the weak link in the chain. Instead of staying in the hotel the four boys sneak out to enjoy themselves at a twist club and Grandfather, trading his clothes for a waiter's suit, heads straight for a gambling club, passing himself off as Lord John McCartney. Again the boys have to rescue him, much to the old man's indignation.

The following day sees the boys plunged into the bustle of the tel-

evision world. Press conferences, rehearsals, make-up, running from place to place, being shepherded by the harassed Norm and got at by the television show's neurotic director (Victor Spinetti), and always in the background is Grandfather, interfering, disrupting and needling Ringo.

Only for a moment are the boys free. They can enjoy themselves playing in a large, open field, but even that does not last. John, however, does make the most of every second; he is always for the here and now. Paul tries keeping things on an even keel and George has a blind doggedness that sees him through. But the strain begins to tell on Ringo.

Grandfather, of course, plays on this, pointing out the barrenness of Ringo's life and finally goading him into walking out into the world, out-

side of the group. The other three boys go out searching for Ringo, leaving Norm to fume and the director to worry himself to near collapse at the possibility of no show.

Meanwhile, Ringo has found the world outside none too friendly and, through a series of encounters and misunderstandings, gets himself arrested. He is taken to the station, where he meets up with Grandfather who has been taken into custody. Grandfather storms at the Police Sergeant (Deryck Guyler) and manages to escape, leaving Ringo behind in the police station.

He gets back to the television theatre and tells the boys, who, pursued again, but this time by the police, go and rescue Ringo and finally they are able to do their show in front of a live audience.

The show does well but as soon as it is finished, again it is the mad dash on to the next plane for the next show. The past thirty-six hours have been a hard day's night. The next thirty-six hours will be the same.

Despite the Oscar nomination, Owen was not asked to provide the script for their second venture, 'Help!' Epstein told Lester that he had employed another scriptwriter for the film.

The original concept for this film related how a doctor told Ringo that he was terminally ill, so Ringo hires a contract killer to murder him when he least expects it. The next day he finds the doctor had mixed up the X-rays and he is not going to die. However, he does not now know how to contact the contract killer. This plot was never used as it was found that another film was being made with virtually the same story.

It was therefore altered to a tale about an Eastern cult which makes sacrifices to their God Kaili. Their sacrificial victims have to wear a special ring, which ends up on Ringo's finger. The Beatles then have to protect Ringo from the fanatics.

Shenson made the mistake of filling the film with character actors, who tended to outshine the Beatles and John Lennon had nothing positive to say about the film and was to describe it as 'crap!'

So this is how the film eventually ran:

In the Eastern Temple of the Goddess Kaili, a human sacrifice is about to be made. But the executioner, the High Priest Clang, is stopped by the beautiful Ahme, priestess of the cult who has discovered that the victim is not wearing the sacrificial ring essential for the ritual.

On the other side of the world the Beatles are performing. Ringo sits on the stage playing the drums and amongst his many rings is the special ring which was a present from an unknown fan of another continent.

In the days that follow there are a series of mysterious events make no sense to the Beatles. At home, on the street, a strange force seems to be directed at Ringo. A gang of thugs descend upon the boys and attempt to amputate Ringo's entire hand and the Beatles realise that it is Ringo's new ring they must be after.

After several more attempts, Clang and his gang nearly succeed in stealing Ringo's whole person, but just in time he is saved by Ahme.

A few days later, while the boys are waiting for a meal in an Indian Restaurant, the dreaded Clang and his henchman Bhuta appear disguised as waiters. They tell Ringo that since they cannot remove the ring from his finger he is to be sacrificed to the goddess himself. The boys flee to the nearest jewellers and ask the man to cut off the offending ring, but the metal breaks the files and the cutting wheel.

The boys call next at a science laboratory run by Professor Foot and his assistant Algernon and they put Ringo through every machine they have, to no avail. The ring resists all the assaults known to science. Foot decides that the ring has properties, which could give the owner the power to rule the world, and he confides to Algernon that he must have it. So the Beatles now have two more enemies who will stop at nothing to retrieve the ring. Ahme once again comes to the rescue and they all flee from the laboratory – to the Alps!

In no time the Beatles' winter sports activities are interrupted by the arrival of Foot and Algernon intent on mayhem to be joined almost at once by Clang and gang. After a frantic chase through snow and ice up mountains and down ski lifts the boys scramble to the nearest railway station and gasp to the ticket man, 'London!'

Back home they confide their troubles to a Superintendent of Scotland Yard and tell him they must have protection in order to record in peace. The next day the boys record two songs on Salisbury Plain, under the protection of the British Army, but Clang and his murderous thugs arrive and put the Beatles to flight. Ahme, in a tank, rescues them in the nick of time.

In London the murder attempts increase and the Beatles decide to leave the country until the heat is off. Heavily disguised they fly off to the Bahamas. But, alas, the world is too small a place for the Beatles, Clang and his gang and the two power-

drunk scientists. Soon, the whole fray is resumed. But Ringo learns the formula, which releases him from the ring. It slips off and he hands it to Clang who hastily hands it on to Foot who tried to pass it on to Algernon and so on down the line.

Ahme and the Beatles at last find peace and the dreaded Kaili will have no more victims.

Although their contract with United Artists committed the Beatles to three films, their experience with 'Help!' had dampened their enthusiasm for film features. They were offered a number of properties including *A Talent For Loving*, a Western which was later filmed with Richard Widmark and Caroline Munro, *The Three Musketeers* in which Brigitte Bardot was to appear as Milady De Winter (Dick Lester was later to film it, together with a sequel), *Up Against It*, a radical tale by playwright Joe Orton, which still hasn't been filmed and J.R.R. Tolkien's *Lord Of The Rings*.

The Beatles believed that the animated film *Yellow Submarine* would fulfil the terms of the contract, but it did not and they ended up discharging the film commitment with *Let It Be*.

Here is the synopsis of the plot for *Yellow Submarine*:

Once upon a time, or maybe twice, there was a place called Pepperland. On a peaceful day in this happy kingdom, a concert by Sgt Pepper's Lonely Hearts Club Band is interrupted by an anti-musical missile attack from the Blue Meanies. The chief Blue Meanie, his assistant Max, and their 99-numbered henchmen turn their splotch guns on the docile Pepperland populace, determined to rid the world of music happiness and love - a world without love is a Blue world!

Old Fred, conductor of the Band, flees to the Lord Mayor, who puts him into the Yellow Submarine for a last-minute escape. The sub surfaces in Liverpool where Ringo wanders aimlessly in boredom. The sub, radar-like, follows Ringo to his house. Fred enters Ringo's house, explains the situation and enlists his aid. They proceed to round up the others. John materialises out of a Frankenstein creature-like figure, Paul is found playing classical music, and George appears out of a haze of transcendental meditation. Armed with a battery of puns and four new songs, the Beatles board the Yellow Submarine and head for Pepperland. They are detoured through the Seas of Time, Science, Monsters, consumer Products, Nowhere, Phrenology, Green and Holes.

They undergo time warps, chase Lucy through her 'sky of diamonds', climb clocks and soup cans, become ancient and infantile, molecularised, actually 'disappear up their own existence' and almost drown in the avalanche of apples, among other adventures.

Characters they encounter on their mad 'Modyssey' include the U.S. Cavalry, Father Mackenzie, assorted monsters (including a vacuum-flask monster), Cowboys, Indians, King Kong and several unidentifiable 'things'. Ringo takes a liking to the super-intellectual Boob (a poetic personification of the 'Nowhere Man') and takes him along on the trip. In the Sea of Green he is captured by a giant blue hand.

A Pepper-powered sneeze propels the Beatles through the Sea of Holes into occupied Pepperland, which has been almost drained of colour. The Lord Mayor is astonished at the resemblance between the Beatles and the original Sgt Pepper Band.

Disguised as Apple Bonkers, they infiltrate the musical instrument compound. Then it is Beatles versus Meanies, with guitars against splotch guns, the ferocious Flying Glove, the Butterfly Stompers, the Hidden Persuaders with guns in their shoes, the snapping Turtle Turks with their mouths in their bellies and the Count Down Clown with his nose-cone nose. A battle is waged to the tune of *All You Need Is Love* and love becomes the overwhelming power. A surprise ending carries the fantastic fracas right into the theatre.

Shenson was to say, "I think if we'd had a sensational script or a great idea, we might have made a third film. But it just wasn't on the cards."

The final film to be made which completed the contract was *Let It Be*.

In the meantime, the Beatles introduced another innovation, *The Magical Mystery Tour*. This was a television film, which they decided to write and produce themselves, using the knowledge they had gleaned from Dick Lester and Walter Shenson. The Beatles reckoned that if *Magical Mystery Tour* proved a success, they would go on to produce their third feature film themselves.

However, the clever and amusing film, depicting a mystery trip in a gaily-painted yellow bus and featuring several new songs, received a critical mauling from the press following its initial screening on BBC2 on Boxing Day in 1967. Yet it received thirteen million viewers on this minority channel, which televised the colour film in black and white.

Magical Mystery Tour was a completely different approach to television shows and could well have led the way for further innovations in this medium but for the hysterical critical bashing. The Rolling Stones had taken inspiration from the Beatles venture to make *The Rolling Stones' Rock 'n' Roll Circus*, which was also a different approach to presenting popular music on television. However, allegedly due to the panning received by *Magical Mystery Tour*, they decided not to show it and a new avenue the television presentation of music was closed due to critics who did not really see the originality of the concept.

Herman's Hermits movies

Herman's Hermits starred in *Hold On (There's No Place Like Space)* in 1966, an MGM colour film produced

Peter Noone in 'Mrs. Brown You've Got A Lovely Daughter'

by Sam Katzman and directed by Arthur Lubin from a screenplay by James B. Gordon. It also featured Shelley Fabares who had co-starred in three Elvis Presley films, *Clambake*, *Girl Happy* and *Spinout*. It was an insubstantial tale in which NASA is considering naming a spacecraft after Herman's Hermits, and has an agent trail them to determine whether they proved suitable subjects for the honour.

MGM issued the soundtrack which contained the numbers: *A Must To Avoid*, *All The Things I Do For You Baby*, *The George And Dragon*, *Got A Feeling*, *Gotta Get Away*, *Hold On*, *Leaning On The Lamppost*, *Make Me Happy*, *We Want You Herman*, *Where Were You When I Needed You?* and *Wild Love*.

The same year they appeared in another MGM film *When The Boys Meet The Girls*, in which they performed *Biding My Time* and *Listen People*.

Their third appearance that year was in *Pop Gear*, also known as *Go Mania*, an American International Pictures movie, which was basically just a series of clips of several British Invasion artists hosted by Jimmy Savile.

In 1968 *Mrs Brown You've Got A Lovely Daughter* was a second starring vehicle for Herman's Hermits. Peter Noone had already had an acting role in *Coronation Street* and had a natural style. The film was shot on location in Manchester and London and was directed by Saul Swimmer and produced by Allen Klein from a screenplay by Thaddeus Vane.

Noone starred as Herman Tully who, with a group of friends (Karl Green, Keith Hopwood, Derek Leckenby, Barry Whitwam) owns a greyhound called Mrs Brown. They want to race it in London and decide to form a pop group in order to pay for the dog's upkeep. They travel to London and stay with a real life Mrs Brown (Mona Washbourne) and her husband (Stanley Holloway). Herman initially falls for a model, but realises his heart belongs to his sweetheart back home (Sheila White).

The soundtrack was issued by MGM and the tracks were: *Daisy Chain*, *Holiday Inn*, *It's Nice To Be Out In The Morning*, *Lemon And Lime*, *The Most Beautiful Thing In My Life*, *Mrs Brown You've Got A Lovely Daughter*, *Ooh She's Done It Again*, *There's A Kind Of Hush All Over The World* and *The World Is For You*.

Cliff Richard movies
Cliff Richard and the Shadows made some enjoyable films in colour during the 1960s. Some of them were also screened in America, although title changes were sometimes used.

The 1964 film *Wonderful Life* was called *Swinger's Paradise* on its American release. In it, Cliff and the Shads are entertainers on an ocean liner and become part of a film crew who make their own movie, paying tribute to the history of movies in general. Among the fourteen songs were *A Girl In Every Port* and *We Love A Movie*.

Previous releases *The Young Ones* (called *Wonderful To Be Young* in America) and *Summer Holiday* were prior to The British Invasion.

His next film was *Finders Keepers* in 1967 was a rather far-fetched story of a group of youngsters who go to Spain to recover a lost atomic bomb. As with his previous musicals, Cliff

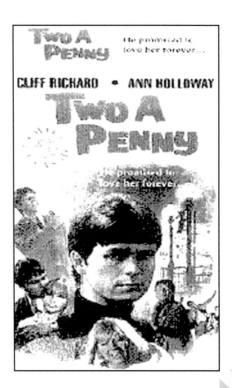

was backed by the Shadows. The songs had a Spanish influence and included *Oh Senorita* and *Paella*, they but were not as strong as the hit material from films such as *The Young Ones* and *Summer Holiday*.

Later the same year Cliff changed direction in *Two A Penny*, a religious film in which all proceeds were donated to Billy Graham's evangelical movement. Cliff portrayed an atheistic drug dealer. He sang several songs including *Twist and Shout* and *Lonely Girl*.

In 1973 he starred in *Take Me High* in which he played a merchant banker who launches a hamburger restaurant in Birmingham.

Although popular in Britain and resulting in hit singles and soundtrack albums, Cliff's pleasant, inoffensive movies were not as high profile in America and usually found themselves as second on the bill, virtually 'B' movies.

Among the films which we could loosely term 'British Invasion films',

there were movies which were vehicles for the artists such as *A Hard Day's Night*, *Catch Us If You Can*, *Ferry 'Cross the Mersey*, *Cuckoo Patrol* and *Mrs Brown You've Got A Lovely Daughter*. There were films that were merely a showcase for a variety of acts such as 'The TAMI Show', *Pop Gear* and *Just For You*, documentaries such as *Don't Look Back* and *The Seekers Down Under*, movies which merely featured a group on the soundtrack, or had an artist compose a soundtrack such as *Wonderwall* and *Up The Junction* and dramas which introduced a pop star into the cast such as *Performance*, *Girl On A Motorcycle* and *To Sir With Love*.

1964 films

Go Go Beat. Also known as *Go Go Big Beat*. Brian Epstein took legal action against this film because the advertisements gave the impression that the Beatles appeared in it. In fact, excerpts were used from a short film called *Mods And Rockers* which was a ballet with tunes by the Beatles, but not performed by them. The Hollies performed *Here I Go Again, Baby That's All*, Lulu sang *Shout* and there were performances by the Four Pennies, the Merseybeats, the Animals, Millie Small and the Wackers.

The film was actually excerpts from three British short films *Swingin' UK*, *UK Swings Again* and *Mods and*

Rockers which had been put together in this eighty-two minute film specially for American release.

Swinging U.K. Disc jockeys Kent Walton, Alan Freeman and Brian Matthews introduce a string of groups including the Merseybeats performing *Fools Like Me* and *Don't Turn Around*, the Four Pennies performing *Juliet* and *Running Scared*, the Wackers performing *Love Or Money*) and Millie Small performing *My Boy Lollipop* and *Baby Let Me Take You Home*. In America it was used as part of a longer film called *Go Go Big Beat*.

It's All Over Town. Yet another dismal British effort, this time featuring the Hollies, Acker Bilk, Frankie Vaughan, the Bachelors, the Springfields and Wayne Gibson & the Dynamic Sounds. Among the numbers are *Down And Out* and *Maraca Bamba* by the Springfields, *Now's The Time* by the Hollies and *Come On Let's Go* by Wayne Gibson & the Dynamic Sounds.

Get Yourself A College Girl. An American movie with another flimsy plot revolving around a girl in an Ivy League College who writes songs under a pseudonym but finds herself in trouble when her identity is revealed. It starred Mary Ann Mobley (a former Miss America who featured in a couple of Presley movies) and Nancy Sinatra and The Dave Clark Five performing *Whenever You're Around* and *Thinking Of You Baby* and the Animals performing *Blue Feeling* and *Around And Around*.

American acts included Freddie Bell & the Bellboys, Donnie Brooks and the Shondells. On its British release it was re-titled 'the Swinging Set'.

Ballad In Blue. Known in America as *Blues For Lovers*. This is an unusual film in that it is a British movie featuring Ray Charles and the Raelettes. Tom Bell and Mary Peach starred as the parents of a blind boy who is befriended by Ray Charles, who happens to be in London. It was directed by American film actor Paul Henried and the numbers featured included *Careless Love, Cry, Hallelujah, I Love Her So, I Got A Woman, Let The Good Times Roll, Light Out Of Darkness, Talkin' About You, That Lucky Old Sun, Unchain My Heart* and *What'd I Say*.

Wonderful Life. See Cliff Richard.

Just for You. South African-born disc jockey Sam Costa lies in bed, presses a button and various pop artists come onto the screen. They include Band Of Angels with *Hide 'n' Seek*, Doug Sheldon with *Night Time*, Roy Sone with *Teenage Valentine*, Peter And Gordon with *Leave Me Alone* and *Soft As The Dawn*, the Applejacks with *Tell Mr When*, Freddie & the Dreamers with *You Were Made For Me* and *Just For You*, Millie with *Sugar Dandy*, Johnny B Great with *If I Had A Hammer*, the Merseybeats with *Milkman*, Louise Cordet with *It's So Hard To Be Good* and the Warriors with *Don't Make Me Blue*. Like a number of these forgettable British films, this included a number of unknown acts which never surface again.

Rhythm 'n' Greens. The Shadows appear throughout in this thirty-two-minute short film, which is a brief history of England, with narration by Robert Morley. The Shadows play *Rhythm 'n' Greens, The Lute Number, The Drum Number, Ranks Chank* and *Main Theme*.

Sounds Of A City. A *Pathe* short filmed in Liverpool and featuring the Swinging Bluejeans, although why the Zephyrs and the Aces, who do not come from Liverpool, are featured, is a mystery.

The System. Known in the States as *The Girl Getters*. A group of lads at a seaside resort devise a system to get girls into bed. Oliver Reed, David Hemmings and Jane Merrow starred. The Searchers provided the title track.

UK Swings Again. The follow up to *Swinging UK*. Disc jockeys Alan Freeman, Kent Walton and Brian Matthews once again introduce a string of acts. With the Animals performing *Baby Let Me Take You Home*, the Hollies with *Here I Go Again* and *Baby That's All* and Lulu & Her Luvvers with *Shout*. Other performers were Brian Poole & the Tremeloes, the Swinging Bluejeans, the Tornadoes and the Applejacks. When it was included in a lengthier film in America called *Go Go Big Beat*, the hosts were Marlon Brando and Rod Steiger.

1965 films

The T.A.M.I. Show Also known as *Gather No Moss* or *Teenage Command Performance*. T.A.M.I. stands for Teenage Awards Musical International and was filmed at a concert held in the Santa Monica Civic Auditorium in California on October 24 1964. Directed by Steve Binder, it was the first full-length concert film to be given a cinema circuit release. The artists who appeared included a mixture of British and American acts: Gerry & the Pacemakers, Billy J. Kramer & the Dakotas, the Supremes, Jan & Dean, the Beach Boys, Chuck Berry, Marvin Gaye, James Brown and the Rolling Stones who perform *Around And Around* and *Off The Hook*.

Ferry Cross The Mersey. A vehicle for Gerry & the Pacemakers. This ended up with the usual trite plot; the progress of a group as they eventually win a music contest (in such cases of course, you can be sure that

THE DAVE CLARK FIVE
"CATCH US IF YOU CAN"
BARBARA FERRIS

the other groups engaged are not better than the one who is supposed to win!). Although the studio sequences were filmed in London, the locations were in Liverpool and included Gerry Marsden at the Cavern and on the Mersey ferry, a scene in Frank Hessy's music store and a climactic beat competition at the Locarno Ballroom.

The basic idea came from a suggestion by Tony Warren, who conceived *Coronation Street*, but they needed someone like Alun Owen to write the script. It remains the only music film of the 60s actually filmed in Liverpool with Liverpool artists and other Mersey acts included Cilla Black performing *Is It Love?*, the Fourmost performing *I Love You Too*, the Black Knights performing *I Got A Woman*)

the Blackwells performing *Why Don't You Love Me?* and Earl Royce & the Olympics performing *Shake a Tail Feather*. Jimmy Savile also makes an appearance.

The Beatles At Shea Stadium. A film taken from a 1966 television broadcast of the Beatles appearance at New York's Shea Stadium in August 1965. This was directed by Dick Fontaine, the man who filmed the Beatles for the very first time when he took a Granada TV team to the Cavern in 1962.

I've Gotta Horse. Known in America as *'Wonderful Day*, it was Billy Fury's second starring vehicle following the 1962 *Play It Cool* and was produced and directed by

Kenneth Hulme, with a screenplay by Hulme and Larry Parnes (Billy's manager). It has lacklustre songs and an awkward plot. The problem with some pop feature films is that songs are specifically written to fit in with the plot and they do not always work. You only have to look at some of Presley's films with songs such as *No Room To Rhumba In A Sports Car*, *Queenie Wahini's Papaya* and *Yoga Is As Yoga Does*. Billy would have fared better singing his actual chart hits.

He stars as a racehorse owner who seems to love his horse more than his musical career and in fact Billy's own racehorse was used in the film. This was his second feature film and the songs included *You've Got To Look Right For The Part*, *Won't Somebody Tell Me Why*, *I've Gotta Horse*, *Stand By Me*, *Do The Old Soft Shoe*, *I Like Animals*, *Find Your Dream* and *I Cried All Night*. Decca issued the soundtrack in Britain.

Billy Fury was Liverpool's first young teen idol. There had been other chart artists from Liverpool including Frankie Vaughan, Michael Holliday and Lita Roza, but they belonged to the sounds of another generation.

Fury never had a success in America on record, although he had two-dozen chart hits in Britain before illness forced his retirement.

Catch Us If You Can. Known in America as *Having A Wild Weekend*. The debut film for the Dave Clark Five was, in some ways, at attempt to make a DC5 equivalent of *A Hard Day's Night* and was directed by John

Boorman. The slim plot revolved around the DC5 as stunt men who, together with a young model, flee commercialism in the form of an 'Eat Meat' commercial and seek a haven in Devon. Like *A Hard Day's Night* it was filmed in monochrome. Peter Nichols wrote the screenplay and the film also featured Barbara Ferris, Robin Bailey, Yootha Joyce and David Lodge.

Epic issued the soundtrack album in America which contained the numbers *Catch Us If You Can, Having A Wild Weekend, I Can't Stand It, Move On, Ol Sol, On The Move, Sweet Memories* and *When*.

Charlie Is My Darling. A colour film produced by Andrew Loog Oldham. It is a documentary following the Rolling Stones for two days on a tour of Ireland. Andrew Loog Oldham asked director Pete Whitehead to make the film after seeing '

Wholly Communion, his documentary on a poetry recital. This first

Stones documentary (there were many others to come) features the group performing *This Could Be The Last Time* and *It's All Right*, while *Get Off My Cloud Heart Of Stone, Satisfaction* and *Going Home* appear on the soundtrack. The Charlie referred to is, of course, Charlie Watts. There are also interviews with the Stones and some of their fans and a backstage rendition of *Maybe It's Because I'm A Londoner*.

Dateline Diamonds. Directed by Jeremy Summers from a screenplay by Tudor Gates. It's a tale about a thief who attempts to use a pirate radio station in his jewellery smuggling operation. The cast included Kenneth Cope, Patsy Rowlands and Kenny Everett while the Small Faces, Kiki Dee and the Chantelles provided music.

Every Day's A Holiday. Re-titled in America as *Seaside Swingers* (this could be due to the fact that there was an American film in 1937 called *Every Day's A Holiday*). Another tired old cliché in which a group of teenagers turn up at a holiday camp in a seaside resort to take part in a television talent competition. Directed by Ray Hill it featured Mike Sarne, John Leyton, Freddie & the Dreamers and the Mojos. Among the numbers performed were *Don't Do That To Me* and *What's Cooking?* by Freddie & the Dreamers, *All I Want Is You* and *Crazy Horse Saloon*

by John Leyton and *A Boy Needs A Girl* by John Leyton and Grazina Frame. The American soundtrack was issued on Mercury.

Mojos in 'Every Day's A Holiday'

Gonks Go Beat. This film is interesting because it has actually become something of a cult movie with people who love really bad films. The Head of the Galaxy is disturbed by the deteriorating relationships on Earth between the boys of Beatland and the girls of Balladisle. He sends Wilko Roger, an ambassador from the planet Gonk to prevent a war between the pop groups and the female balladeers. War is prevented in a Romeo and Juliet fashion when Helen, a girl balladeer falls for Steve, a member of a group. Lulu & the Luvvers, the Nashville Teens, the Graham Bond Organisation, Alan David, Elaine & Derek, Ray Lewis & the Trekkers, the Long & the Short, the Troles and the Vacqueros provided the music.

Billy Fury in 'Play It Cool'

Go Go Mania. Also known as *Pop Gear.* Directed by Frederic Goode for American International Pictures, this is mainly a compilation of clips of British Invasion bands, with short introductions by disc jockey Jimmy Savile. The Beatles are seen performing *Twist And Shout* and *She Loves You* from a Pathe News clip of their Ardwick Apollo, Manchester appearance on November 20th 1963. Other artists include the Animals performing *House Of The Rising Sun* and *Don't Let Me Be Misunderstood*, Peter And Gordon performing 'World Without Love', Billy J. Kramer performing 'Little Children', and 'Herman's Hermits performing *I'm Into Something Good.* Other acts included the Spencer Davis Group, the Nashville Teens, Susan Maughan, the Rockin' Berries, the Four Pennies, the Fourmost, the Honeycombs and Sounds Incorporated.

Help! See the Beatles.

When The Boys Meet The Girls. An MGM film, which meant, of course, an appearance by Herman's Hermits who perform *Biding My Time* and *Listen People.* The film starred Connie Francis and Sam The Sham & the Pharoahs and was actually a reworking of the George and Ira Gershwin musical *Girl Crazy.*

Three Hats for Lisa. Joe Brown starred as Johnny Howjego in this musical set in London. Sidney Havers directed it from a screenplay by Leslie Bricusse and Talbot Rothwell. Youngsters wishing to please an Ital-

ian film star agree to her challenge for them to steal three hats on her behalf. The hats were a policeman's helmet, a businessman's bowler and a bearskin cap from a palace guard.

Brown has appeared in six movies, including *What A Crazy World, Spike Milligan Meets Joe Brown* and *Mona Lisa.* A British hit artist, he never found success in America as part of The British Invasion.

Be My Guest. A family inherits a seaside hotel and their son's rock group helps to promote it. This is another trifling tale with David Hemmings as the son. Steve Marriott also appears for the second time with Hemmings and the film was produced and directed by Lance Comfort from a screenplay by Lyn Fairhurst. Music was by Jerry Lee Lewis,

the Nashville Teens, the Zephyrs and the Nightshades and the numbers included *Be My Guest, No One But Me, She Laughed, Somebody Help Me* and *Watcha Gonna Do.*

Cuckoo Patrol. A vehicle for Freddie & the Dreamers, directed by Duncan Wood from a screenplay by Lew Schwarz. A review in the BFI (British Film Institute) Magazine described it as "a plotless and incredibly unfunny farce with the further embarrassment of grown up men impersonating boy scouts." The group are supported by a number of British character actors including John Le Mesurier, Kenneth Connor, Victor Maddern and Arthur Mullard in the tale of a group of scouts who thwart a plot by thieves during an outing.

Don't Look Back. The film of Bob Dylan's 1965 British tour, directed by D.A. Pennebaker, which also features Donovan, Marianne Faithfull, Alan Price and Joan Baez, with Donovan performing *To Sing For You.* A ciné verité style documentary, which was to influence films such as *Monterey Pop* and *Woodstock.*

Hold On. See Herman's Hermits.

What's New Pussycat? Feature film starring Peter O'Toole and Peter Sellers with Tom Jones singing *What's New Pussycat* and Manfred Mann performing *My Little Red Book.*

Primitive London. Also known as *Swinging London.* Directed by Arnold Louis Miller, it is a documentary focussing on the raunchier side of the capitol; wife swapping, strip clubs, girls sitting in a bathtub to shrink their jeans and so on. Billy J. Kramer appeared as a spokesman for the Swinging city.

Thunderbirds Are Go! A feature film based on the popular television puppet series by Gerry Anderson, which included music by Cliff Richard & the Shadows, who appear as marionettes.

1966 films
The Family Way. Not really a film associated with the British Invasion acts, although Paul McCartney penned the score for the movie. It starred Hayley Mills, Hywel Bennett and John Mills.

Blow Up. A film of Italian director Michaelangelo Antonioni's vision of *Swinging London.* David Hemmings, the lead in several forgettable British pop films of the early 1960s, starred as a David Bailey-style photographer. The Yardbirds are seen performing *Stroll On* in a London club, which ends with Jeff Beck smashing up the equipment and being pursued by fans. It is one of the few filmed sequences which shows the Yardbirds performing with their two lead guitarists at the time, Beck and Jimmy Page. There was a jazz score by Herbie Hancock.

The Seekers At Home. A film celebrating the Seekers' first return to Australia following their string of hits from their London base. They were filmed in Canberra, Sydney and Melbourne and at Surfer's Paradise and the Barossa Valley. The film had them performing fourteen songs: *A World Of Our Own, You Can Tell The World, Nobody Knows The Trouble I've Seen, Morningtown Ride, Sinner Man', Open Up Them Pearly Gates, Just A Closer Walk With Thee, We Shall Not Be Moved, 'Yesterday', I Was Born About 10,000 Years, Whistling Rufus, The Eriskay Love Lilt, Someday, One Day, I'll Never Find Another You, A World Of Our Own* and *The Carnival Is Over.*

The Big TNT Show. An American International film with Phil Spector as musical director. It was filmed at a concert at the Moulin Rouge club in Los Angeles in 1966. It featured Joan Baez, Bo Diddley, the Byrds, Ray Charles, Donovan performing *My Sweet Joy, Summer Day Reflection* and *Universal Soldier* and Petula Clark performing *Downtown, You're The One* and *My Love.*

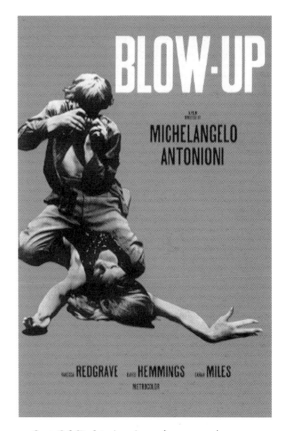

Out Of Sight. An American movie in which a secret organisation called F.L.U.S.H. intends to wipe out rock groups. Freddie & the Dreamers performed *Funny Over You* and *A Love Like You.* The other artists were Gary Lewis & the Playboys, Dobie Gray, the Knickerbockers, the Turtles and the Astronauts.

The Ghost Goes Gear. The tale of a group whose manager needs money to finance his ancestral home, which turns out to be a haunted house. It ends with a pop concert at a garden party. On it's release the film was cut to half its length and issued as a forty-one-minute movie. Music is provided by Steve Winwood, the Three Bells (a female vocal trio from Liverpool), with Acker Bilk performing *Stranger On The Shore* and Dave Berry singing *The Crying Game*.

Just For You. Another run-of-the-mill British pop film with several groups, including the Applejacks, Bachelors, Peter & Gordon, Freddie & the Dreamers and the Merseybeats and introduced by Sam Costa. It was completely altered for its American release. Costa was replaced by American disc jockeys Arnie Ginsberg and Bob Foster and much of the British musical footage dropped and replaced with clips of the Chiffons, the Rocking Ramrods, Casey Payton, Freddie Cannon and the Vagrants. It was also given a new name, *Disk-O-Tek Holiday*.

The Pretty Things. A fourteen-minute short directed by Caterina Arvet promoting The Pretty Things, another really excellent British band who never benefited from the British Invasion but are remembered for their classic albums such as *S.F. Sorrow* and *Parachute*.

Mods And Rockers. A twenty-five minute short featuring a ballet set in a café where a choreographed battle takes place between Mods and Rockers with a group called the Cheynes performing the Beatles numbers *Please Please Me*, *I Wanna Be Your Man* and *From Me To You*.

1967 films
Here We Go Round The Mulberry Bush. A film that featured the music of the Spencer Davis Group, Traffic and Stevie Winwood on the soundtrack. It was directed by Clive Donner, produced by Larry Kramer and based on the book by Hunter Davies, the Beatles official biographer. It is basically a rites of passage tale of a young lad and his first sexual encounters in the new town of Stevenage. Barry Evans, Judy Geeson, Adrienne Posta and Angela Scoular starred. The soundtrack album was released by United Artists and featured the numbers *Every Little Thing*, *Just Like Me*, *Picture Of Her*, *Possession*, *Taking Out Time*, *Virgin's Dream* and *Waltz For Caroline* by the Spencer Davis Group, *It's Been A Long Time* by Andy Ellison and *Am I What I Was Or Was I What I Am? Here We Go Round The Mulberry Bush* and *Utterly Simple* by Traffic. United Artists released the soundtrack on both sides of the Atlantic.

Smashing Time. Two northern girls arrive in 'Swinging London' and make their mark. Liverpool's Rita Tushingham starred alongside Lynn Redgrave and Michael York. Lots of 'Swinging London' images; mini skirts, pop groups, hip photographers etc. The soundtrack was issued on Stateside in Britain and ABC in America and the songs were *Baby Don't Go*, *Carnaby Street*, *Day Out*, *It's Always Your Fault*, *New Clothes*, *Smashing Time*, *Trouble*, *Waiting For My Friend* and *While I'm Still Young* by Keith West & Tomorrow.

Money Go Round. A film in which Sheila White and Jeremy Bulloch (in the future to become Bobba Fett in the *Star Wars* trilogy), are taken round the London Stock Exchange. Music is provided by the Liverpool band the Kubas, who toured with the

'To Sir With Love'

Beatles. They perform *Ballad Of the Stock Exchange*, *Champagne and Caviar*, *Money-Go-Round* and *Stock-taking Stockbroker*.

Two A Penny. See Cliff Richard.

Festival. A film of the Newport Jazz Festivals between the years 1961 to 1966. The only British Invasion artist featured is Donovan.

The Beatles At Shea Stadium. A film taken from a 1966 television broadcast of the Beatles' appearance at New York's Shea Stadium in August 1965.

Poor Cow. Directed by Ken Loach and starring Carol White and Terence Stamp. Donovan composed the music, which included *Colours*, *Be Not Too Hard* and *Poor Love.*

The Image. David Bowie was paid thirty pounds to appear in this short film in which he is soaked with buckets of water while clinging to a window ledge.

Finders Keepers. See Cliff Richard.

To Sir With Love. A hugely popular film, particularly in America. Sidney Poitier starred as a black teacher who seeks to gain the respect of a group of East End youngsters. Lulu appeared in the film and also had a chart-topping success in America with the film's title song. The Mindbenders also appear and perform *Off And Running* and *Stealing My Love From Me.* The soundtrack was released by Fontana on both sides of the Atlantic.

Julie Christe

Tonite Let's All Make Love In London. This was subtitled *A Pop Concerto for Film.* Produced and directed by Peter Whitehead, it is a documentary about 'Swinging London' which features the Pink Floyd performing 'Interstellar Overdrive', Twice As Much performing 'Night Time Girl' and Vashti performing 'Winter Is Blue'. *Interstellar Overdrive* was the title of a poem by Alan Ginsberg and Floyd recorded the number in January 1967. The soundtrack also features Eric Burdon & the New Animals, Chris Farlowe, the Small Faces and the Rolling Stones. The soundtrack album was issued in Britain by Instant and contains the numbers *Out Of Time*, *Paint It Black* and *Here Comes The Nice.* Among the celebrities featured in short interviews are Michael Caine, Julie Christie, Alan Aldridge, Alan Ginsberg, David Hockney, Lee Marvin, Mick Jagger and Vanessa Redgrave. The Stones are seen in a studio performing *Lady Jane* and *Standing In The Shadows.*

'Tonite Let's All Make Love in London'

The Touchables. A 20th Century Fox colour film directed by Robert Freeman and produced by John Bryan. With Esther Anderson, Judy Huxtable, Kathy Simonds and Marilyn Richard as four mini-skirted girls known as the Touchables. An unusual film in which the four girls kidnap a pop star, Christian, played by David Anthony, and imprison him in a plastic bubble for their pleasure. Robert Freeman, the photographer who photographed early Beatles album sleeves, directed the film.

The soundtrack album was issued in Britain on Stateside and in America on 20th Century Fox. The tracks were: *Respect* by Ferris Wheel, *All Of Us* by Nirvana, *Good Day Sunshine* by Roy Redman and *Blues For A Frog* and *Dancing Free* by Wynder K. Frog.

It preceded an American film the next year with a virtually identical plot. *Three In An Attic* was about three girls who kidnap a handsome young man and imprison him in an attic for their pleasure.

It's A Bikini World. A Trans American film directed by Stephanie Rothman. A Beach movie with a guest appearance from a British band, The Animals, who perform *We Gotta Get Out Of This Place*. American acts included the Castaways, the Gentrys, the Toys and Pat and Lolly Vegas.

Privilege. Directed by Peter Watkins, with songs composed by Mark Leander and Mark London and starring Paul Jones and Jean Shrimpton. Paul Jones performed *Free Me*, *I've Been A Bad Bad Boy* and *Privilege*. The George Bean group performed

Jerusalem and *Onward Christian Soldiers*. The former vocalist with Manfred Mann starred as a pop singer manipulated by the government who force him to promote an evangelical crusade. Leading 60s model

Jean Shrimpton 'the Shrimp' looked lovely, but was a wooden actress. The soundtrack was issued in Britain on HMV and in America on UNI.

Up The Junction. Peter Collinson directed this tale of a Chelsea girl slumming it across the Thames in Battersea and featured Suzy Kendall, Dennis Waterman and Adrienne Posta. It was the top box office success of the year in Britain and was based on a much grittier television pay by Nell Dunn. The score was by Manfred Mann and the soundtrack was issued in Britain by Fontana and in America by Mercury.

Magical Mystery Tour. See the Beatles.

How I Won The War. A film directed by Richard Lester, director of the Beatles' films, with a guest appearance by John Lennon.

What's Happening? A fifty-three-minute documentary by Albert and David Maysles focussing on the Beatles first visit to America in February 1964, the start of the British Invasion. This is where it all began, with scenes of them arriving in New York, appearing on the *Ed Sullivan Show* and travelling to Washington.

1968 films

The Committee. A film starring Paul Jones with a score by the Pink Floyd and Arthur Brown performing *Nightmare*. An odd tale, fifty-eight minutes in length, it was based on a short story by Max Steuer, who also co-directed with Peter Sykes. A hitchhiker decapitates a driver who bores him, then sews the head back on again and is then driven to a strange mansion where he faces a sinister committee.

Cream's Farewell Concert. Directed by Tony Palmer, produced by Robert Stigwood and filmed at the group's Royal Albert Hall concert on November 26th 1967. The documentary includes the numbers *Spoonful*, *Politician*, *Sunshine Of Your Love*, *White Room*, *Toad* and *I'm So Glad*. John Peel introduced them with the words, "Tomorrow they'll be Eric Clapton, Jack Bruce and Ginger Baker, but tonight they are Cream."

All My Loving. A fifty-five-minute documentary on the history of pop music by Tony Palmer, condensed from the television series of the same name.

The Deadly Bees. A horror story starring Suzanna Leigh about a ferocious swarm of bees. It featured a group called the Birds performing *That's All I Need For You.* Roy Wood was a member of the band at the time.

Mrs Brown You've Got A Lovely Daughter. See Herman's Hermits.

The Bliss Of Mrs Blossom. Starring Shirley McLaine and Richard Attenborough it included the New Vaudeville Band playing *I'm Beginning To Fall In Love* in a party sequence. The story revolved around the wife of a bra manufacturer who keeps a lover in the attic.

Ringo Starr in 'Candy'

Yellow Submarine. See the Beatles.

Wonderwall. Directed by Joe Massott and starring Jane Birkin, the music score was by George Harrison and the soundtrack album issued on *Apple Records.* A touch of British psychedelia of the time, with Indian musicians and Liverpool group the Remo Four recorded by George.

Candy. A film based on the controversial novel by Terry Southern and Mason Hoffenburg, with a host of stars including Marlon Brando, Richard Burton, Walter Matthau and Ringo Starr. The soundtrack includes

music by the Byrds and Steppenwolf. It looked as if Ringo would become the Beatle most associated with films and he was to appear in a number of features including *The Magic Christian*, *Blindman*, *That'll Be The Day* and *Caveman*. However, it was George Harrison who almost revived the British film industry with his Hand Made Films and movies such as *The Life Of Brian*, *The Long Good Friday*, *Mona Lisa* and *Withnail and I* who is now regarded as the movie Beatle.

Girl On A Motorcycle. Also known as *Naked Under Leather.* This film was based on a novel by Andre Pieyre de Mandiaques and is the tale of the bored wife of a schoolteacher who rides a motorcycle from Alsace to Heidelberg, naked under her leather outfit, to liaisons with her lover. During her long journey through the French countryside she recalls her erotic encounters with her lover. It starred Marianne Faithfull and Alain Delon and had such excruciating dialogue as "Your body is like a violin in a velvet case. Your toes are like tombstones." The soundtrack was issued in Britain by Polydor and in America by *Tetregrammatron.*

The Guru. Rita Tushingham and Michael York team up again. York plays a musician, obviously based on George Harrison, who goes to India to meet his guru, filmed at a time when the Beatles and the Maharishi

'Wonderwall'

Mahesh Yogi had been making lots of newspaper copy. The music was by Ustad Vilayat Khan.

The Lone Ranger. A twenty-two-minute short about a drifter entering a town. Pete Townshend supplied the music.

Otley. A film with a 'Swinging London' setting, shot around the Portobello Road area and starring Tom Courtney. The Herd and busker Don Partridge provided music. The soundtrack was issued in Britain on RCA and in America on Colgems.

Performance. Due to its controversial nature, this film was held up for two years and not released until 1970. James Fox starred as a gangster on the run who hides in the house of a rock star and his two girl friends. Mick Jagger played the pop star and Anita Pallenberg and Michele Breton his birds. The music was written and arranged by Jack Nitzsche. Randy Newman sang *Gone Dead Train*, Mike Jagger sang *Memo From Turner*, the Last Poets performed *Wake Up Niggers*, Merry Clayton sang *Performance* and *Poor White Hound Dog* and Buffy Sainte-Marie sang *Dyed, Dead And Red*. The soundtrack was issued both sides of the Atlantic by Warner Brothers.

Mick Jagger was to star in a couple of further feature films, but it is a pity the Rolling Stones did not make *Only Lovers Left Alive* a post-apocalypse type tale which it was announced they would film.

Pop Down. A loony plot in which travellers from outer space land on earth to study humans. The film starred Diane Keen and Zoot Money (as Sagittarius). Brian Auger and Julie Driscoll, Idle Race, Dantalion's Chariot, Don Partridge and Blossomtoes provided the music. It was unfortunate that nearly all the pop films that had a sci-fi slant were so ridiculous. Another was to emerge in 1970 starring Olivia Newton John. The film was called *Toomorrow* and she was a member of a group of that name. It was the intention to promote

'Monterey Pop'

the fantasy group as an actual band following the release of the film. As the film was a flop, however, *Toomorrow* disbanded.

The story told of the pop group being kidnapped by aliens called Alphoids. Paul McCartney considered a similar plot for Wings, but abandoned the idea, even though Willie Russell had prepared a script.

San Francisco. A short about the city in which Pink Floyd play *Interstellar Overdrive.*

Work...Is A Four Letter Word. Cilla Black's only co-starring role in a feature film. She appears opposite David Warner in a black comedy about psychedelic mushrooms.

1969 films

Monterey Pop. A film of the Monterey Pop Festival, which took place in 1967. The only British Invasion artists were the Who who performed *My Generation* and Eric Burdon & the Animals who performed *Paint It Black.*

Popcorn – An Audio Visual Experience. Directed by Peter Clifton, it is a film of the 60s counter-culture featuring British and American artists, with scenes that include Twiggy, surfers in the Pacific, an atom bomb blast and hippies in Katmandu. The British artists are The Bee Gees performing *To Love Somebody*, Joe Cocker performing *A Little Help From My Friends*, the

Rolling Stones performing *Jumpin' Jack Flash* and *Two Thousand Light Years From Home*, the Spencer Davis Group performing *Gimme Some Lovin* and the Small Faces performing *Itchykoo Park*. Emperor Rosko, an American disc jockey, based in Britain, was also featured.

Sympathy For the Devil. Also known as *One Plus One*. Directed by Jean Luc Goddard. A film about the Rolling Stones recording *Sympathy for the Devil*, but intercut with scenes of revolutionaries, with black militants who gather in a junkyard and someone reading *Mein Kampf* aloud in a bookstore. Regarded by many as pretentious, but with some good scenes of the Stones.

More. A drama starring Mimsy Farmer and Klaus Grunberg about the effects of the 'Summer of Love' drug culture, with a score by the Pink Floyd. The soundtrack was issued in Britain on Columbia and in America on Tower.

Adventures Of The Son Of Exploding Sausage. A bizarre musical comedy featuring the Bonzo Dog Doo Dah Band.

Girls. A French film by Just Jaeckin with a soundtrack penned and performed by Eric Stewart of 10cc.

Experience. A British short featuring the Jimi Hendrix Experience at the Saville Theatre, London. Brian Epstein owned the theatre and the Beatles often attended the shows.

Rope Ladder To The Moon. A fifty-minute documentary by Tony Palmer about Jack Bruce. It tells how the poor boy from Glasgow won a scholarship to the Edinburgh Academy of Music and became a rock star member of Cream. The music is taken from the Bruce album 'Songs For A

Tailor' and 'Goodbye Cream'.

The Virgin Soldiers. A tale of British conscripts involved in the war in the jungles of Malaya. David Bowie appeared as one of the soldiers and the theme tune 'the Virgin Soldiers March' was composed by Ray Davies of the Kinks.

What's Good For The Goose. A feature film starring Norman Wisdom and Judy Geeson. Set in the Merseyside seaside resort of Southport, it also featured the Pretty Things. Phil May was to comment "We went up there for a week and just didn't do anything. Then we did one number and after that they kept writing new scenes for us. It seemed that they just wrote the script as they went along. Eventually we ended up doing five numbers, *I'll Never Be Me*, *What's Good for The Goose*, *Eagle's Sun* and a couple of others."

Be Glad for The Song Has No Ending. A documentary about the Incredible String Band'.

'Experience' at the Saville Theatre

The 1950s saw the birth of the rock movie, beginning with the dramatic Bill Haley 'Rock Around the Clock' opening to 'The Blackboard Jungle' in 1955. This made way for the floodgates to open to a torrent of rock, pop, calypso and twist movies, together with films in which current pop singers were featured.

The first British Invasion movies such as 'A Hard Days Night' largely eclipsed this style

'The Girl Can't Help It'

of 'teen flick' although US 'Beach' movies and of course most of Elvis' films continued throughout most of the '60's using a similar formula. continued to be made.

There were hundreds of American Rock movies made between 'Blackboard Jungle'

and 'A Hard Days Night'. These are the main ones:

'Rock Around The Clock' (1956) which featured Bill Haley and the Comets, The Platters, Tony Martinez and his Band and Freddie Bell and his Bellboys.

'Don't Knock The Rock' (1956) which featured Bill Haley and his Comets, Little Richard, the Treniers, Dave Appell and his Applejacks, Jovada and Jimmy Ballard, plus Alan Freed.

'Shake Rattle And Rock' (1956) which featured Fats Domino, Joe Turner, Tommy Charles, Choker Campbell and Anita Ray.

'The Girl Can't Help It' (1956) featured Julie London, Ray Anthony, Fats Domino, the Platters, Little Richard, Gene Vincent and his Blue Caps, the Treniers, Eddie Fontaine, The Chuckles, Abbey Lincoln, Johnny Olenn, Nino Tempo and Eddie Cochran.

'Rock Pretty Baby' (1956) which featured Sal Mineo and John Saxon.

'Rumble On The Docks' (1956) which featured James Darren and Freddie Bell and his Bellboys 'April Love' (1957) featured Pat Boone and Shirley Jones.

'Rock Rock Rock' (1957) which featured Tuesday Weld (with Connie Francis singing her songs) Teddy Fandazzo of The Three Chuckles, the Moonglows, Chuck Berry, Jimmy Cavallo and his House Rockers, the Flamingos, the Johnny Burnette Trio, Laverne Baker, Cirino and the Bowties, Frankie Lymon and the Teenagers and the Coney Island Kids.

'Rock You Sinners' (1957) which featured Art Baxter and the Rockin' Sinners, Tony Crombie and the Rockets, Dickie Bennett, Joan Small, George 'Calypso' Browne, Don Sollash and the Rockin' Horses, 'Curly' Pat Berry and The Blue Jacks.

'The Big Beat' (1957) which featured Charlie Barnet, Buddy Bregman, Alan Copeland, Gogi Grant, the Del Vikings, the Diamonds, Fats Domino, the Four Aces, Harry James, Freddie Martin, the Lancers, the Mills Brothers, Russ Morgan and Jeri Southern.

'Summer Love' (1957) which featured John Saxon, Molly Bee and Rod McKuen.

'Bop Girl' (1957) which featured Bobby Troup, the Goofers, Lord Flea and his Calypsonians, Nino Tempo, the Titans, the Cubanos and the Mary Kaye Trio.

'Calypso Heat Wave' (1957) which featured The Treniers, The Tarriers, The Hi-Los and Johnny Desmond.

'Carnival Rock' (1957) which featured the Blockbusters, Susan Cabot, David Houston, Bob Luman, the Platters and the Shadows.

'Jamboree' (1957) which featured Fats Domino, Buddy Knox, Jerry Lee Lewis, Jimmy Bowen, Charlie Gracie, the Four Coins, Count Basie and his Orchestra with Joe Williams. Jodie Sands, Carl Perkins, Slim Whitman, Lewis Lyman and the Teenchords, Ron Coby, Connie Francis, Andy Martin, Frankie Avalon and Rocco & his Saints.

'Mister Rock And Roll (1957) which featured Alan Freed, Teddy Randazzo, Lionel Hampton, Frankie Lymon and the Teenagers, Laverne Baker, Ferlin Husky, Shaye Cogan, Brook Benton, Little Richard and Clyde McPhatter.

'Rock All Night' (1957) which featured the Blockbusters and The Platters.

'Untamed Youth' (1957) which featured Eddie Cochran.

'Rockabilly Baby' (1957) which featured Les Brown.

'Harlem Rock And Roll' (1957) which featured Duke Ellington, Nat King Cole, Lionel Hampton, the Clovers, Joe Turner, Ruth Brown and the Delta Rhythm Boys.

'Kona Coast' (1957) which featured Duane Eddy.

'Rock A Bye Baby' (1958) which featured

Connie Stevens and Gary Lewis.

'Sing Boy Sing' (1958) which featured Tommy Sands.

'Rock Baby, Rock It' (1958) which featured Johnny Carroll and Roscoe Gordon.

'High School Confidential' (1958) which featured Jerry Lee Lewis and Ray Anthony.

'Go Johnny Go' (1958) which featured Alan Freed, Eddie Cochran, Jimmy Clanton, Ritchie Valens, Harvey of the Moonglows, Chuck Berry, Jo-Ann Campbell, the Flamingos, the Cadillacs and Jackie Wilson.

'Hot Rod Gang' (1958) which featured Gene Vincent and the Blue Caps.

'Let's Rock' (1958) which featured Julius LaRosa, Wink Martindale, Danny and the Juniors, Paul Anka, Della Reese, Roy Hamilton, the Tyranes and the Royal Teens.

'Mardi Gras' (1958) which featured Pat Boone, Tommy Sands and Gary Crosby.

'Country Music Holiday (1958) which featured Ferlin Husky, Faron Young, the Jordanaires, Oscar and Lonzo, the LaDell Sisters and Drifting Johnny Miller.

'Hound Dog Man' (1959) which featured Fabian and Dodie Stevens.

'Hey Boy! Hey Girl!' (1959) which featured Louis Prima and Keely Smith, Sam Butera and the Witnesses.

'Juke Box Rhythm' (1959) which featured Jack Jones, the Earl Grant Trio, the Nitwits, Johnny Otis and the Treniers.

'Girl's Town' (1959) which featured Paul Anka.

'Senior Prom' (1959) which featured Louis Prima and Keely Smith, Sam Butera and the Witnesses, Ed Sullivan, Mitch Miller, Connie Boswell, Bob Crosby, Toni Arden, Freddie Martin, Jose Melis and Les Elgert.

'Gidget' (1959) which featured The Four Preps.

'College Confidential' (1959) which featured Conway Twitty, Randy Sparks and Cathy Crosby.

'All The Young Men' (1960) which featured James Darren.

'Platinum High School' (1960) which featured Conway Twitty.

'All Hands On Deck' (1960) which featured Pat Boone.

'Because They're Young' (1960) which featured James Darren, Duane Eddy and the Rebels and Dick Clark.

'Swinging Along' (1961) which featured Ray Charles, Bobby Vee and Roger Williams.

'Come September' (1961) which featured Bobby Darin.

'Hey Let's Twist' (1961) which featured Joey Dee and the Starliters, Jo-Ann Campbell and Teddy Randazzo.'

'Where The Boys Are' (1961) which featured Connie Francis.

Twist Around The Clock' (1961) which featured Chubby Checker, Dion, Vicki Spencer, Clay Cole and The Marcels.

'Teenage Millionaire' (1961) which featured Chubby Checker, Jimmy Clanton, Jackie Wilson, Dion, Bill Black's Combo, Mary Johnson, Vicki Spencer and Jack Larson.

'Love In A Goldfish Bowl' (1961) which featured Tommy Sands and Fabian.

'Disneyland After Dark' (1962) which featured Bobby Rydell and Annette Funicello.

'Two Little Bears' (1962) which featured Brenda Lee.

'Two Tickets To Paris' (1962) which fea-

tured Joey Dee and the Starliters and Gary Crosby.

'Don't Knock The Twist' (1962) which featured Chubby Checker, Vic Dana, Gene Chandler, Linda Scott, The Carroll Bros and The Dovells.

'Follow The Boys' (1962) which featured Connie Francis.

'State Fair' (1962) which featured Pat Boone, Bobby Darin and Ann-Margret.

'Lonely Boy' (1962) which featured Paul Anka.

'Hootenany Hoot' (1963) which featured the Brothers Four, Sheb Wooley, Johnny Cash, the Gateway Trio, Judy Henske, George Hamilton IV, Joe and Eddie, Cathie Taylor and Chris Crosby.

'Bye Bye Birdie' (1963) which featured Bobby Rydell.

'For Those Who Think Young' (1964) which featured James Darren and Nancy Sinatra. 'Girl's Town' (1959) which featured Paul Anka.

'Senior Prom' (1959) which featured Louis Prima and Keely Smith, Sam Butera and the Witnesses, Ed Sullivan, Mitch Miller, Connie Boswell, Bob Crosby, Toni Arden, Freddie Martin, Jose Melis and Les Elgert.

'Gidget' (1959) which featured The Four Preps.

'College Confidential' (1959) which featured Conway Twitty, Randy Sparks and Cathy Crosby.

'All The Young Men' (1960) which featured James Darren.

'Platinum High School' (1960) which featured Conway Twitty.

'All Hands On Deck' (1960) which featured Pat Boone.

'Because They're Young' (1960) which featured James Darren, Duane Eddy and the Rebels and Dick Clark.

'Swinging Along' (1961) which featured Ray Charles, Bobby Vee and Roger Williams.

'Come September' (1961) which featured Bobby Darin.

'Hey Let's Twist' (1961) which featured Joey Dee and the Starliters, Jo-Ann Campbell and Teddy Randazzo.'

'Where The Boys Are' (1961) which featured Connie Francis.

Twist Around The Clock' (1961) which featured Chubby Checker, Dion, Vicki Spencer, Clay Cole and The Marcels.

'Teenage Millionaire' (1961) which featured Chubby Checker, Jimmy Clanton, Jackie Wilson, Dion, Bill Black's Combo, Mary Johnson, Vicki Spencer and Jack Larson.

'Love In A Goldfish Bowl' (1961) which featured Tommy Sands and Fabian.

'Disneyland After Dark' (1962) which featured Bobby Rydell and Annette Funicello.

'Two Little Bears' (1962) which featured Brenda Lee.

'Two Tickets To Paris' (1962) which featured Joey Dee and the Starliters and Gary Crosby.

'Don't Knock The Twist' (1962) which featured Chubby Checker, Vic Dana, Gene Chandler, Linda Scott, The Carroll Bros and The Dovells.

'Follow The Boys' (1962) which featured Connie Francis.

'State Fair' (1962) which featured Pat Boone, Bobby Darin and Ann-Margret.

'Lonely Boy' (1962) which featured Paul Anka.

'Hootenany Hoot' (1963) which featured The Brothers Four, Sheb Wooley, Johnny Cash, The Gateway Trio, Judy Henske, George Hamilton IV, Joe and Eddie, Cathie Taylor and Chris Crosby.

'Bye Bye Birdie' (1963) which featured Bobby Rydell.

'For Those Who Think Young' (1964) which featured James Darren and Nancy Sinatra.

The Fabulous Fabian In His First Motion Picture ...With That "Blue Denim" Girl!

JERRY WALD'S production of

HOUND·DOG MAN

COLOR by DE LUXE CINEMASCOPE

FABIAN · CAROL LYNLEY
STUART WHITMAN · ARTHUR O'CONNELL
DODIE STEVENS DON SIEGEL · FRED GIPSON and WINSTON MILLER

Until the impact of the Beatles and the British Invasion, British hits were basically confined to Britain, Europe and some Commonwealth countries, whilst America remained the world's biggest market.

Despite this, during the years of The British Invasion, several American artists based themselves in Britain and it proved to be a successful move. The first such artist was P.J. Proby, who was born James Marcus Smith in Texas on November 6th 1938.

He attended a military academy and his sister dated Elvis Presley. Eddie Cochran's girlfriend dubbed him P.J. He chauffeured Paul Newman around Hollywood and also dated Dean Martin's daughter.

American producer Jack Good, who was based in Britain, invited him to the U.K. to appear on the television special 'Around The Beatles', and he hit No. 3 in the charts with the single *Hold Me*. He followed up with two further Top Ten hits *Together* and *Somewhere* and also charted with *I Apologise* and *Maria*.

Proby's entire career crumbled due to an incident on stage in Croydon in January 1965 when his trousers split dramatically and Tom Jones replaced him. Due to the incident, he was also banned from touring by a number of theatre chains. His recording career foundered and he later became bankrupt for a second time as he had already been declared a bankrupt in America.

Controversy dogged Proby over the years. He loosed off an air pistol at his third wife and pursued a farmer's fourteen-year-old daughter, who later became his fifth wife. In addition to his legal marriages, he had six common-law wives.

In 1968 Proby became engaged to Vanessa Forsyth, but discovered he already had two wives. On learning his second marriage was probably bigamous, he said: "How the hell was I to know the divorce had not come through?" Not surprisingly, Forsyth then left him.

He moved to the north of England and became a shepherd in Bolton and a muck spreader in Huddersfield, before returning to London and a job as a janitor in Hammersmith. He once faced a possible stiff sentence for firing an air gun with pellets and was fined sixty pounds for taking an axe to his unpaid, live-in secretary. The flamboyant singer drank five bottles of bourbon a day, but renounced alcohol when he had a heart attack.

Jack Good came to his rescue in 1970 when he featured Proby in the musical *Catch My Soul*. He later appeared as Elvis in the stage production *Elvis On Stage*, but was sacked due to his eccentric behaviour. In 1978 he was hired to appear in *Elvis The Musical* in London's West End, but was again fired for trying to rewrite the script. In 1984 Proby fell off the stage during a Rock 'n' Roll Legends tour.

Appearing on the cabaret circuit for a time, he based himself in the north of England again and began recording for a record label in Manchester. After further years in the wilderness. Proby stepped back into the limelight in the 1990s when he appeared in the West End in another musical as Elvis Presley. He also had a part in the Roy Orbison tribute show *Only The Lonely*, singing old hits. For a while he was romantically linked with singer Billie Davis.

He continues to emerge on the music scene from time to time and in November 2003 embarked on the 'Sixties Gold Tour' of Britain on a bill with Herman's Hermits, the Troggs, Mike Pender's Searchers and the Ivy League. He is also recording a new album.

The Walker Brothers were another American act that proved immensely popular in Britain. Scott Engel, who was born in Hamilton, Ohio on January 9th 1944, was originally bass guitarist with a group in California called the Routers. He then teamed up with John Maus and Gary Leeds in a trio they decided to call the Walker Brothers.

Walker Brothers

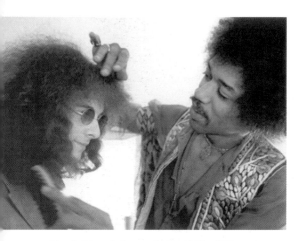

Jimi Hendrix and Noel Rodding

Maus, who was born in New York City on November 4th 1944 and Leeds who was born in Glendale, California on September 3rd 1944 had both been members of a group called the Dalton Brothers.

They decided to move to England and settled in London in February 1965, but their debut single *Pretty Girls Everywhere* failed to click, although their second single *Love Her* became a success and the trio soon became major stars with a string of further hits. Their British chart singles included *Make It Easy On Yourself*, *My Ship Is Coming In*, *The Sun Ain't Gonna Shine Anymore* '(Baby) You Don't Have To Tell Me*, *Another Tear Falls*, *Deadlier Than The Male*, *Stay With Me Baby* and *Walking In The Rain*.

Conflicts between Scott and John eventually resulted in the trio splitting up. Gary charted with *You Don't Love Me* and *Twinkie Lee*, John with *Annabella* and Scott with *Jackie*, *Joanna* and *Lights Of Cincinnati*.

The trio reformed briefly in 1976, hitting the charts with *No Regrets*.

In 1992 a CD collection, *No Regrets – the Best Of the Walker Brothers 1965-1976* reached No. 4 in the U.K. chart.

In 1996 Scott Engel recorded his first new album in eleven years, *Tilt* and performed a track on the television show *Later with Jools Holland*. It was his first such appearance in over a decade and the album entered the chart at No. 27.

Scott still resides in west London.

John Maus lives near San Diego, California with his third wife Randy and daughter Nicholle. He is an inspector for a software company.

Gary Leeds lives in east London and in 1994 was working as a motorcycle courier.

Those two acts never had any success in their home country, although the next artist to begin his climb to fame from London did. He was Jimi Hendrix.

Jimi was born James Marshall Hendrix in Seattle, Washington on November 27th 1942 and first enlisted as a paratrooper, but was discharged due to a back injury. He was left-handed but taught himself to play guitar upside down. On leaving the service he became a backing musician for numerous artists including Little Richard, Sam Cooke, B.B.King and the Isley Brothers.

Hendrix moved to New York, where he formed his own band, Jimmy James & the Blue Flames. In 1966 he was discovered playing in New York's Café Wha by Chas Chandler of the Animals, who became his manager, took him to London and teamed him with Mitch

Mitchell and Noel Redding to form the Jimi Hendrix Experience. He began to make an impact with records such as *Hey Joe* and *Purple Haze* and the group made their U.S. debut at the Monterey Pop Festival in June 1967. A series of best selling albums and singles established Hendrix as one of the premier rock guitarists in the world.

Sadly, he became addicted to drugs, trying as many as possible from alcohol to LSD, sniffing cocaine and heroin, popping pills. He was arrested in Toronto, Canada in 1969 for possessing heroin but was acquitted. The group split up that year and Hendrix appeared at the Woodstock festival before forming a new group, the Band of Gypsies. It was not a successful outfit and disbanded within a relatively short time.

Hendrix was found dead on September 18th 1970 in London, having choked to death by inhalation of vomit due to barbiturate intoxication. He was aged twenty-seven and had once said, "Once you're dead, you've got it made."

Noel Redding, bass guitarist with the Jimi Hendrix Experience, died of unknown causes at his home in Ireland in May 2003.

Another American artist whose career received a boost while he was based in Britain was James Taylor, who was born in Boston on March 12th 1948. He had begun writing songs when committed to a psychiatric hospital for several months suffering from depression.

1966 saw him join a New York Band, the Flying Machine, but by

Jimi Hendrix with Brian Jones

1968, in an attempt to rid himself of his heroin addiction, he moved to London and met up with Peter Asher, who signed him to the Beatles record label *Apple Records*.

He became one of the initial artists signed to the label and when Asher began producing Taylor's debut al-

bum, Paul McCartney played bass on the track *Carolina On My Mind*. It is interesting to note that another song on the 'James Taylor' album was called *Something In the Way She Moves* which George Harrison used as the first line of his song *Something* the following year.

Taylor was disturbed by what he considered was *Apple*'s lack of pro-motion of his records and he returned to America and left the *Apple* label in 1969. Peter Asher remained as his producer when Taylor signed to the *Warner Brothers* label. Ironically for *Apple*, Taylor immediately had a ma-

James Taylor

...jor hit with his first Warner album *Sweet Baby James* and his million-seller single *Fire and Rain*. Taylor was to enjoy chart success in America throughout the 1970s.

He continues to perform and record and from January to November 2003 was on an Australian, European and American tour.

The American artist, based in Britain, to make the most impact on the U.K. charts was Suzi Quatro, born in Detroit, Michigan on June 3rd 1950. Producer Mickie Most discovered Suzi in Detroit in 1969 and under his wing she was to have fifteen chart hits during the 1970s and sold over forty million records.

The singer/bass guitarist, who dressed in black leather jump-suits topped the charts with numbers such as *Can The Can* and *Devil Gate Drive*. Her last hit was *Heart Of Stone* and her only American chart entry was *Stumblin' In*, a duet with Chris Norman of Smokie, in 1979.

Suzi enjoyed a degree of success as an actress, appearing on television as Leather Tuscadero in *Happy Days* and in U.K. dramas such as *Minder* and comedies such as *Absolutely Fabulous*. She also starred in the 1986 stage production of *Annie Get your Gun.*

She married Len Tuckey, the lead guitarist with her band and the couple had two children, Richard and Laura. They settled in a sixteenth-century house in Essex.

Len and Suzi were later divorced and she married Rainer Haas, a German millionaire promoter. She continues to live in Essex during the week, commuting to stay with her husband at weekend at their home in Hamburg.

Suzi still appears at festivals and pops up regularly on television and radio. During 1998 she was celebrating the silver anniversary of her first hit by recording an album of new material. In the same year she was pleased to see her fifteen-year-old daughter following in her footsteps as a singer.

In 2000 she began her own BBC radio series *Rocking With Suzi Q* and toured Australian, Europe and the U.K. In 2003 she started working on a new album, tentatively titled *Naked Under Leather* (a reference to the Marianne Faithfull film, *Girl On A Motorcycle*) and a DVD of her life, *48 Crash,* is in preparation.

The impact American artists based in Britain had did not have the same effect as that the British groups had on the American charts, but it is an interesting chapter in the story of the Anglo-American music relationship.

Suzi Quatro

Ed Sullivan with the Beatles

The Ed Sullivan Show ran from June 20th 1948 until June 6th 1971. Although the CBS Sunday Night show was originally called *Toast Of The Town*, ex-journalist Sullivan had been the host since the beginning and on September 25th 1955 the name of the show was changed to *The Ed Sullivan Show*.

Sullivan had been sports editor of the Evening Graphic, a New York newspaper, in the 1920s. In 1930 he began his own radio show and later began hosting a show for CBS called *Ed Sullivan Entertains*. He also acted as MC at dinners and shows and was spotted by a CBS executive who

thought that he would be ideal to host the new *Talk Of The Town* TV series.

It became a prime time Sunday evening show and his guests includ-

Elvis and Sullivan

ed senators, variety acts, sports stars, astronauts, opera singers, Hollywood actors and rock stars. he show was considered so important that many stars actually made their television debuts on the show. They included Bob Hope, Louis Armstrong, Humphrey Bogart, Walt Disney, Clark Gable, Grace Kelly, Fred Astaire, Margot Fonteyn, James Cagney, Julie Andrews and Yul Brynner.

His biggest-rating show of the 1950s took place in 1956 when Elvis Presley made his debut on the programme. However, Sullivan told his cameramen to photograph Elvis from

Gerry & the Pacemakers

the waist up only, commenting "We had a lot of Lutherans, a lot of clergy and nuns in our viewing audience. It was a Sunday night show."

It was by accident that he came across Beatlemania when he was at Heathrow Airport and, as a result, booked the Beatles, with their first show bringing in the largest television audience ever to that date. It was also the beginning of regular appearances on the prestigious show by other British groups and singers.

Here is a basic rundown of The British Invasion appearances beginning with the Beatles' debut on the show on February 9th 1964, which was show number 798. For details of all Beatles appearances, see 'the Beatles on the Ed Sullivan show' at the end of this listing.

799. Beatles second appearance.

780. Beatles third appearance.

782. The Dave Clark Five made their debut on this March 8th 1964 show, becoming the first British group to appear on the *Ed Sullivan Show* following the Beatles original triumphal appearances. They performed *Glad All Over*. The main theme of the show was *A Salute To American Composers* with Juliet Prowse dancing and various singers performing American standards such as *Old Man River*, *The Sunny Side Of the Street* and *Singing In The Rain*.

783. The Dave Clark Five performed *Do You Love Me*, *Bits And Pieces* and *Glad All Over* on this March 15th 1964 show whose other guests were Peter O'Toole, Topo Gigio, Carmel Quinn, Pat O'Brian, Jackie Vernon and the Volantes.

786. The Searchers made their debut on this April 5th 1964 show performing *Ain't This Just Like Me* and *Needles And Pins*.

789. Gerry & The Pacemakers made their Sullivan debut on May 3rd 1964 performing *Don't Let The Sun Catch You Crying* and *I'm The One*. The other guests on the show were Stevie Wonder, Louis Gossett Jr, Bill Dana, May Barnes, the Claytons, Vaughn Meader and Bibbi Oscarwall.

790. Dusty Springfield and Gerry & the Pacemakers appeared on this May 10th 1964 show. Gerry performed *I Like It* and *Don't Let The Sun Catch You Crying*. Dusty performed *Stay A While* and *I Only Want To Be With You*. Bobby Rydell also performed the Lennon & McCartney number *World Without Love*. The other guests were the Brooks Sisters, Phyllis Diller, Sid Gary, Doug Hart, Jackie Mason and Itzhak Perlman.

792. Screened on May 24th 1964 with the Beatles on film performing *You Can't Do That* and being interviewed by Ed Sullivan in London.

793. The Dave Clark Five performed *Can't You See That She's Mine* and *Do You Love Me* on this May 31st 1964 edition. The other guests were Bill Cosby, Helen Hayes, Abbe Lane, Peter Linda Hayes and Mary Healey.

794. Billy J. Kramer & the Dakotas made their debut on this June 7th 1964 show performing *Pride*, *Little Children* and *Bad To Me*. The other guests were Alec Guinness, Nipsey Russell, Robert Horton, Tessie O'Shea and Leo Bassi.

799. The guests on the July 26th 1964 show were Helen Shapiro, Steve Lawrence, Geula Gill, Mana Negalia and los Chavales de Espana.

Helen never had an American hit yet had eleven chart entries in Britain between 1961 and 1964, including two chart toppers *You Don't Know*

Helen Shapiro

and *Walkin' Back To Happiness*. Although her last British hit *Fever* preceded this Sullivan appearance it only reached No. 38 in the British charts and was her last entry.

The London singer was only 14 when she had her first chart hit. She also starred in the film 'It's *Trad Dad*, which was directed by Richard Lester who went on to direct *A Hard Day's Night*, using some of the innovations he introduced in the Shapiro film. The Beatles were also on the support bill when she was sixteen and headlining her own British tour. John and Paul wrote a song for her, Misery', which her recording manager turned down. In a Mersey Beat interview she recalled 'John and Paul always used to be writing numbers together on the coach. I remember them playing *From Me To You* to me, and asking me what I thought of it. I told them I thought it was terrific – and I'm glad to say I was right".

In 1963 she recorded an album in Nashville, Tennessee, but the single chosen for her, 'Woe Is Me', only reached the latter end of the Top 40 in Britain. Her success might have continued if *It's My Party* had been chosen as her single instead. Helen recorded the original version of the song, which was then recorded by American teenager Lesley Gore who topped the American charts and entered the British top ten with the number.

Although her chart days were over, Helen continued her career as a singer, turning to a jazz repertoire and was at one time managed by the Beatles former publicist, Tony Barrow.

805. The Animals made their debut on this October 18th 1964 show performing *I'm Crying* and *The House Of The Rising Sun*. The other guests on the show were Van Johnson, Jackie Mason, Totie Fields, Rita Pavone, John Byner and Joan Sutherland.

806. The Rolling Stones made their debut on this October 25th 1964 bill performing *Around And Around* and *Time Is On My Side*. The other guests were Jack Jones, Stiller & Meara, London Lee and the Kim Sisters.

807. The Dave Clark Five performed *Anyway You Want It* on this show on November 1st 1964. The other guests were Rex Harrison, Alan King, Marilyn Michaels, Dolores Gray, Richard Hearne and Rolando.

809. Peter & Gordon made their debut on this November 15th 1964 bill performing *I Don't Want To See You Again* and '500 Miles'. The other guests were Sammy Davis Jr, Kaye Stevens, The Kessler Twins, Jackie Vernon, Charlie Drake, Trio Hoganas and Brizio.

Charlie Drake was a popular British comedian appearing in television and films. He had had a previous American chart entry *My Boomerang Won't Come Back*, which reached no 21 in February 1962.

818. The Animals performed *Don't Let Me Be Misunderstood* on this January 24th 1965 edition. The other guests were Alan King, Shari Lewis, Allen & Kossi, George Kirby and Bach Yen. The show was repeated on August 15th 1965.

821. The Dave Clark Five performed *Everybody Knows*, *Because* and *Anyway You Want It* on this Feb-

Ed Sullivan and the Animals

ruary 14th 1965 bill. The other guests were Steve Lawrence, Victor Borge, Dick Martin, Dan Rowan, the Israeli Ballet, Topo Gigio, the Mattison Trio and John's balancing act. The show was repeated on August 8th 1965.

825. Petula Clark made her debut on this March 14th 1965 show performing *Downtown* and *I Know A Place*. The other guests were Pat O Brien, Nancy Walker & Bert Lahr, the Clancy Brothers and Tommy Makem, Steve Rossi, Jimmy Roselli, Dorothy Donegan and the Olympiades.

829. Gerry & the Pacemakers appeared on this show on April 12th 1965 performing *Ferry 'Cross The Mersey*, *It's Gonna Be Alright* and *Why, Oh Why*. The other guests were Maurice Chevalier, Soupy Sales, London Lee, Jose Torres, Felicia Sanders, the San Francisco Ballet, Stephenson's Dogs and Jorgen and Conny. The show was repeated on July 25th 1965.

831. Freddie & the Dreamers made their debut on April 25th 1965 per-

Billy J Kramer & Dakotas

forming *I'm Telling You Now* and *Do The Freddie* The other guests were Sean Connery, Xavier Cugat, Eydie Gorme, Leon Bibb, Allen & Rossi, Shelly Berman and Topo Gigio.

832. The Rolling Stones, Dusty Springfield and Tom Jones appeared on the May 2nd 1965 bill. The Stones performed *The Last Time*, *Little Red Rooster* and *Someone To Love*. Dusty performed *All Cried Out* and Tom Jones performed *It's Not Unusual*. The other guests were Morecambe & Wise, Leslie Uggams, and Totie Fields.

834. Petula Clark appeared on this May 15th 1965 edition performing '*I Know A Place* and Heart. Rudolf Nureyev and Margot Fonteyn performed three excerpts from 'Swan Lake', comedian Alan King did a routine about kids and parents. There was also comedian Sue Carson, The

West Point Glee Club, the Elwardos, juggler Ugo Garrido, the Beach Boys performing 'Help Me Rhonda' and pop singer Frankie Randall.

835. The Bachelors performed *Marie* and *I Believe* on this show on May 22nd 1965 and Kathy Kirby performed *I Can't Stop Loving that Man Of Mine*. Rudolph Nureyev and Morgot Fonteyn performed Khachaturian's ballet 'Gayne'. There was also stand-up comedian Bob King, Pernell Roberts sang a Western medley, Liza Minelli *All I Need Is One Good Break* and *Sing Happy*, The Fredians, an acrobatic trio and Guy Lombardo sang *Red Roses For A Blue Lady* and 12th Street Rag.

836. The Animals performed '*Bright Lights, Big City*' and *Bring It On Home To Me* on this May 30th 1965 bill. The other guests were Anthony Newley, Connie Francis, Wayne Newton, Bert Lahr, Stiller & Meara, Jackie Vernon, Pat Hemming, Marty Gunty and the De Mille Aerialists.

Newley was a major star in Britain in the late 1950s and Brian Epstein chose him to open the Whitechapel branch of his NRMS Store. George Harrison also met Newley during a visit to America to see his sister Louise and commented, "America was really great. I met Tony Newley over there. He'd never heard of any of our numbers so I played him some of our records. When I left he said he wanted to record 'I Saw Her Standing There." Newley was as good as his word and recorded the number as a single which was released in America in October 1963, becoming

the second cover of a Beatles number to he issued in the States.

Newley died of cancer in April 1999.

837. Herman's Hermits performed *Mrs Brown You've Got A Lovely Daughter* and *I'm Henry VIII, I am* on this June 6th 1965 show. The other guests were Tommy Steele, Trini Lopez, Roberta Peters, John Byner and Georgie Kaye.

Steele was Britain's premier rock 'n' roll performer of the 1950s. George Martin was originally asked to consider signing him and watched him perform at the 2 O's coffee bar in London, but he decided against it. Decca's Dick Rowe saw Steele and immediately signed him up and Steele had a string of British hits, but never entered the American charts.

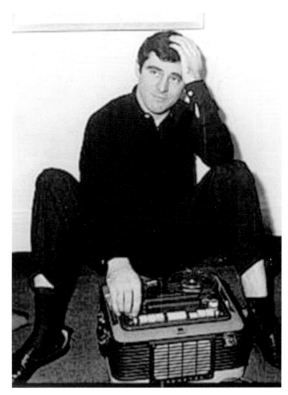

Anthony Newly

838. Tom Jones performed *It's Not Unusual* and *Watcha Gonna Do* and The Seekers performed *A World Of Our Own* on this June 13th 1965 edition. The other guests were Dee Dee Sharp, Sid Caesar, London Lee, Jean Paul Vignon, Allen & Rossi and Rudi Schweitzer.

839. The Dave Clark Five performed *Glad All Over*, *Come Home* and *I Like It Like That* on this June 20th 1965 edition. The guests were Cab Calloway, Juliet Prowse, Soupy Sales, Totie Fields, Arthur Hayes, the Malmo Girls and Elizabeth & Collier.

840. Billy J. Kramer & the Dakotas performed *From A Window* and *Bad To Me* on this June 27th 1965 show. The other guests were Tony Bennett, Jackie Vernon, the Belafonte Folk Singers, the Kim Sisters, Topo Gigio and Johnny Hart.

841. Gerry & the Pacemakers performed *I Like It*, *You'll Never Walk Alone* and *I'm The One* on this August 29th 1965 edition. The other guests were Morecambe & Wise, Rich Little, Jerry Vale, The Womenfolk and the Kessler Twins.

842. The Beatles and Cilla appeared on this September 12th 1965 show.

845. Tom Jones performed *With These Hands* on this October 3rd 1965 show. The other guests were Peter sellers, Judy Garland, Sophie Tucker and Jackie Vernon. The show was repeated on August 7th 1966.

846. Petula Clark performed *Round Every Corner* and *A Foggy Day In London Town* on this October 10th 1965 show. The other guests were

Diana Ross & the Supremes, Woody Allen, Wayne Newton, Kate Smith and the Step Brothers.

847. On this October 17th 1965 show The Animals performed *Work Song*. The other guests were Sam The Sham & the Pharoahs, Pat Boone, Sid Caesar, Totie Fields, Joyce Jameson, Guy Marks, the McGuire Sisters, the Gima Brothers and Lou Johnson.

848. Herman's Hermits performed *Just A Little Bit Better* and *Jezebel* on the October 24th 1965 show. The other guests were Marvin Gaye, Duke Ellington, the Smothers Brothers, Richard Pryor and Helen Hayes. The show was repeated on June 19th 1966.

851. The Dave Clark Five performed *Over And Over* and *Catch Us If You Can* on the November 14th 1965 show. The other guests were Woody Allen, Bert Lahr, Jerry Vale and the Barry Sisters.

853. Petula Clark performed *My*

Tommy Steele

The Rolling Stones on Ed Sullivan Show

Love and *Mademoiselle de Paris* on this November 28th 1965 show. The other guests were Glenn Yarborough, Victor Borge, Sammy Kaye and Sally Ann Howes.

854. Tom Jones performed *Thunderball* on this show on December 5th 1965. The other guests were Martha & the Vandellas, Robert Goulet, Jane Powell, Shelley Burman and Bobby Ramsen.

855. The Dave Clark Five performed *Catch Us If You Can* on this December 12th 1965 show. The other guests were the Byrds, Al Hirt, Alan King, Wayne Newton, Barnara McNair and the Swingle Singers.

862. The Animals performed *We Gotta Get Out Of This Place* and *Inside Looking Out* on this February 6th 1966 show. The other guests were Simon & Garefunkel, Rosemary Clooney, Peter Greenaro, Tony Lema, Alan King, Pompoff Theom, Gino Tonetti and Nancy Walker.

863. The Rolling Stones performed *Satisfaction*, *As Tears Go By* and '19th Nervous Breakdown on this Febru-

ary 13th 1966 show. The other guests were Ethel Merman, Hal Holbrook and Wayne Newton. The show was repeated on July 10th 1966.

864. The Dave Clark Five performed *Over And Over* and *At The Scene* on this February 20th 1966 show. The other guests were Diana Ross & the Supremes, Richard Kiley, Jerry Stiller, Anne Meara, Allan Sherman and Ugo Garrido. The show was repeated on July 24th 1966.

865. Petula Clark performed *A Sign Of The Times*, *My Love* and *I Want To Hold Your Hand* on this February 27th 1966 show. The other guests were Nancy Sinatra, Gary Lewis & the Playboys, Richard Pryor, Alan King, Blossom Seeley and the Trio Rennos. The show was repeated on September 4th 1966.

866. Tom Jones performed *More* on this March 6th 1966 show. The other guests were Frankie Avalon & Annette Funicello, John Byner and Ray Milland. The show was repeated on July 3rd 1966.

869. Cilla Black was said to have performed *Love's Just A Broken Heart* on this March 27th 1966 show. The other guests were Debbie Reynolds, Kirk Douglas, Ed Ames, Totie Fields and Woody Herman.

872. On this April 17th 1966 show The Animals performed *Shake* and *Don't Bring Me Down* and Petula Clark performed *A Sign Of The Times* and *Just Goodbye*. The other guests were Jimmy Durante, Sonny King,

Myron Cohen, Franko Corelli, Dorothy Kirsten, Laurence & Carroll and Getta Morelli.

873. The Dave Clark Five performed *Catch Us If You Can* and *Try Too Hard* on this April 24th 1966 show. The other guests were Allan Sherman, Roberta Peters and Shelley Bermann.

876. The Bachelors were scheduled to appear on this show on May 16th 1966, but it is unclear what actually happened. It was said that the American Musicians Union had put its foot down about the number of British artists who were being given a permit to perform in the States. It seems from this time on that British artists appeared less frequently on the *Ed Sullivan Show* than in the past. The Musicians Unions on both sides of the Atlantic were concerned at the number of musicians crossing the Atlantic either way and tried to get a tit for tat exchange. This did limit the

number of British artists going to America and possibly restricted the expansion of The British Invasion.

Britain is only a small island and America is a vast country with a massive population, so naturally there were far more musicians and far more outlets in America than in Britain and having a system of limited exchange was not balanced in favour of the British acts.

It is possible that this restriction on the appearances of British acts in America could have affected the Bachelors impressive chart run. Between May 1964 and May 1966 they had six chart entries: *Diane*, *I Believe*, *No Arms Can Ever Hold You*, *Marie*, '*Chapel In The Moonlight* and *Love Me With All Of Your Heart*.

Although an Irish trio from Dublin, they were based in England and recorded for a British label so, strictly speaking, they can be classed as part of the British Invasion.

Sullivan and the Bachelors

879. The Beatles were featured in promotional films of *Rain* and *Paperback Writer* on the June 5th 1966 show. The guests were Richard Pryor, Robert Goulet, Bobbie Norris, Charlotte Rae and Torie Fields.

880. The Dave Clark Five performed *Look Before You Leap* and *Please Tell Me Why* on the June 12th 1966 show. The other guests were Jerry Lewis, Wayne Newton, Jackie Vernon, Peter Gennaro and Joey Adams.

884. The Rolling Stones performed *Have You Seen Your Mother, Baby, Standing in The Shadow*, *Paint It Black* and *Lady Jane* on the September 11th 1966 show. The other guests were Louis Armstrong, Robert Goulet, Red Skelton and Joan Rivers.

885. Herman's Hermits performed *My Reservation's Been Confirmed* on the September 18th 1966 show. The other guests were Peanuts, Red Buttons, Jackie Mason, Nancy Ames, Renata Tebaldi and Franco Corolli and the Muppets.

888. Petula Clark, Richard Pryor, Allan & Rossi, Wayne & Shuster, Manuela Vargas and Berosini Chimes appeared on this show on October 9th 1966.

893. The New Vaudeville Band, Noel Harrison, Johnny Hart, Joan Sutherland and the McGuire Sisters appeared on the November 13th 1966 show.

Noel Harrison was the son of actor Rex Harrison and was later to release a single *Windmills Of Your Mind*, which was a top ten hit in Britain, but it did not register in the American charts.

894. The Dave Clark Five performed *Sitting Here Baby* and a promo film of their '19 Days' was also screened on the November 20th 1966 show. The other guests were Barbara McNair, Bobby Vinton, Henny Youngman, Nancy Walker, Charles Nelson Reilly, Peter Gennaro and Franco Corelli.

900. The New Vaudeville Band performed *Winchester Cathedral*, *Whispering* and *Shine* on the January 1st 1967 show. The other guests were Joan Rivers, Peter Nero, Lana

Ed Sullivan with Peter Noone from Herman's Hermits

Cantrell, George Kaye, the Castro Brothers, Les Ballets Africains, Sandra Balesti, the Three Haues, Hendra & Ullet and the Tovarich Troupe.

902. The Rolling Stones performed *Ruby Tuesday* and *Let's Spend Some Time Together*. This was an adaptation of *Let's Spend The Night Together*, which had to be altered for the show because of censorship. Petula Clark performed *Elusive Butterfly* and *Colour My World*. The

January 15th 1967 show also featured Allan Sherman, the Muppets, Alan King, the Sisters of St Benedict, the Michael Bennett Dancers and the Monroes.

912. The Dave Clark Five performed *I've Got To Have A Reason* and *You Got What It Takes* on the March 26th 1967 show. The other guests were Eddie Albert, Pat Buttrum, the Muppets, London Lee, Sergio Franchi and Anna Moffo.

920. Petula Clark performed a medley of *I Know A Place*, *Je Me Sens Bien*, *My Love*, *Downtown*, *Don't Sleep In The Subway* and *This Is My Song*. The Seekers performed *Georgy Girl*. The May 21st 1967 show also featured Alan King, Birgit Nilsson, Ronald Turin, Claude Levellee', Peter Gennaro and Les Feux Follets. The show was repeated on July 30th 1967.

927. Petula Clark sang *I'll Be Loving You Eternally* and *How Can I Be Sure?* on the show on September 10th 1967. The other guests were the Young Rascals, Red Skelton, Eddie Fisher and Buddy Hackett.

933. Lulu performed *To Sir With Love* on the October 22nd 1967 show. The other guests were Eddie Fisher, Jerry Stiller, Anne Meara, Mike Douglas, Norm Crosby, the McGuire Sisters and Tommy Cooper.

935. Shirley Bassey appeared on the November 5th 1967 show along with Tony Bennett, Rodney Dangerfield, Woody Herman, Totie Fields and Allen & Rossi.

938. The Beatles were featured via a promotion film of *Hello Goodbye* on the November 26th 1967 show.

The other guests were Connie Francis, All Hirt, the New Doodletown Pipers, John Byner, Jane Morgan and Morecambe & Wise. The show was repeated on August 11th 1968.

954. The Bee Gees performed *Words* on the March 17th 1968 show. The other guests were Lucille Ball, George Hamilton, Fran Jeffries, Jerry Stiller, Tony Sandler and Ralph Young.

958. Tom Jones performed *It's Not Unusual*, *Danny Boy* and *Delilah* on the April 21st 1968 show. The other guests were Patty Duke and Totie Fields.

971. On the October 27th 1968 show Mary Hopkin performed *Morning Of My Life* and *Those Were The Days*. The other guests were Helen Hayes, Ed Ames, the Doodletown Pipers, Dewey 'Pigmeat' Markham and the Kuban Cossacks.

973. Tom Jones, Vicki Carr, Wayne & Schuster, Scoey Mitchell and Valconte & Valconte appeared on this November 10th 1968 show. Jimi Hendrix was originally booked, but he cancelled. Jimi was one of a number of American artists who went to Britain to kick-start their careers. Others included P.J. Proby, the Walker Brothers, James Taylor and Suzi Quatro.

975. Dusty Springfield sang *Son of A Preacher Man* on this November 24th 1968 show. Other guests were Jackie Mason, Nancy Wilson, Morey Amsterdam and the New Doodlestown Pipers.

976. Engelbert Humperdinck performed *Les Bicyclettes De Belsize* and *Marry Me* on this December 1st

1968 show. The other guests were Herb Alpert & His Tijuana Brass, Tiny Tim, Jack Carter and Scoey Mitchell.

984. Shirley Bassey sang *Goin' Out Of My Head* on this January 26th 1969 show. The other guests were Tommy James & the Shondells, George Hamilton, Joe Namath and John Byner.

996. Joe Cocker & His Grease Band performed *Feelin' Alright* on this April 27th 1969 show, although his impact was marred by the fact that he was obscured by dancers as he sang. The number eventually reached No. 59 in the American charts. The other guests were Connie Francis, Alan King, John Byner, Lovelace Watkins and the Martins.

Cocker was a singer from Sheffield who also had a Beatles association with *I'll Cry Instead* being one of his

Joe Cocker & the Grease Band

early recordings. His biggest British hit was *With A Little Help From My Friends*, which topped the charts. He was invited to *Apple* where George sang *Old Brown Shoe* and *Something* to him and Cocker went on to record 'Something'. Paul McCartney also played Joe some songs and he said he would like to record *Golden Slumbers*, but Paul offered him *She Came In Through The Bathroom Window* and it became the number that brought him his first American Top 50 chart placing on January 10th 1970. He then settled in America where he had a string of chart hits.

The Grease Band comprised Cocker (vocals), Chris Stainton (bass), Tommy Eyre (keyboards), Kenny Slade (drums) and Alan Spenner and Henry McCullough (guitars).

1000. Mary Hopkin performed *Goodbye* on this May 25th 1969 show. The other guests were Sam & Dave, Theodore Bikel, Louise Nye, the Primo Family and Lucera Tena.

1011. Shirley Bassey performed *I'll Never Fall In Love Again* and *This Is*

Mary Hopkin

My Life on this October 1969 show. The other guests were Lee Marvin, Woody Allen, Oliver, Jo Anne Worley, the Castro Brothers, Topo Gigio and the Yale Glee Club. The show was repeated on August 23rd 1970.

1014. Petula Clark performed *Fool On The Hill* on this November 2nd 1969 show. The other guests were Pearl Bailey, Buck Owens, the Band, David Frye, Lucho Navarro and Trio Rennos.

1017. The Rolling Stones performed *Gimme Shelter*, *Love In Vain* and *Honky Tonk Woman* on this November 23rd 1969 show. The other guests were Ella Fitzgerald, Robert Klein, Ed Ames, Topo Gigio, Peter Gennero, the Hawthorn Tigers and Eddie Albert.

1021. The penultimate show of the decade on December 21st 1969 was a tribute to 'The Swinging, Soulful Sixties', part of which was devoted

Shirley Bassey

to British Invasion artists. Petula Clark sang *Downtown* and was interviewed. There was clip of the Beatles performing at Shea Stadium from August 15th 1965 and clips of the Dave Clark Five, the Animals, Herman's Hermits and the Rolling Stones.

It is puzzling why the Sullivan show continued to promote the Dave Clark Five time after time, which was a great contribution to their American success, while hardly utilising the Beatles again following their initial three appearances. It is not clear whether it was Brian Epstein and the Beatles themselves who were reluctant to appear again.

Obviously, the *Ed Sullivan Show* team decided on the Dave Clark Five as the British band they were going to promote over any other. Perhaps it is because they were so clean cut. Although the programme used the Rolling Stones on a handful of occasions, they had to censor the group during one of their performances.

It is also noticeable that the show had the same group of comedians and speciality acts appearing regularly, as if they had particular favourites.

The British acts used most often after the DC5 were not even groups, they were Petula Clark and Tom Jones.

Despite the fact that the *Ed Sullivan Show* continued to produce high ratings, CBS cancelled it declaring that they wanted to modernise their schedule. The show eventually went off the air on June 6th 1971.

Sullivan died on October 13th 1974.

Dave Clark Five

The Beatles on
'*The Ed Sullivan Show*'

The Beatles made four live appearances on the show and were featured on further shows in filmed excerpts.

Their first appearance was on show number 778 on February 9th 1964. Apart from the Beatles, the other guests were Charlie Brill, Georgia Brown, Davy Jones, Fred Kapps, Mitzi McCall, Tessie O'Shea and members of the Broadway cast of the musical *Oliver*, including Davy Jones, later to become a member of the Monkees.

The opening credits were shown as the curtains rose and the commercials were for Aero Shave and Griffin Liquid Wax Shoe Polish. The Beatles then performed *All My Lovin'*, *Til There Was You* and *She Loves You*.

A commercial for Anacin Pain reliever followed and then magician Fred Kapps performed a card and salt-shaker trick. Davy Jones, Georgia Brown and other cast members of *Oliver* then appeared and sang *I'd Do Anything*.

The next commercial was for Cold-Water All, a laundry detergent. Then impressionist/comedian Frank Gorshin (some may remember him as *The Riddler* in the *Batman* TV series) gave impressions of film stars involved in politics: Broderick Crawford, Dean Martin, Anthony Quinn, Marlon Brando, Burt Lancaster, Kirk Douglas, Alfred Hitchcock and Alec Guinness.

A Pillsbury commercial preceded Tessie O'Shea, who had been appearing on Broadway in *The Girl Who Came to Supper*. She sang a medley of show tunes including 'I Got Rhythm' and 'The Tender Trap', then took up a banjo to perform 'Two Ton Tessie (From Tennessee)'.

The comedy team of Mitzi McCall and Charlie Brill appeared in an office sketch in which a casting agent interviewed several aspiring actresses, all played by Mitzi.

The Beatles returned to perform *I Saw Her Standing There* and *I Wanna Hold Your Hand* and were followed by Wells & the Four Fays, an acrobatic troupe who performed physical comedy and stunts.

A commercial for Pillsbury pancakes followed and then Sullivan made his closing comments, announcing the following week's show.

The following show, numbered 779 and co-starring the Beatles with film actress Mitzi Gaynor, was broadcast on February 16th 1964 from the Deauville Hotel in Miami Beach, Florida. The opening titles featured images of racehorse and a man diving off a high diving board. George Fenniman then talked about Lipton Tea, one of the sponsors of the show. Sullivan then spoke briefly with Fenniman, who then introduced a Lipton tea commercial. The advert was taped at the hotel swimming pool and Fenniman was encouraging women to try the tea.

The Beatles then performed *She Loves You*, *This Boy* and *All My Loving*. Boxers Sonny Liston and Joe Louis then bowed to the audience prior to another Lipton Instant Tea commercial.

The comedy team Allen and Rossi then did a boxing sketch with Steve Rossi interviewing Marty Allen as 'Rocky Allen'. Steve Rossi then sang *Strike up The Band* while Allen wore a Beatles wig.

Mitzi Gayner them performed *Too Damned Hot*, with four male dancers. She went on to sing a blues medley which included *Birth Of The Blues*, *St. James Infirmary*, *When The Saints Go Marching In*, *Joshua Fit The Battle Of Jericho* and a reprise of *When The Saints Go Marching In*'

A Kent cigarette commercial was next, followed by a tape of Ed Sullivan at Hialeah Racetrack introducing the Nerveless Nocks, four male sway pole acrobats who performed their gymnastics on the taped segment.

Stand up comedian Myron Cogwen then told jokes about a elderly women in Miami who end up at the racetrack, Krushev promising more consumer goods to the Russian people, one about a Minister and Rabbi playing cards and ending up with a joke about a CIA agent in Yugoslavia.

A Pillsbury commercial followed and then the Beatles sang *I Saw Her Standing There*, *From Me To You* and *I Want To Hold Your Hand*.

After this Sullivan had a brief chat with the Beatles and a commercial for Lipton Iced Tea followed. Next came an appearance by comedic unicyclists the Valantis, then a Kent cigarette commercial and Ed Sullivan's closing comments on who was appearing the following week.

The February 23rd 1964 show, numbered 780 was the Beatles third appearance in succession. Apart from the Beatles the guests were Acker Bilk, Gordon MacRae, Sheila MacRae, Morecambe & Wise, Dave Barry and Morty Gunty.

After the opening credits the commercials were for Chef Boy and Aero Shave and then the Beatles performed *Twist And Shout* and *Please Please Me*. Gloria Bleezarde then sang *Safety In Numbers*, a comedy song about people being identified by numbers rather than names.

The next commercial was for Anacin followed by the marionettes Pinky & Perky. Puppets Caterpillar and Crow then sang *You Must Have Been A beautiful Baby* followed by Cow and other puppets singing *Speedy Gonzales.*

Morcambe & Wise then appeared in a sketch about a man who collects Louis XIV brandy glasses. Acker Bilk then played 'Acker's Lacquer' on his clarinet, with support from the Hugh Lambert Dancers.

The Cold Water All laundry detergent advert followed after which Gordon and Sheila MacRae parodied *The Gary Moore Show* and then did a production number with dancers while they sang 'The sweetest Sounds'. They then did impressions of Frank Fontaine, Carol Channinbg, Zsa Zsa Gabor, Lucille Ball and Red Skelton, ending with Gordon MacRae singing *If I Ever Would Leave You.*

Commercials for Pillsbury Danish Rolls and crescent rolls followed.

Comedian Dave Barry made his bow with a joke about his daughter's wedding, followed by ones about his teenage son, his nine year-old son watching television and teenagers being taller than their parents. He then sang *Sonny Boy.*

Cab Calloway performed *St James Infirmary* and *Old Man River.*

A commercial for Lipton Iced Tea followed and then comedian Morty Gunty told jokes about three poisoned scientists giving their last requests, his wife's interior decorator and his experiences as a teacher.

The Beatles sang *I Want to Hold Your Hand,* then a commercial for Pillsbury Bavarian layer cakes and Pillsbury pancake mix followed

while Sullivan made his closing comments.

The next Beatles appearance was not live, but was a filmed segment, and was featured on show number 792 on May 24th 1964. The film included a clip from their movie *A Hard Day's Night* of them performing *You Can't Do That,* a number which ended up on the cutting room floor. Ed Sullivan was then seen interviewing the Beatles on the set of the film in London.

Other guests on that particular

show were Liza Minelli, Duke Ellington, Jean-Paul Vignon, Shirley Verrett and Morecambe & Wise.

Their fourth and final live appearance took place at the beginning of Season 19 on show number 842 on September 12th 1965. Apart from the Beatles, the guests were Cilla Black, Soupy Sales and Allen & Rossi. The Beatles had actually recorded their performance on August 14th.

Following the opening comments by Ed Sullivan there was a Lipton tea commercial with George Fenneman. Soupy Sales then reminisced with Sullivan about the recent summer.

Cilla Black performed *September In The Rain* and was followed by the magician Fantasio, a sleight-of-hand artist who was taped in Las Vegas.

Commercials for Pillsbury crescent rolls and chocolate chip cookies followed and Sullivan then introduced each individual member of the Beatles who greeted him as each walked past. They performed *I Feel Fine, I'm Down* and *Act Naturally.* Sullivan then asked the audience to calm down. A commercial for Burlington-Lees carpets followed.

Steve Rossi next sang *Try To Remember,* then appeared with his partner Marty Allen as the comedy team Marty and Rossi. Rossi began to sing *When You're Smiling* but was constantly interrupted by his partner. He then sang *We Love You,* a variation on *She Loves You,* with Allen dancing in the audience.

The next commercials were for Advanced All detergent and Lux beauty soap, then Cilla Black appeared and sang *Goin' Out Of My Head* and was briefly interviewed by Sullivan.

Soupy Sales then sang a novelty song about a new dance called *The Mouse,* encouraging audience participation.

A Lipton tea advertisement with 'weatherman bob' followed and then the Beatles appeared once again and performed *Ticket To Ride, Yesterday* and *Help.*

After an Anacin commercial Ed Sullivan made his closing comments and announced the following week's guests. The closing titles saw the Beatles performing 'Help' once again, with George Fenneman then

doing another Lipton tea commercial and Dick Van Dyke promoted his sitcom.

This edition of *The Ed Sullivan Show* was the final show to be shot in monochrome.

The Beatles appearance on show number 879 on June 5th 1966 was simply a screening of two of their promotional videos for *Rain* and *Paperback Writer*. The guests on the show were Richard Pryor, Robert Goulet, Bobbie Norris, Charlotte Rae and Totie Fields.

Their final *Ed Sullivan Show* appearance of the decade was show number 1021 on December 21st 1969, a special edition called *The Swinging Soulful Sixties*. The guests were the Beatles, Diana Ross & the Supremes (her final appearance with the group), Petula Clark and Barbra Streisand.

Sullivan began by reviewing the decade, using tapes from previous shows. The first section was called *Broadway Theatre Songs* and in-

cluded Richard Burton's soliloquy from *Hamlet*, Robert Goulet singing a song from the musicals *Camelot* and *Happy Face* and Gwen Verdon singing *If My Friends Could See Me Now* from *Sweet Charity*.

The next section was called *Beatle-mania* and presented excerpts from the Beatles at Shea Stadium on August 15th 1965.

The third section was called *British Acts* and featured Petula Clark performing 'Downtown', followed by an interview, then there were clips if the Dave Clark Five, the Animals, Herman's Hermits, the Rolling Stones and Petula Clarks. Next, David Frost looked at the headlines from the 1960s and also some of the movies.

The next section focussed on Diana Ross & the Supremes with Sullivan discussing with Ross the trends of popular music in the 1960s. There was then a medley of Supremes numbers: *Baby Love, Stop! In The*

Name Of Love, Come See About Me, My World Is Empty Without You, You Can't Hurry Love, The Happening, Keep Me Hangin' On, Reflections, Love Child and *I Hear A Symphony*. The Supremes then sang Someday *We'll Be Together*.

There were then clips of Barbara Streisand performing *I Cried A River*, her Las Vegas act and clips from *Funny girl*. There was an excerpt of Herb Alpert performing *Taste Of Honey* and Judy Garland singing *Smile*.

The history of the Beatles on *The Ed Sullivan Show* is puzzling. It launched them on the path to tremendous fame in America and their first three appearances were dazzling. Then it all seemed to fizzle out for the rest of the decade, with one brief recorded live appearance and then some clips and promos during the next six years, while the Dave Clark Five, for instance, appeared an incredible seventeen times. There were also regular appearances from Petula Clark and Tom Jones.

The *Ed Sullivan Show* was obviously the biggest entertainment show on American television at the time, but there is no explanation as to why, following their major impact on the show in 1964, the Beatles never really bothered to appear again. Was this due to Brian Epstein or did the Beatles not want to appear on the show again? It is puzzling, particularly as regular live appearances, which they could surely have had, would have boosted their album releases and North American tours even more.

All of the singles below entered the American charts between 1964 and 1969, the era referred to as the British Invasion. Since there were three American charts - Billboard, Cashbox and Record World, we will refer to positions in the Billboard chart.

There are a couple of entries which have been left out as they do not exactly fit into the category of British Invasion such as comedian Charlie Drake with *My Boomerang Won't Come Back*, Rolf Harris with *Tie Me Kangaroo Down, Sport*, Sounds Orchestral with *Cast Your Fate To The Wind 111* and Irish actor Richard Harris with *MacArthur Park*. Also excluded are artists who originally had their hits in Britain such as Irish group, Them (although Irish group the Bachelors have been included because they were based in Britain) and South African singer, Danny Williams.

The Animals

The House Of The Rising Sun topped the charts on August 15th 1964. *I'm Crying* reached No. 19 on October 17th 1964. *Don't Let Me Be Misunderstood* reached No. 15 on March 6th 1965. *Bring It On Home To Me* reached No 32 on May 29th 1965. *We Gotta Get Out Of This Place* reached No 13 on September 4th 1965. *It's My Life* reached No. 23 on December 4th 1964. *Inside Looking Out* reached No.34 on April 2nd 1966. *Don't Bring Me Down* reached No. 12 on June 4th 1966 (released under the name Eric Burdon & the Animals). *See See Rider* reached No. 10 on October 1st 1966. *Help Me Girl* reached No. 29 on December 31st 1966. *When I Was Young* reached No. 15 on April 22nd 1967. *San Franciscan Nights* reached No. 9 on August 19th 1967. *Monterey* reached No 15 on December 30th 1967 and *Sky Pilot (Parts 1 & 2)* reached No. 14 on June 22nd 1968.

During the years of their American chart entries there were some changes in personnel and the Animals were later to disband. Their success in America lasted far longer than a number of the other British bands.

The Animals' initial releases were of the 'taking coals to Newcastle' nature. *The House Of The Rising Sun'* was a traditional American song while *Bring It On Home To Me* had been a hit for Sam Cooke in 1962 and *See See Rider (aka C.C. Rider)* had been recorded by several American artists including Chuck Willis, LaVern Baker and Bobby Powell.

The Bachelors

Diane reached No 10 on May 16th 1964. *I Believe* reached No 33 on August 1st 1964. *No Arms Can Ever Hold You* reached No 27 on January 30th 1965. *Marie* reached No 15 on July 3rd 1965. *Chapel In The Moonlight* reached No 32 on November 6th 1965. *Love Me With All Of Your Heart* reached No 38 on May 14th 1966.

Shirley Bassey

Goldfinger reached No 8 on February 22nd 1965.

The Bee Gees

New York Mining Disaster 1941 reached No. 14 on June 10th 1967. *To Love Somebody* reached No. 17 on July 29th 1967. *Holiday* reached No. 16 on October 21st 1967. *(The Lights Went Out In) Massachusetts* reached No. 11 on November 25th 1967. *I've Gotta Get A Message To You* reached No. 8 on September 7th 1968. *I Started A joke* reached No. 6 on January 4th 1969. *First Of May* reached No 37 on December 4th 1969.

The Bee Gees were a phenomenal band and, like the Beatles, supreme songwriters. They were to continue to have an amazing string of international hits for decades. Among their American chart-toppers were *How Can You Mend A Broken Heart*, *Jive Talkin'*. *You Should Be Dancing*, *How Deep Is Your Love*, *Stayin' Alive*, *Night Fever*, *Too Much Heaven*, *Tragedy* and *Love Inside Out*.

Madeline Bell.

I'm Gonna Make You Love Me reached No. 26 on March 9th 1968.

Cilla Black

You're My World reached No. 26 on July 25th 1964.

Arthur Brown
(The Crazy World Of)

Fire reached No. 2 on September 29th 1968.

Chad & Jeremy

Yesterday's Gone reached No. 21 on June 13th 1964. *A Summer Song* reached No. 7 on September 19th 1964. *Willow Weep For Me* reached No. 15 on December 12th 1964. *If I Loved You* reached No. 23 on March

13th 1965. *Before and After* reached No. 17 on May 29th 1965. *I Don't Wanna Love You Baby* reached No. 3 on August 28th 1965. *Distant Shores* reached No. 30 on August 13th 1966.

The Dave Clarke Five

Glad All Over reached No. 6 on March 7th 1964. *Bits And Pieces* reached No. 4 on April 11th 1964. *Do You Love Me* reached No. 11 on May 9th 1964. *Can't You See That She's Mine* reached No. 4 on June 20 1964. *Because* reached No. 3 on August 8th 1964. *Everybody Knows (I Still Love You)*, reached No. 15 on October 17th 1964. *Any Way You Want It* reached No 14 on December 5th 1964. *Come Home* reached No. 14 on February 27th 1965. *Reelin' And Rockin'* reached No. 23 on May 8th 1965. *I Like It Like That* reached No. 7 on July 10th 1965. *Catch Us If You Can* reached No. 4 on September 4th 1965. *Over And Over* reached No. 1 on November 20th 1965. *At The Scene* reached No. 18 on February 19th 1966. *Try Too Hard* reached No. 12 on April 23rd 1966. *Please Tell Me Why* reached No. 28 on July 2nd 1966. *You Got What It Takes* reached No. 7 on April 15th 1967. *You Must Have Been A Beautiful Baby* reached No. 35 on July 1st 1967.

Obviously, the group with more appearances on 'The Ed Sullivan Show' than any other band also tried to emulate the Beatles by releasing a large volume of records within a short time - seven singles alone in 1964.

The Dave Clarke Five were the first close rivals of the Beatles at the start of the British Invasion. However,

they also covered a number of previous American releases. The Contours had had a hit with *Do You Love Me*, although the DC5 version was almost a carbon copy of the version by Liverpool band Faron's Flamingos. *Reelin' And Rockin'* was a Chuck Berry number, although Berry's version had never charted. *I Like It Like That* was a number by American songwriter Chris Kenner, who had also penned *The Land Of A 1,000 Dances* and was a DC5 hit in the U.S. but not in Britain. *Over And Over* was another song by a US writer Bobby Day which had been a minor hit for him although the flipside of Day's single *Rockin' Robin* is a more popular number. *You've Got What It Takes* had been a previous hit by Motown artist Marv Johnson.

Petula Clark

Downtown reached No. 1 on January 2nd 1965. *I Know A Place* reached No. 3 on April 3rd 1965. *You'd Better Come Home* reached No. 22 on August 31st 1965. *Round Every Corner* reached No. 21 on October 30th 1965. *My Love* reached No. 1 on January 15th 1966. *A Sign Of The Times* reached No. 11 on April 2nd 1966. *I couldn't Live Without Your Love* reached No. 9 on August 30th 1966. *Who Am I?* reached No. 21 on October 29th 1966. *Colour My World* reached No. 16 on December 31st 1966. *This Is My Song* reached No. 3 on March 19th 1967. *Don't Sleep In The Subway* reached No. 5 on June 17th 1967. *The Cat In The Window (The Bird In The Sky)* reached No. 26 on September 16th 1967. *The Other Man's Grass Is Always Greener*

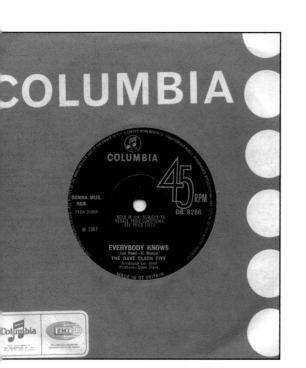

reached No. 31 on December 30th 1967. *Kiss Me Goodbye* reached No. 15 on March 2nd 1968. *Don't Give Up* reached No. 37 on August 24th 1968.

Cream

Sunshine Of Your Love reached No. 5 on February 24th 1968. *White Room* reached No. 6 on October 19th 1968. *Crossroads* reached No. 28 on Feburary 8th 1969.

David & Jonathan

Michelle reached No. 18 on January 29th 1966.

The Spencer Davis Group

Gimme Some Lovin' reached No. 7 on January 28th 1967. *I'm A Man* reached No. 10 on April 8th 1967.

Deep Purple

Hush reached No. 4 on August 24th 1968. *Kentucky Woman* reached No. 38 on December 12th 1968. Their hits were not confined to the 1960s.

Donovan

Catch The Wind reached No, 23 on June 12th 965. *Sunshine Superman* reached No. 1 on August 13th 1966. *Mellow Yellow* reached No. 2 on November 19th 1966. *Epistle To Dippy* reached No. 19 on February 25th 1967. *There Is A Mountain* reached No. 11 on August 26th 1967. *Wear Your Love Like Heaven* reached No. 23 on December 9th 1967. *Jennifer Juniper* reached No. 26 on March 3rd 1968. *Hurdy Gurdy Man* reached No. 5 on June 29th 1968. *Lalena* reached No. 33 on October 19th 1968. *To Susan On The West Coast Waiting*

reached No. 35 on March 1st 1969. *Atlantis* reached No. 7 on April 26th 1969. *Goo Goo Barabajagal (Love Is Hot)* reached No. 36 on August 30th 1969.

The Equals

Baby, Come Back reached No. 32 on September 29th 1968.

Adam Faith.

It's Alright reached No. 31 on February 20th 1965.

Marianne Faithfull

As Tears Go By reached No. 22 on December 19th 1964. *Come And Stay With Me* reached No. 26 on March 27th 1965. *This Little Bird* reached No. 32 on June 26th 1965. *Summer Nights* reached No. 24 on September 4th 1965.

Georgie Fame

Yeh Yeh reached No. 21 on February 2nd 1965. *The Ballad Of Bonnie & Clyde* reached No. 7 on March 2nd 1968. *Yeh Yeh* was another American cover, which had previously been released by Mongo Santamaria.

Don Fardon

(The Lament Of The Cherokee) Indian Reservation reached No. 20 on September 21st 1968.

Flying Machine

Smile A Little Smile For Me reached No. 5 on October 18th 1969.

The Fortunes

You've Got Your Troubles reached No. 7 on September 11th 1965. *Here*

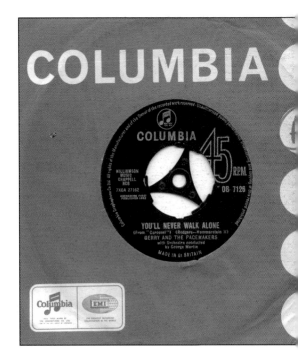

It Comes Again reached No. 27 on November 27th 1965. *Here Comes That Rainy Day Feeling Again* reached No. 15 on June 19th 1971.

The Foundations
Baby, Now That I've Found You reached No. 11 on January 13th 1968. *Build Me Up Buttercup* reached No. 3 on January 18th 1969.

Freddie & The Dreamers
I'm Telling You Now reached No. 1 on March 27th 1965. *I Understand (Just How you Feel)* reached No. 36 on April 24th 1965. *Do The Freddie* reached No. 18 on May 15th 1965. *You Were Made For Me* reached No. 21 on May 15th 1965.

Gerry & The Pacemakers
Don't Let The Sun Catch You Crying reached No. 4 on June 6th 1964. *How Do You Do It?* reached No. 9 on August 8th 1964. *I Like It* reached No 17 on October 17th 1964. *I'll Be There* reached No. 14 on January 9th 1965. *Ferry Cross The Mersey* reached No. 6 on February 13th 1965. *It's Gonna Be Alright* reached No. 23 on April 24th 1965. *Girl On A Swing* reached No. 28 on October 8th 1966. Although Gerry & The Pacemakers' repertoire comprised over 250 songs, many of them American rock and roll numbers. Marsden's hits were not covers of American records; some compositions were by songwriter Mitch Murray, others by Gerry himself. His most famous British recording was *You'll Never Walk Alone*, taken from the Rodgers & Hammerstein musical, although Gerry's interpretation

of the number was adapted to his own style

Herman's Hermits
I'm Into Something Good reached No. 13 on November 14th 1964. *Can't You Hear My Heartbeat* reached No. 2 on February 20th 1965. *Mrs Brown You've Got A Lovely Daughter* reached No. 1 on April 17th 1965. *Silhouettes* reached No. 5 on the same date. *Wonderful World* reached No 4 on June 5th 1965. *I'm Henry VIII, I Am* reached No. 1 on July 10th 1965. *Just A little Bit Better* reached No. 7 on September 25th 1965. *A Must To Avoid* reached No 8 on January 1st 1966. *Listen People* reached No 3 on February 26th 1966. *Leaning On The Lamp Post* reached No. 9 on April 16th 1966. *The Door Swings Both Ways* reached No. 12 on July 23rd 1966. *Dandy* reached No. 5 on October 15th 1966. *There's A Kind Of Hush* reached No 4 on March 4th 1967. *No Milk Today* reached No. 35 on March 18th 1967. *Don't Go Out Into The Rain (You're Going To Melt)* reached No. 18 on July 8th 1967. *Museum* reached No. 39 on September 19th 1967. *I Can Take Or Leave Your Loving* reached No 22 on February 3rd 1968.

It was producer Mickie Most who had the group record *I'm Into Something good*, which had been penned by Gerry Goffin and Carole King for Earl-Jean, an ex-member of the Cookies. *Silhouettes* was also the cover of an American number, which had previously been recorded by the Rays, Steve Gibson & the Redcaps and the Diamonds. *Wonderful World*

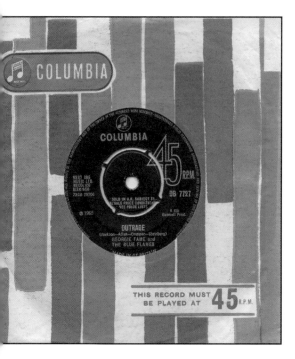

was the Sam Cooke classic, which had already been a hit on both sides of the Atlantic. Peter Noone's cheery demeanour ideally suited to typically London cockney type songs *I'm Henry VIII, I Am* and *Mrs Brown You've Got A Lovely Daughter*. American writer P.J. Sloan was later commissioned to write a number for the group and provided them with their hit *A Must To Avoid*.

The Hollies

Look Through Any Window reached No. 32 on January 8th 1966. *Bus Stop* reached No. 5 on August 20th 1966. *Stop Stop Stop* reached No 7 on November 12th 1966. *On A Carousel* reached No. 11 on April 15th 1967. *Pay You Back With Interest* reached No. 28 on June 24th 1967. *Carrie Anne* reached No. 9 on July 8th 1967. *Jennifer Eccles* reached No. 40 on May 18th 1968. The group continued to have hits in the American charts until the 1980s, including *He Ain't Heavy, He's My Brother*, *Long Cool Woman (In A Black Dress)* and *The Air That I Breathe*.

The Hollies had also originally looked to American hits for some of their releases including *Just Like Me*, which had previously been recorded by the Coasters and brought the group their first British hit, *Searchin'* which was another Coasters cover, *Stay* another of their British hits had been an American chart topper for Maurice Williams and the Zodiacs in 1960 and Doris Troy had originally recorded *Just One Look*.

The Honeycombs

Have I the Right? reached No. 5 on October 10th 1964.

Mary Hopkin

Those Were The Days reached No. 2 on December 19th 1968. *Goodbye* reached No 3 on March 5th 1969. The following year saw her final chart entry with *Temma Harbour* at No. 39.

Engelbert Humperdinck

Release Me (And Let Me Love Again) reached No. 4 on April 29th 1967. *There Goes My Everything* reached No. 20 on July 15th 967. *The Last Waltz* reached No. 25 on October 14th 1967. *Am I That Easy to Forget* reached No. 18 on January 6th 1968. *A Man Without Love* reached No 19 on June 1st 1968. *Les Bicyclettes De Belsize* reached No. 31 on November 23rd 1968. *I'm A Better Man* reached No. 38 on September 29th 1969.

Humperdinck had two further American hits in 1970.

Tom Jones

It's Not Unusual reached No. 10 on May 1st 1965. *What's New Pussycat?* reached No. 3 on July 3rd 1965. *With These Hands* reached No. 27 on September 18th 1965. *Thunderball* reached No. 25 on January 1st 1966. *Green, Green Grass Of Home* reached No. 11 on January 21st 1967. *Detroit City* reached No. 27. *Help Yourself* reached No. 35 on October 5th 1968. *Love Me Tonight* reached No. 13 on June 7th 1969. *I'll Never Fall In Love Again* reached No 6 on August 9th 1969.

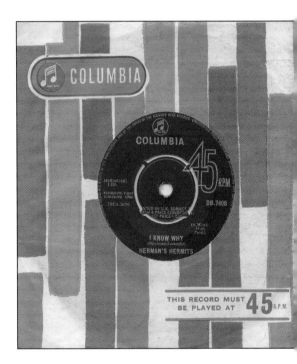

Tom continued to have American chart entries throughout the following decade.

Jonathan King

Everyone's Gone To The Moon reached No. 17 on October 23rd 1965.

The Kinks

You Really Got Me reached No. 7 on October 24th 1964. *All Day And All Of The Night* reached No. 7 on January 16th 1965. *Tired Of Waiting For You* reached No. 6 on March 27th 1965. *Set Me Free* reached No. 23 on July 10th 1965. *Who'll Be The Next In Line* reached No. 34 on September 4th 1965. *A Well Respected Man* reached No. 13 on January 8th 1966. *Dedicated Follower Of Fashion* reached No 36 on June 18th 1966. *Sunny Afternoon* reached No. 14 on August 27th 1966. *Lola* reached No. 9 on September 9th 1970 and the group continued to have American hits until the 1980s.

Billy J Kramer with the Dakotas

Little Children reached No. 7 on May 2nd 1964. *Bad To Me* reached No. 9 on June 13th 1964. *I'll Keep You Satisfied* reached No. 30 on August 15th 1964. *From A Window* reached No. 23 on September 19th 1964.

Leapy Lee

Little Arrows reached No. 16 on November 9th 1968.

Led Zeppelin

Whole Lotta Love reached No. 4 on December 6th 1969. They continued to have hits for the next decade.

Lulu

To Sir With Love reached No. 1 in the charts on September 23rd 1967. *Best Of Both Worlds* reached No. 32 on January 6th 1968. Lulu had a further American hit in 1970 and another in 1981.

Magic Lanterns

Shame, Shame reached No. 29 on November 30th 1968.

Manfred Mann

Do Wah Diddy Diddy reached No. 1 on September 12th 1964. *Sha La La* reached No. 12 on November 28th 1964. *Pretty Flamingo* reached No. 29 on July 23rd 1966. *Mighty Quinn* reached No. 10 on March 9th 1968.

Do Wah Diddy Diddy had originally been a hit for the Exciters under the original title *Do-Wah-Diddy*, *Sha La La* had also been a hit for an American girl group, the Shirelles. Although not a hit for them in the U.S. Manfred Mann had also covered Tommy Roes hit *Sweet Pea* which charted for them in Britain.

The Mindbenders

Game Of Love reached No. 1 on March 27th 1965. *A Groovy Kind Of Love* reached No. 2 on April 30th 1966.

The Moody Blues

Go Now! reached No.. 10 on March 27th 1965. *Tuesday Afternoon (Forever Afternoon)* reached No. 24 on August 24th 1968. They had further hits which stretched into the 1980s. *Go Now!* had been penned by Jerry Leiber and Mike Stoller and previ-

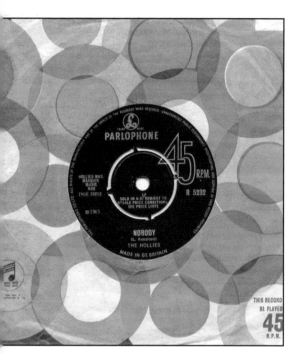

ously recorded by American artist Bessie Banks.

The Nashville Teens
Tobacco Road reached No. 14 on October 10th 1964.

The New Vaudeville Band
Winchester Cathedral reached No 1 on November 5th 1966.

Peter & Gordon
A World Without Love reached No. 1 on May 16th 1964. *Nobody I Know* reached No. 12 on July 11th 1964. *I Don't Want To See You Again* reached No. 16 on October 24th 1964. *I Go To Pieces* reached No 9 on January 23rd 1965. *True Love Ways* reached No. 14 on May 8th 1965. *To Know You Is To Love You* reached No. 24 on July 24th 1965. *Woman* reached No. 14 on March 12th 1966. *Lady Godiva* reached No. 6 on November 5th 1966. *Knight In Rusty Armour* reached No 15 on January 14th 1967. *Sunday For Tea* reached No. 31 on April 15th 1967.

Peter & Gordon benefited from Peter Asher's friendship with Paul McCartney and were able to start their career recording Lennon & McCartney numbers. They then began to cover previous American hits. *I Got To Pieces* had previously been recorded by Del Shannon and *To Know Him Is To Love Him* was by Phil Spector and his original group the Teddy Bears.

Procol Harum
A Whiter Shade Of Pale reached No. 5 on July 1st 1967. *Homburg*

reached No. 34 on November 11th 967. The group had a further hit in 1962 with *Conquistador*.

Cliff Richard
Although Cliff had his first American chart entry with *Living Doll* in 1959, he only had one chart entry during the 1960s. *It's all In The Game* reached No. 25 on January 18th 1964, a few weeks before the Beatles topped the chart for the first time. Between 1976 and 1982 he had a further six American chart entries.

Julie Rogers
The Wedding reached No. 10 on December 5th 1964.

The Rolling Stones
Tell Me (You're Coming Back) reached No. 24 on August 1st 1964. *It's All Over Now* reached No. 26 on August 22nd 1964. *Time Is On My Side* reached No. 6 on November 7th 1964. *Heart Of Stone* reached No. 19 on January 30th 1965. *The Last Time* reached No. 9 on April 10th 1965. *(I Can't Get No) Satisfaction* reached No 1 on June 19th 1965. *Get Off Of My Cloud* reached No. 1 on October 16th 1965. *As Tears Go By* reached No. 6 on January 8th 1966. *19th Nervous Breakdown* reached No. 2 on March 5th 1966. *Paint It Black* reached No. 1 on May 21st 1966. *Mother's Little Helper* reached No. 8 on July 16th 1966. *Lady Jane* reached No. 24 on August 6th 1966. *Have You Seen Your Mother, Baby, Standing In The Shadow?* reached No. 9 on October 8th 1966. *Ruby Tuesday* reached No. 1 on February 4th 1967.

Dandelion reached No. 14 on September 23rd 1967. *She's A Rainbow* reached No. 25 on January 13th 1968. *Jumpin' Jack Flash* reached No. 3 on June 15th 1968. *Honky Tonk Woman* reached No. 1 on July 26th 1969.

The Stones continued to have hits in the American charts into the 1980s, including chart toppers such as *Brown Sugar*, *Angie* and *Miss You*.

Crispian St Peters
The Pied Piper reached No. 4 July 9th 1966. *You Were On My Mind* reached No. 36 on July 22nd 1967.

The Searchers
Needles And Pins reached No. 13 on March 21st 1964. *Don't Throw Your Love Away* reached No. 16 on June 20th 1964. *Some Day We're Gonna Love Again* reached No. 34 on December 9th 1964. *Love Potion Number Nine* reached No 3 on December 19th 1964. *What Have They Done To The Rain* reached No. 29 on February 20th 1965. *Bumble Bee* reached No. 21 on April 10th 1965.

The Searchers were undoubtedly one of the best of the Mersey groups and John Lennon regarded *Sweets For My Sweet* (a British chart-topper but not an American release) the best record to come out of Liverpool at the time. Their jangly guitar style also influenced the Byrds. Despite their great vocal and instrumental style, their

major flaw, which resulted in them not being a major rival to the Beatles, was that they did not compose their own songs and their recordings were basically covers of American num-

bers, several of which had already been previously recorded by other artists.

Sweets For My Sweet had been a hit for the Drifters. *Needles and Pins* had been penned by Sonny Bono and Jack Nitzsche and recorded by Jackie de Shannon. *Love Potion Number Nine* was an American hit for the clovers in 1959 and LaVern Baker had previously recorded *Bumble Bee*.

The Silkie
You've Got To Hide Your Love Away reached No. 10 on November 6th 1965. This was a Lennon & McCartney number.

The Small Faces
Itchycoo Park reached No. 16 on January 13th 1968.

Whistling Jack Smith
I Was Kaiser Bill's Batman reached No 20 on May 13th 1967.

Dusty Springfield
I Only Want To Be With You reached No. 12 on February 15th 1964. *Stay Awhile* reached No 38 on May 2nd 1964. *Wishin' And Hopin'* reached No. 6 on July 11th 1964. *You Don't Have To Say You Love Me* reached No. 4 on June 4th 1966. *All I See Is You* reached No. 20 on October 1st 1966. *I'll Try Anything* reached No. 40 on April 22nd 1967. *The Look Of Love* reached No. 22 on October 14th 1967. *Son Of A Preacher Man* reached No. 10 on December 14th 1968. *The Windmills Of Your Mind* reached No. 31 on May 24th 1969. *A Brand New Me* reached No. 24 on November 29th 1969.

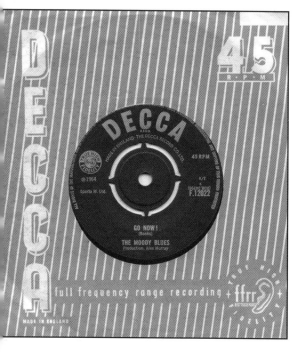

Status Quo
Pictures Of Matchstick Men reached No 12 on June 29th 1968.

The Swinging Bluejeans
Hippy Hippy Shake reached No. 24 on March 28th 1964. Most of the Bluejeans' recordings were covers of American rock numbers. *Hippy Hippy Shake* had originally been recorded by Chan Romero, *Good Golly Miss Molly* by Little Richard, *You're No Good*, which was a minor American hit for them was previously recorded by Betty Everett and *Don't Make Me Over* had been recorded by Dionne Warwick.

Thunderclap Newman
Something In The Air reached No. 37 on October 25th 1969.

The Tremeloes
Here Comes My Baby reached No. 13 on May 6th 1967. *Silence Is Golden* reached No. 11 on July 15th 1967. *Even The Bad Times Are Good* reached No. 36 on March 19th 1977.

The Troggs
Wild Thing reached No. 1 July 9th 1966. *With A Girl Like You* reached No. 29 on September 3rd 1966. *Love Is All Around* reached No 7 on March 23rd 1968.

Unit Four Plus Two
Concrete And Clay reached No 28 on May 29th 1965.

Vanity Fare
Early In The Morning reached No 12 on December 20th 1969. They had

a bigger hit the following year with *Hitchin' A Ride*.

Ian Whitcomb
You Turn Me On (Turn On Song) reached No. 8 on June 19th 1965.

The Who
Happy Jack reached No. 24 on May 20th1967. *I Can See for Miles* reached No. 9 on October 28th 1967. *Call Me Lightning* reached No. 40 on May 4th 1968. *Magic Bus* reached No. 25 on August 31st 1968. *Pinball Wizard* reached No. 19 on May 3rd 1969. *I'm Free* reached No. 37 on August 23rd 1969. The group continued to have hits in America until the early 1980s.

The Yardbirds
For Your Love reached No. 6 June 5th 1965. *Heart Full Of Soul* reached No. 9 on August 21st 1965. *I'm A Man* reached No. 17 on November 20th 1965. *Shapes Of Things* reached No. 11 on April 9th 1966. *Over Under Sideways Down* reached No. 13 on July 16th 1966. *Happenings Ten Years Ago* reached No. 30 on December 24th 1966.

The Zombies
She's Not There reached No. 2 on November 7th 1964. *Tell Her No* reached No. 6 on January 30th 1965. *Time Of The Season* reached No. 3 on February 22nd 1969.

The Beatles had originally started out with a repertoire based on hits by American rock 'n' roll artists and gradually developed their own unique and distinctive material, mainly penned by Lennon & McCartney. On their first album they included a number of covers from rock 'n' roll hits and Motown numbers.

The initial British Invasion releases saw the artists covering American numbers although gradually, like the Beatles, a number of the acts began to pen their own material. This is most obvious with artists such as the Kinks, Donovan and the Bee Gees. In fact, the Beatles almost heralded the dearth of the songwriter. So many American hits had been penned by the writers in the famous Brill Building in New York and artists in general, both in Britain and America, had previously relied on songwriters to provide them with material. After Lennon & McCartney, things were never the same and if the advent of the Beatles caused a reduced market for solo singers, they also reduced the market for songwriters as groups and artists began to pen their own material.

The additional impact in 1964 was due to the fact that the British acts had a number of British hits already behind them when they made their American debut and, in most case, these were released in rapid succession. Take Billy J. Kramer, for instance, with all of his American hits within a six-month period.

There were so many British records rush released in 1964 on the heels of the Beatles that it must have seemed as if the British began to completely dominate the American charts. The impact began to fade after the first few years and the American Musicians Union also curtailed a lot of potential tours and appearance by British groups.

64 British artists entered the American charts between 1964 and 1969, while during the 1970s that increased to 100 and British acts continued to enjoy success on record in America during succeeding decades.

The British acts who charted in America during the 1970s were:

Ace. Argent. Ashton, Gardner & Dyke. Average White Band.

Bad Company. Bay City Rollers. Blue Haze. David Bowie. Brotherhood Of Man. Polly Brown. Buggles.

Christie. City Boy. Eric Clapton. Climax Blues Band. Joe Cocker.

Roger Daltrey. Kiki Dee. Derek & The Dominos. Dire Straits. David Dundas.

Edison Lighthouse. Dave Edmunds. Electric Light Orchestra. Emerson, Lake & Palmer. David Essex.

Faces. Fancy. First Class. 5000 Volts. Flash. Fleetwood Mac. Foghat. Peter Frampton. Free.

Genesis. Gary Glitter. Ian Gomm. Gonzalez.

Albert Hammond. George Harrison. Hot Chocolate. Hotlegs.

Joe Jackson. Jethro Tull. Elton John.

Mac & Katie Kissoon.

John Lennon. Nick Lowe.

Manfred Mann's Earth Band. Marmalade. Dave Mason. Matthews' Southern Comfort. Ian Matthews. Paul McCartney. John Miles. Mott The Hoople. Mungo Jerry.

Graham Nash. Nazareth. New Seekers. Olivia Newton John. Paul Nicholas. Maxine Nightingale.

Nigel Olsson.

Robert Palmer. Paper Lace. Alan Parsons Project. Pilot. Pipkins. Police.

Suzi Quatro & Chris Norman. Queen.

Gerry Rafferty. Chris Rea. Roxy Music. Rubettes.

Leo Sayer. Hurricane Smith. Smokie. Ringo Starr. Stealers Wheel. Cat Stevens. Al Stewart. Rod Stewart. Supertramp. Sweet. Sweet Sensation.

10cc. Ten Years After. T. Rex. Bonnie Tyler.

Uriah Heep.

White Plains. Roger Whittaker. Peter Wingfield. Wings. Gary Wright.

Yes.

The Beatles were to have a total of **21 chart-toppers** between **1964** and **1970**. Their complete **record** of American hits is:

I Want To Hold Your Hand reached No.1 on January 25 1964

I Saw Her Standing There reached No. 14 on January 25 1964

She Loves You reached No 1 on February 1 1964.

Please Please Me reached No. 3 on February 22 1964.

My Bonnie reached No. 26 on March 7 1964.

Twist And Shout reached No. 2 on March 21 1964.

Can't Buy Me Love reached No. 1 on March 28 1964.

Do You Want To Know A Secret? reached No. 2 on April 11 1964

Thank You Girl reached No. 35 on April 25 1964.

Love Me Do reached No. 1 on May 2 1964.

P.S.I. Love You reached No.12 on May 16 1964.

A Hard Day's Night reached No. 1 on July 18 1864.

Ain't She Sweet reached No. 19 on August 1 1964.

And I Love Her reached No. 12 on August 8 1964.

I'll Cry Instead reached No. 25 on August 15 1964.

Matchbox reached No. 17 on September 19 1964.

Slow Down reached No. 25 on September 26 1964.

I Feel Fine reached No. 1 on December 5 1964.

She's A Woman reached No. 4 on December 12 1964.

Eight Day's A Week reached No.1 on February 27 1965.

I Don't Want to Spoil The Party reached No. 39 on March 20 1965.

Ticket to Ride reached No. 1 on May 1 1965.

Help! reached No. 1 on August 14 1965.

Yesterday reached No. 1 on October 2 1965.

We Can Work It Out reached No. 1 on December 18 1865.

Day Tripper reached No. 5 on December 25 1965.

Nowhere Man reached No. 3 on May 3 1966.

Paperback Writer reached No. 1 on June 11 1966.

Rain reached No. 23 on June 25 1966.

Yellow Submarine reached No. 2 on August 27 1966.

Eleanor Rigby reached No. 11 on September 9 1966.

Penny Lane reached No. 1 on March 3 1967.

Strawberry Fields Forever reached No. 8 on March 11 1967.

All You Need Is Love reached No. 1 on July 29 1967.

Baby You're A Rich Man reached No. 34 on August 12 1967.

Hello Goodbye reached No. 1 on December 9 1967.

Lady Madonna reached No. 4 on March 23 1968.

Hey Jude reached No. 1 on September 14 1968.

Revolution reached No. 12 on September 14 1968.

Get Back reached No. 1 on October 5 1968.

Don't Let Me Down reached No. 35 on October 5 1968.

The Ballad Of John And Yoko reached No. 8 on June 21 1969.

Come Together reached No. 1 on October 18 1969.

Something reached No. 1 on October 18 1969.

Let It Be reached No. I on March 21 1970.

The Long And Winding Road reached No. 1 on May 23 1970.

About the Author

Bill Harry was born in Liverpool and attended Liverpool College of Art with John Lennon and Stuart Sutcliffe. He coined the phrase 'Mersey Beat' and founded the newspaper of the same name. He also arranged for Brian Epstein to visit the Cavern where he saw the Beatles for the first time.

As news editor/feature writer for *Record Mirror* and pop columnist for *Weekend* magazine, his columns also appear in the Fleetway publications *Marilyn* and *Valentine*. He writes for *Record Retailer*, *Music Now* and is the British correspondent for German magazines *OK* and *Star Club News*. He has acted as personal PR to many artists including the Hollies, Kinks, Pink Floyd, Beach Boys, Led Zeppelin, David Bowie, Supertramp, Suzi Quatro, Kim Wilde and many more.

Bill has to date published many books: *Arrows* (Everest Books); *Mersey Beat: The Beginning of the Beatles* (Omnibus Press); *Heroes of the Spaceways* (Omnibus Press); *The Beatles Who's Who* (Aurum Press); *The Book of Lennon* (Aurum Press); *Beatlemania* (Virgin Books); *Beatles For Sale* (Virgin Books); *Paperback Writers* (Virgin Books); *Book of Beatles Lists* (Javelin Press); *Ask Me Why* (Javelin Press); *The McCartney File* (Virgin Books); *Sgt Pepper's Lonely Hearts Club Band* (Atalanta Press); *The Ultimate Encyclopedia of the Beatles* (Virgin Books); *The Best Years of the Beatles* (Headline); *The Encyclopedia of Beatles People* (Blandford Press); *Whatever Happened To...(*Blandford Press); *The Beatles Encyclopedia* (Virgin Books); *The John Lennon Encyclopedia* (Virgin Books); *The Paul McCartney Encyclopedia* (Virgin Books). *The George Harrison Encyclopedia* (Virgin Books).

Photo Credits courtesy of

Mersey Beat Archives
Bill Harry
The Beat Goes On
Flying Music
EMI Records
Rocket Records
Polydor Records
The British Film Institute
Simon Landis